Tabbed Divider Guide

SO-CFM-450

Research is a dynamic process with its roots in antiquity. For that reason we have incorporated into *Bookmarks* a photo essay depicting the evolution of research through the ages, from ancient libraries to online databases. On every tabbed divider in this text, you'll find a photograph and brief discussion of the historical, cultural, and social dimensions of research. With this photo essay, and with other images throughout *Bookmarks*, we aim to tell a story about research and writing—one that connects your work to the ever-changing ways we discover and report information. A selected few of the tabbed-divider photos follow; for the full story, examine each of the dividers. Notice, too, that the tabbed dividers also direct you to frequently consulted sections in *Bookmarks*.

Babylonian clay tablet (*see p. 183: the divider for "Authoring Your Own Web Site"*)

Scholars in the Library of Alexandria (*see p. 41: the divider for "Finding Information"*)

Faculty and students of New College, Oxford (*see p. 95: the divider for "Evaluating Sources"*)

Ben Franklin opening the first subscription library (*see p. 161: the divider for "Handling Quotations"*)

The first general purpose electronic calculator (*see p. 233: the divider on "Using MLA Documentation"*)

Student using the Internet (*see p. 203: the divider on "Using COS Documentation"*)

The Library of Congress (*see p. 325: the divider on "Using CBE Documentation"*)

Turn this page for more on Web resources ⟶

More Web Resources

"Bookmarks: Web Sites Worth Knowing"

You'll find this feature on the reverse side of all tabbed dividers. It supplies more valuable URLs to consult for your projects, with a helpful screen shot and annotations about the sites. This example appears on p. 96.

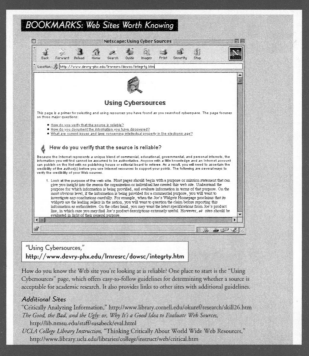

Research Central, the Web site for this text at
http://www.awlonline.com/researchcentral

This companion Web site offers annotated links to essential Web resources, easy-to-use Web page templates specially designed for publishing research projects on the Web, and exercises on source evaluation and Web design.

Longman English Pages Web site at
http://longman.awl.com/englishpages

The English Pages Web site provides continuously updated resources for reading, writing, and research practice in four areas: Composition, Literature, Technical Writing, and Basic Skills. Features include "Simulated Searches" for finding and evaluating information on the WWW, "The Faces of Composition," with first-person authentic essays written for a wide variety of situations, and annotated links to everything from an online library to scholarly manuscripts.

BOOKMARKS

A Guide to
Research and Writing

by

John Ruszkiewicz
University of Texas at Austin

Janice R. Walker
Georgia Southern University

 LONGMAN

An Imprint of Addison Wesley Longman, Inc.

New York • Reading, Massachusetts • Menlo Park, California • Harlow, England
Don Mills, Ontario • Sydney • Mexico City • Madrid • Amsterdam

Senior Development Editor: Sharon Balbos
Supplements Editor: Donna Campion
Project Manager: Bob Ginsberg
Design Manager: Wendy Ann Fredericks
Text and Cover Designer: Wendy Ann Fredericks
Front Cover Illustration: © Jeff Nishinaka/Artville
Back Cover Photo: © Damir Frkovic/Masterfile
Art Studio: ElectraGraphics, Inc.
Photo Researcher: Kelly Mountain, Mountain Resources
Technical Desktop Manager: Heather A. Peres
Senior Print Buyer: Hugh Crawford
Electronic Page Makeup: Carole Desnoes
Printer and Binder: Von Hoffmann Press, Inc.
Cover Printer: Von Hoffmann Press, Inc.

For permission to use copyrighted material, grateful acknowledgment is made to the copyright holders on pp. 333–334, which are hereby made part of this copyright page.

Library of Congress Cataloging-in-Publication Data

Ruszkiewicz, John J., date -
    Bookmarks : a guide to research and writing / John Ruszkiewicz.
Janice R. Walker.
        p.   cm.
    Includes index.
    ISBN 0-321-02393-5
    1. Report writing Handbooks, manuals, etc. 2. Report writing—
Computer network resources Handbooks, manuals, etc. 3. Research
Handbooks, manuals, etc. 4. Research—Computer network resources
Handbooks, manuals, etc. I. Walker, Janice R. II. Title.
LB2369.R88   1999
808'.027—dc21   99-34699
                                                                      CIP

Please visit our website at http://www.awlonline.com/researchcentral/

ISBN 0-321-02393-5

12345678910—VH—02010099

Contents

PART
I

Beginning
Research
1

1 Sizing Up Your Research Project   2

2 Managing Your Project   9

3 Finding a Topic   19

PART

Working
with
Sources
87

PART
IV

Developing
the Project
133

PART

V

Documentation
201

26 CBE Documentation 327

Preface

What's a *bookmark*? A decade ago, the answer would have been simple—a strip of metal, fabric, or paper inserted between the pages of a book to hold a reader's place. But, today, a bookmark can also be understood as a feature in a Web browser, a way to store Web addresses one expects to consult often. Someone familiar with the World Wide Web might even use the term as a verb: *to bookmark*.

What has happened to this simple word provides a rationale for *Bookmarks: A Guide to Research and Writing.* Just as electronic technology has complicated the meaning of *bookmark*, it has similarly transformed every aspect of *research* for college writers and instructors. So we offer *Bookmarks* as a new generation research handbook, one built on the assumption that students need to know how electronic sources, materials, and methods are altering their relationship to knowledge.

And yet we insist that not everything has changed. Bookmarks still do hold readers' places, and research still does often involve familiar activities such as finding topics, browsing indexes, summarizing and paraphrasing sources, and organizing ten-page papers. For this reason, we have carefully designed *Bookmarks* as a bridge between old and new traditions—a guide for researchers who expect to work regularly in both print and electronic environments.

It will be obvious that *Bookmarks* has been written with the presence of technology assumed. Throughout the volume, for example, we refer to research "projects," not papers, and we treat Web pages, brochures, and multimedia presentations as plausible options for reporting research findings in many situations. We take technology seriously because it creates new opportunities for undergraduates to do serious research in both their local and professional communities. At both the University of Texas at Austin and the University of South Florida, we have watched students using the Web and other technologies grow as writers and researchers, and we have been excited by their achievements.

We've also been chastened, occasionally, by Web projects that were more glitter than substance—offered by writers who have failed to read, organize, document, or edit carefully. While much of *Bookmarks* is genuinely new, the framework for describing research processes and the detailed chapters on documentation draw on materials refined over more than a decade. The result, we are confident, is a research guide that offers writers state-of-the-art advice about college research: the best of an older tradition merged with a thoughtful assessment of the new.

Our focus in this book is on offering **comprehensive, practical advice for student researchers**, including:

❑ An opening section **encouraging students to think of themselves as researchers** (Section 1a). More than twenty manageable chapters explain the process of research.

❑ Specific advice for **sizing up research projects and assignments** (Section 1b). In particular, writers learn how to read and interpret assignments.

❑ A full chapter on **project management** (Chapter 2), offering suggestions for setting up calendars and timelines. There is fresh advice, too, for working on collaborative projects.

❑ A chapter on **field research** (Chapter 8). Not all research occurs in the library or online, so *Bookmarks* includes suggestions for conducting interviews, using questionnaires, and making systematic observations.

❑ A complete chapter on **handling quotations** (Chapter 20), offering guidelines for selecting and using quotations.

Bookmarks pays unusual **attention to rhetorical matters**, offering:

❑ A full chapter on **finding a topic** (Chapter 3) as well as a chapter that helps writers to **focus and narrow** their theses (Chapter 5).

❑ A stasis approach to establishing the **purpose of a research project** (Chapter 4). **Stasis questions** also steer the development of thesis sentences and other aspects of the research process.

❑ A chapter on **drafting the project** (Chapter 18) that helps researchers develop cogent arguments for a particular audience.

Bookmarks emphasizes the process of **evaluating and working with sources**, research skills especially critical for success today. We include:

❑ A full chapter on **evaluating sources** (Chapter 11). The chapter includes a chart that explains the differences between research materials.

❑ A thorough discussion of **intellectual property issues** (Chapter 15). The chapter also provides guidelines for using academic sources responsibly.

❑ A full chapter on **keyword searches** (Chapter 7). The chapter helps writers manage electronic indexes and search engines efficiently.

❑ A chapter on **positioning sources** (Chapter 12). Writers learn how to detect and assess the biases in the materials they are using.

❑ A full chapter on **summarizing and paraphrasing** (Chapter 14).

A key feature of *Bookmarks* is its extraordinarily **comprehensive coverage of documentation** formats, including **Columbia Online Style (COS)**. This new system of documentation for electronic sources is presented authoritatively by its creator (Chapter 22). In addition, *Bookmarks* includes detailed treatment of **MLA, APA, CMS, and CBE** documentation styles (Chapters 23–26)—with comprehensive indexes to documentation items and clear examples of citations as they should appear both in the body of a paper and in the list of Works Cited or References. And *Bookmarks* includes complete **sample papers** in MLA, APA, and CMS styles, as well as excerpts from papers illustrating COS and CBE styles. Handy checklists help writers set up important items in research papers including title pages, works cited sheets, and abstracts.

Bookmarks itself exemplifies the way technology is reshaping the writing process. The book features a **strong visual component**, with a **photo essay** telling the story of research throughout the ages. It begins inside the front cover and continues on each tabbed divider. **Screen shots of useful Web sites** appear on the reverse of all tabbed dividers. These sites comprise a useful feature entitled "Bookmarks: Web Sites Worth Knowing" which guides researchers to reliable and intriguing sources online. Additional **photographs and diagrams** throughout the volume illustrate the research process.

A full-color, illustrated **guide to creating Web pages** (p. 185) offers succinct, practical advice for creating and evaluating Web projects.

Two complete sets of exercises follow each of Chapters 1–21. The first set introduces writers to specific research skills ("Getting Involved") and the second leads them step-by-step through their own academic work ("Managing Your Project").

Tabbed dividers throughout *Bookmarks* enhance access to frequently consulted topics, and a **glossary of terms** inside the back cover provides easy reference for new or unfamiliar terminology.

Supplements

Bookmarks for Instructors by Craig Branham of St. Louis University

This instructor's manual offers practical suggestions for designing and teaching research-intensive courses with *Bookmarks*. Rich with references to related readings, it includes discussion of alternatives to the research paper, students' concerns and attitudes about research, intellectual property issues, and ways to present the Internet as a research tool and publishing medium. The text also features several sample documents, including a syllabus, some assignment sheets, and an Acceptable Use policy.

Web Site for *Bookmarks: Research Central* at *http://www. awlonline.com/ researchcentral* created by Craig Branham of St. Louis University

This companion Web site supports *Bookmarks* with interactive resources for both students and their instructors. For student researchers, the site offers annotated links to essential Web resources, easy-to-use Web page templates specially designed for publishing research projects on the Web, and exercises on source evaluation and Web design. For instructors, the site features a registry where instructors can share links to their class sites and students' work and find potential collaborators.

The English Pages Web Site at *http://longman.awl.com/englishpages*

This site provides instructors and students with continuously updated resources for reading, writing, and research practice in four areas: Composition, Literature, Technical Writing, and Basic Skills. The site features "Simulated Searches" which recreate the process of finding and evaluating information on the WWW. It also includes "The Faces of Composition," a portion of the site with authentic essays showing students how others have applied what they've learned in composition—investigation, collaboration, inquiry, and debate—to a wide variety of situations. And the site includes helpful annotated "Links" to an online library, scholarly manuscripts, and the like. These links provide the best information on the widest variety of writing issues and research topics.

Daedalus Online

This is the next generation of the well-received and highly regarded *Daedalus Integrated Writing Environment* (DIWE). Developed by top composition scholars, *Daedalus Online* employs standard Web-based utilities to facilitate a shared writing process among students using **any** word processor from **any** computer that connects to the Internet, with secure, 24-hour availability.

Students using *Daedalus Online* can now easily explore online composition resources, employ prewriting strategies, partake in computer-mediated real-time conferencing, and post feedback to an asynchronous discussion board. They can use these features to tighten meaning, style, and expression in their writing.

Daedalus Online offers a comprehensive suite of online course management tools, which allows instructors to create and post assignments effortlessly, link these assignments to online educational resources, tie these lessons to integrated top-selling Longman textbooks, and customize materials to fit with any instructional preference.

To get more information about *Daedalus Online* or to order an examination copy of any Longman textbook visit *http://www.awlonline.com/daedalus* or contact your Addison Wesley Longman sales representative.

The Essential Research Guide **Laminated Card**

Students can carry around this handy laminated card for reference at all times. The card contains, on one side, an extremely informative grid on evaluating sources—everything from scholarly books to popular magazines to various types of Web sites—and on the other, a Web guide listing Web sites across the disciplines along with editing and proofreading symbols.

Acknowledgements

Many people contributed to the development of Bookmarks. In particular, we would like to thank the following reviewers, who have given us the benefit of their expertise: Allen Bradshaw, Mesa Community College; Craig Branham, St. Louis University; Cheryl M. Clark, Miami-Dade Community College; Alisa Cooper, South Mountain Community College; Gerard Donnelley-Smith, Clark College; Charlene A. Dykman, University of Houston; Jill D. Evans, Kettering College of Medical Arts; Gloria Floren, MiraCosta College; Jim Frazer, University of Arkansas; Bill Hart-Davidson, Purdue University; Ted E. Johnston, El Paso Community College; Traci Kelley, University of Minnesota, Crookston; Scott A. Leonard, Youngstown State University; Hilbert Levitz, Florida State University; Joe McCarren, Slippery Rock University; Lawrence McCauley, The College of New Jersey; John McLaughlin, East Stroudsburg University of Pennsylvania; Gerald Nelms, Southern Illinois University at Carbondale; Debora A. Person, University of Wyoming; Randall L. Popken, Tarleton State University; Dean Rehberger, Michigan State University; Donna Reiss, Tidewater Community College; James Stokes, University of Wisconsin, Stevens Point; Molly Turner-Lammers, Dakota State University; Traci Hales Vass, University of Colorado, Denver; and Ken Zimmerman, Lane Community College. Thanks also to faculty members Jason Craft, Sharan Daniel, Jeff Jackanicz, Chris LeCluyse, Michelle Neely, Andrew Osborne, Madison Searle, Joel Silverman, and Joanna Wolfe at the University of Texas at Austin and Lori Amy, Mary Hartley, Ellen Hendrix, Mike Pemberton, and Mark Richardson at Georgia Southern University for their comments on the cover design.

We would also like to thank our colleagues working in both libraries and online environments for their professional guidance on this project. Much of what we present in *Bookmarks* is based on information gathered over decades of teaching and research—both in dusty stacks and in front of terminals. The faculty and especially the graduate students at the University of Texas at Austin's Computer Writing and Research Labs deserve a special round of thanks. This facility of the Division of Rhetoric and Composition has pioneered many of the electronic research and pedagogical strategies described in *Bookmarks*. A special thanks as well to the Information Literacy Committee of the University of South Florida library for helping to keep us informed of student and faculty concerns about research and writing from sources in the information age.

We are grateful, too, to the editorial team at Addison Wesley Longman, especially to Anne E. Smith, who recognized the potential of this project immediately and found a way for us to do it. Sharon Balbos handled the all-important editorial responsibilities with patience and skill, adroitly assembling the complicated parts of this project—including the innovative photo essay. Bob Ginsberg gets credit for the smooth production of *Bookmarks*—all writers who work with Bob know that their books are in the best of hands. Thanks, too, to Kelly Mountain of Mountain Resources, who helped us assemble the photographs for *Bookmarks;* to David Munger for his contributions in compiling and verifying the information presented on useful Web sites; to Heidi Beirle, who helped devise the mini-essays that accompany photos on the front of all tabbed dividers; and to Jennifer Bracco who finalized the credits.

Last, but certainly not least, we would like to thank our students in dozens of research-based writing courses for helping us to understand how college research projects typically begin, develop, advance, collapse, and recover. We hope that the practical knowledge we gained from them is evident throughout this project.

JOHN RUSZKIEWICZ
JANICE R. WALKER

To the Writer

Welcome to *Bookmarks: A Guide to Research and Writing.* This textbook provides a fresh perspective on undergraduate research because the work you'll do in college has changed. Papers are not just papers anymore. Today, instructors expect you to delve deeply into new research materials and use a wide variety of innovative resources—both textual and graphic. They aren't surprised by illustrations, charts, and graphics in papers—in fact, they anticipate them. Some instructors may even encourage you to put your work online. And yet these same teachers will likely assume that you also command all the traditional research skills, from reading an assignment sheet carefully to formatting a Works Cited page properly.

Bookmarks provides comprehensive yet easy-to-understand information to guide you through such contemporary college projects. It will help you choose a topic, find and evaluate sources, and prepare your research project efficiently, using up-to-date research and writing tools. Whether your path leads you to printed or electronic sources or to conduct your own field research, *Bookmarks* can do more than help you avoid the pitfalls of a research project. It can make the project an exciting introduction to genuine research.

Bookmarks provides ready access to the materials you will need. The chapters are arranged in a step-by-step sequence that helps you work systematically. The opening sections introduce preliminary skills such as reading an assignment sheet, discovering what is in your library, and choosing a topic. There's also an essential chapter on managing a research project (Chapter 2)—don't miss it. Then the research process advances, chapter by chapter, right through the completion and editing of a final project. The concluding section offers a comprehensive guide to the major systems of documentation, with a full chapter given to each type including COS, MLA, APA, CMS, and CBE.

But you may treat *Bookmarks* as a reference tool as well. Use the tabbed dividers, the comprehensive table of contents, and the index to locate any information you need from *Bookmarks*. The part openers and chapter introductions can give you a glimpse at the material contained in each section, and the convenient glossary of terms inside the back cover will explain unfamiliar terminology. Throughout the book you will find comprehensive treatment of electronic research forms, including illustrations of suggested Web sites, a full-color insert on authoring a Web site, and important information on intellectual property for the modern researcher.

Be sure to visit the companion Web site for this text, called *Research Central,* at http://www.awlonline.com/researchcentral. This site provides additional templates for you to use to make creating your own Web site easy and fun. The site also offers a valuable annotated listing of links to essential Web resources to help you find information online.

And visit the Longman *English Pages* Web site at http://longman.awl.com/englishpages. This site offers continuously updated resources for reading, writing, and research practices. The site includes simulated searches, sample essays, and links to helpful research sources.

As we hope you'll discover, undergraduate research is becoming more exciting because it is, more and more, real research with consequences for readers beyond individual classrooms. We sincerely hope that you enjoy using *Bookmarks* as much as we have enjoyed working with students like you to develop it.

JOHN RUSZKIEWICZ
JANICE R. WALKER

Until recently, most college research projects have been designed to introduce students to academic standards for research—that is, to the procedures for gathering, assessing, and reporting information. The resulting research papers were —and remain—important exercises in handling information responsibly.

But not many students wrote such research papers expecting to publish them or to share them with anyone except teachers and classmates. Few undergraduates had the time, resources, or incentive to reach deeply into scholarly archives or to develop interesting projects on their own. What's more, there was no audience for such work and no easy way for a writer to reach a public intrigued by the questions a college student might pursue.

But times have changed. Students in college courses can now find tools, media, and audiences to support their serious academic efforts. Thanks to the Internet, students and instructors anywhere in the world can visit each other's online courses and Web projects. And anyone with modest computer skills can do things on computers that skilled technicians couldn't imagine a decade ago.

So if just a few years ago, a research paper was typically a ten-page effort with a dozen sources—six books and six articles—a research project today can be that very same paper, or that paper moved to a Web site, or a Web site itself, or a hypertext, a multimedia project, a MOO, a CD-ROM, a listserv, or any combination of these forms.

College researchers now can address readers beyond the walls of their classrooms, "publishing" their work themselves and reaching audiences potentially vaster than those claimed by most printed journals. Of course, the electronic tools that make all this possible can be expensive, creating new challenges and literacies. Yet the new technologies do not supplant the need for clear, powerful, and responsible writing.

Throughout this guide to college research, we will be walking a fine line to preserve the best parts of an older tradition while making room for new kinds of inquiry and writing, whether you are preparing a traditional paper, an electronic project, or something in between. That's what this book is about.

PART

I

Beginning Research

CHAPTER 1
Sizing Up Your Research Project

CHAPTER 2
Managing Your Project

CHAPTER 3
Finding a Topic

CHAPTER 4
Establishing a Purpose

CHAPTER 5
Narrowing Your Topic

1

Sizing Up Your Research Project

In college, your research will ordinarily have two dimensions: you will discover information, and you will talk about it. The dialogue might be just a conversation you have with an instructor or colleagues, or it might occur in a listserv online. Eventually you might address an entire professional group when you publish your findings in a journal or on a Web site. But, clearly, research doesn't become real knowledge until your discoveries are shared, digested, tested, and reformulated by a community of people. New ideas usually bring an intellectual community to life; the discussions which follow then spur more ideas and more discoveries.

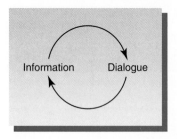

Consider what happened after Dolly, a sheep, was cloned in 1997. This discovery by Scottish scientists—that it was possible to clone life forms as complex as mammals—immediately settled some questions, but it raised just as many new ones for scientists, politicians, theologians, and ordinary citizens to ponder. Should human beings be cloned? Would a cloned person have a soul? Would it be ethical to clone people just to harvest body parts? Could cloning help people who are unable to have children? Certainly, the dialogue begun by Dolly will be churning long after she's stuffed and mounted in a museum.

Your research projects may not be quite so consequential as the one that produced Dolly. But they can have real significance if the process of discovery you initiate continues after a paper is turned in or a project submitted. College projects can open conversations that last a lifetime; many students find themselves redirecting their careers or changing majors as a result of the topics they've selected for college projects. That's normal and proper.

Cloned by scientists in Scotland in 1997, Dolly created a firestorm in the media and raised questions about the ethics of this type of medical research. Will humans be cloned next?

Today many newer research paths are consciously open-ended because developments in electronic technology have made us more aware than ever that intellectual conversations never cease. So if you think of research as an active process of creating knowledge rather than a passive one of reporting information, you'll be more comfortable with another notion: that almost every college paper and project should be supported by research. The information explosion of recent years makes this prospect genuinely exciting. Today, in the library or online, you can locate (and quickly too) more useful material than you can digest on almost every subject or question. Just as important, you'll have real opportunities to explore your subject with other writers locally and across the world. You may even be able to select the medium by which to share what you discover and create in a research assignment, exploring the rhetoric of document design, hypertext, or multimedia.

Of course, along with these new opportunities come new responsibilities: as the researcher, you'll find it is more important than ever that you choose your sources wisely and that you accurately credit the sources you choose to include in your project. For more information on evaluating your sources, see Chapter 11. Citation formats are covered in Part V.

1 a   Think of yourself as a researcher and writer

Many of us imagine both researchers and writers as people different from ourselves. That may be because of the stereotypes we see of scientists, professors, and other professional people in films and on television. So consumed by their work that they barely find time to eat or fall in love, they come across as lab-coated eccentrics—comically inept, absentminded, or disconnected from the problems of the "real world." Can you think of a scientist or academic in a Hollywood movie—old or recent—who wasn't somehow peculiar?

But like all stereotypes, this one has problems. For one thing, all of us are capable of research and do it most of the time, often unself-consciously. The youngster who absorbs everything she can about the Chicago Bulls, the guy who can offer informed opinions about any car on the road, the amateur botanists who have yet to find wildflowers they can't identify have all sought out, evaluated, and cataloged information on their favorite subjects. Like the rest of us, they have acquired a surprising level of exper-

Images from popular culture can reinforce stereotypes such as that of the lab-coated, slightly mad scientist, here represented by actor Brent Spiner in the film *Independence Day*. However, in real life any of us might be a researcher.

tise on topics that matter to them. Likely, they could—if asked—write about these subjects with authority and even passion. And that's what professional researchers do. Research develops from curiosity—the simple need to learn things and to share those discoveries with others.

The stereotype of the isolated researcher is also flawed because it suggests that research is done chiefly by exceptional and eccentric individuals. The fact is that while research may take patience, skill, method, and some training, it's not beyond the talents of anyone intrigued enough by a subject or a problem to do something about it. People learn to do research just as they learn to write, and they get better at both skills the more they practice them. Just as important, people in the professional world usually do research as part of a team. They work toward common goals, argue about how to get there, collaborate on their reports, and (usually) share the credit.

So don't begin a research project—especially one that will involve writing—by demeaning your talent and possibilities. Expect to be challenged and to work hard. Expect to involve others in your work. But also expect to succeed.

1b Size up an assignment carefully

You won't be surprised to find that college research projects will vary from course to course, major to major. Some assignments may focus on facts you are asked to locate and report clearly. Other assignments may push beyond existing materials, requiring that you do research in libraries, in databases, in laboratories, on the Internet, or in the field. Research of this kind may involve performing a controlled scientific experiment, constructing a survey, or theorizing about the social implications of a literary work. In other words, research can involve vastly more than reading a source and repeating what you find in it.

In most cases, a college research project assignment will be spelled out on an assignment sheet. Read the sheet carefully, making sure you understand what you may do. Pay attention to key words in the assignment. Are you being asked to analyze, classify, define, discuss, evaluate, review, explain, compare, contrast, prove, disprove, persuade, survey? Each of these terms means something different.

Be sure to understand the scope of the project. If you are expected to prepare a paper, consider how much you can cover within the specified page limits. In general, the shorter the project, the more specific the subject should be. The nature of fieldwork projects, Web projects, surveys, and other types of research may be described in different ways—by the kind of subjects you should interview, the types of survey questions you may formulate, or the number of Web pages or links you must support. When you

CHART
Key Research Terms

Analyze. Examine. Break your subject into its parts or components. Discuss their relationship or function.

Classify. Define. Place your subject into a more general category. Distinguish it from other objects in that category. What are its significant features? What makes it unique? recognizable?

Discuss. Talk about the problems or issues your subject raises. Which issues are the most significant? What actions might be taken? Look at the subject from several points of view.

Evaluate. Think about the subject critically. What criteria would you use to judge it? How well does it meet those standards? How does it compare to similar subjects?

Review of the literature. Examine a field or subject to see what the key issues are and what positions have been staked out by various researchers.

Explain. Show what your subject does or how it operates. Provide background information about it. Put your subject in its historical or political context so readers understand it better.

Compare. Show how your subject resembles other things or ideas.

Contrast. Show how your subject differs from other things or ideas.

Prove. Provide evidence in support of an idea or assertion.

Disprove. Provide evidence to contradict or undermine an idea or assertion.

Persuade. Come to a conclusion about your subject and explain why you believe what you do. Use evidence to convince others to agree, or provide good reasons for someone to think or act in a particular way.

Survey. Measure opinion on a question by using appropriate methods to guarantee an adequate, random, and representative sample of the population.

---

are in doubt about the requirements of a project, particularly when you are working collaboratively, ask your instructor for more information.

1c Examine the details of the assignment

Your first priority early in a project is to understand the nature and scope of an assignment (see Section 1b). But instructors often expect more than a bare minimum of effort when they ask you to do research. So you should go over the assignment sheet as if it were a contract, annotating and highlighting its key features. Consider issues such as the following.

Scope. An instructor may give you options for presenting a project—as a conventional paper, an oral report, an electronic presentation, a Web project. Understand the range of those options in terms of what you must do and at what length. Find out whether the project has word or page limits or time limits at *both* ends (no less than, no more than). Most instructors don't want to read twenty-page papers when the assignment calls for just four or five pages.

Due dates. There may be several due dates for different parts of the project: topic proposal, annotated bibliography, outline, first draft, final draft. Take each due date seriously, and assume that an assignment is typically due at the *beginning* of class on the date appointed, not by the end of the class or later in the school day.

Presentation. Note exactly what your final paper or project must include. The instructor may require items such as a cover sheet, an abstract, appendices, bibliographies, illustrations, charts, links, and so on. Highlight such requirements so you don't forget them. Check, too, whether your instructor expects you to turn in all your materials at the end of a project, including notes, drafts, photocopied sources, and peer editing sheets. If so, keep this material in a folder or envelope or keep an electronic copy on disk from the start of the project. Don't wait until the last minute to get organized.

Format. Take care to notice any specific requirements the instructor may have for margins, placement of page numbers, line spacing, titles, headings, illustrations, graphics, and so on or any specific formats required for electronic projects. If an instructor doesn't give specific directions for such items for a paper, model it on one of the documents in this book. We provide samples of papers that follow various conventions, depending on purpose and discipline: Columbia Online Style (COS) for projects using electronic sources; Modern Language Association (MLA) style for projects in English and the humanities; American Psychological Association (APA) style for projects in psychology and the social sciences; the *Chicago Manual of Style* (CMS) for projects in the humanities and other fields; and the Council of Biology Editors (CBE) style for projects in the natural sciences.

Assume that any final paper will be typed or printed; don't submit handwritten work unless your instructor specifically permits it. For a project submitted electronically, make sure it is in the required format as well.

Documentation. Be sure you understand your instructor's preferences for documenting a project. For example, some instructors may specify MLA, APA, or COS documentation; others may give you the option of choosing any system, providing that you handle it consistently. Make a decision about your documentation system early because you'll want to use it for your bibliography and note cards or in electronic files. Many students put off the fine tuning of their documentation until their final drafts, but that's a mistake because you should get feedback on your documentation much earlier. So commit yourself to getting the notes right at the beginning.

Collaboration. Some instructors encourage or require collaboration on research projects. If that's the case with your project, learn the ground rules to see how the work can be divided and what reports and self-assessments may be required from project participants. Pay attention, too, to how the project itself will be evaluated.

1d Consider the forms your project might take

Even a conventional research paper may take a variety of forms. A paper written to the specification of MLA documentation will likely use sources to back up or expand specific statements; one written to APA standards may follow the form of a research report, beginning with an abstract and concluding with a References list. You may be expected to use charts and graphics in these papers and to format them correctly.

But projects today may take many other shapes. You might, for example, be asked to design a brochure or information packet for a community group. The style of the brochure will need to fit the target audience, and graphics will be an essential part of the message. Or your project may entail a class presentation that includes an oral presentation supplemented by media, including slides or overhead projections prepared by a computer program such as *PowerPoint.* How you deliver complex information in this setting represents a distinct rhetorical challenge.

Or perhaps your project—possibly a collaborative one—involves creating a Web site or multimedia project that both presents information on a subject and opens electronic forums for discussion. You'll also want to lead readers to other sources through appropriate links and citations. The pages you create have to be visually attractive, rich in content, and reasonably quick to load.

GETTING INVOLVED

1. Describe in detail a scientist, researcher, or academic from a film or television program you have seen recently. Does the researcher fit or escape the stereotype of "researcher" described in this chapter? Some films you might consider: *Dr. Strangelove, A Clockwork Orange, Back to the Future, Frankenstein* (any version), *Independence Day.*

2. Describe a subject about which you might be said to have expert knowledge. The subject can be in any realm, from baseball cards to horticulture. Explain how you acquired knowledge of your subject. Could you write a book about the subject? How would you prepare to write such a book—what additional research might you have to do?

3. Working with a group, identify specific places on your campus or in the immediate community where research of some kind is going on every day. Describe the type of information produced or sought and the way that information is reported and shared. Be creative. Don't assume that research goes on only in academic environments.

4. People often form opinions or urge action on the basis of faulty information. Describe a problem in your local community (school, town, workplace) that might be clarified if people had better information or shared it more effectively. For example, students on a campus might be complaining that their fees for courses and activities are too high. But just how high are those fees? Are they out of line with fees at comparable institutions? Have the fees been rising

at a rate faster than inflation? In this case, researching the facts about fees might make any claims about fees better informed. But consider also how such information might be effectively shared. Or explore why there is not effective dialogue on the subject currently. Look for similar cases or situations in your community.

MANAGING YOUR PROJECT

1. If you have received an assignment sheet for a project, photocopy the sheet and then annotate it thoroughly. Highlight the actual assignment and the due dates. Note the special features the project must have. What parts of the assignment emphasize information? What parts encourage dialogue, conversation, or collaboration?

2. Identify the two or three parts of the assignment that you expect will cause you the most difficulty, and then explain to yourself exactly why you are nervous about those requirements or expectations. For each such problem, consider what steps you might take to make the difficulty more manageable. Will more reading help? Could the instructor or a librarian help? Might the project be easier if you found someone to collaborate with you?

Managing Your Project

In creating a college research project, you might follow the order outlined by this guide, from Chapter 1, "Sizing Up Your Research Project," to Chapter 21, "Completing Your Project." Each chapter describes an aspect of college research that may be important to your work. But few projects follow a simple sequence from start to finish—the separate stages of any given project, even basic steps such as choosing appropriate sources or organizing your information, will almost certainly overlap.

In addition, the activities within a project won't all require the same level of effort or time. For one project, you may devote just a few afternoons to gathering the information but then spend weeks summarizing the sources you've found. On another project, you might invest days designing, distributing, and tallying a survey of student opinion but then find that all your results can be reported on a simple graph—perhaps one that is computer generated. Because of such wide variations, no research guide can offer more than a provisional sequence or timetable for your activities.

But because projects do have to move forward, you can't afford to leave the management of any major research effort to chance. A successful project will require conscious planning. Following are some suggestions for organizing a research project.

2a Establish the hard points of your project

Hard points are those features of a project you can't change—usually described in the actual assignment. For instance, if an instructor asks for a ten-page paper on genetic engineering using CBE style, due in two weeks, you quickly have four hard points.

1. Format: ten-page paper
2. Topic: genetic engineering
3. Documentation: CBE
4. Due date: two weeks from today

All four points will shape your planning, but perhaps none more so than the due date. You know that researching and writing ten pages in two weeks is a lot of work.

Many college assignments will have only one due date—the day the project must be submitted. When that's the case, you'll have to schedule the remainder of the project yourself. But do take that final due date seriously. Instructors rarely show much, if any, tolerance for late projects—particularly when there has been plenty of time to complete them.

Some instructors, however, may give you a whole series of due dates for a major project, asking that you submit items such as the following at specific times.

❑ Project proposal, prospectus, or thesis

❑ Annotated working bibliography

❑ Storyboards (for projects with graphics)

❑ First draft

❑ Web site design specifications

❑ Responses to peer editing

When you are given multiple due dates, these items can be arranged in sequence to form a timeline into which the remaining hard points of your project can be fitted.

```
PROJECT              ANNOTATED              FIRST              FINAL
PROPOSAL    --->     BIBLIOGRAPHY    --->   DRAFT    --->      DRAFT
OCT. 2               OCT. 16                OCT. 23            NOV. 6
```

Research projects that aren't related to specific academic courses also will have hard points—again, most of them due dates. If you are preparing a report on spending by your student government, your hard point for the project might be a debate scheduled several days prior to campus elections—when your findings might have an impact on potential voters. If your work isn't completed by then, it may lose much of its power.

So when you receive an assignment, quickly identify its hard points, clarifying any questions about them immediately with your instructor or project supervisor.

2b Define the stages of your project

If you've never done a full research project before, you might find yourself guessing about many of these steps. But your hard points can provide a starting point. Let's imagine, this time, that you've been asked to work with two other students. Your job is to prepare a Web site describing the student government services for the first-year students who attend summer orientation programs. It's April 15 and orientation sessions begin June 15. Here are your hard points.

1. Format: Web site

2. Topic: student government services

3. Audience: first-year students

4. Due date: June 15—two months after start-up

To meet these goals, you probably would have to do the following:

❑ Gather information about student government services.

❏ Decide what information to present to first-year students.

❏ Decide how to present information: as text? graphics?

❏ Design a plan for a Web site.

❏ Create the Web site.

❏ Test the Web site.

Each goal in the plan would have to be met before your site would be ready for your target audience.

Other kinds of projects would follow vastly different paths. If you are gathering information in a library, you might have to allow time for creating a bibliography, locating documents, and then taking notes from them. If you are planning a field project that involves interviews, you have to determine *whom* to interview about *what,* prepare the questions, actually conduct the interviews, and then review and report your findings.

At the outset, however, there is no sure way of knowing all the elements a project might involve. The best you can do is estimate your work. In planning a project, it will certainly help to talk to more experienced researchers, to librarians, to instructors, and to colleagues. You might also review sample research projects, asking yourself, "What did the authors have to do to create this work or get these results?"

Finally, you might review the activities that research projects typically require. Following are some of those responsibilities. No project would include all the items listed, and many might include tasks and activities not mentioned here. Use the list to stimulate your own thinking and to help you arrange your activities in a rough sequence.

STAGE 1: BEGINNING RESEARCH

❏ Sizing up the research assignment/project

❏ Establishing purpose and audience

❏ Choosing a topic or defining the project

❏ Creating a management plan

❏ Preparing a topic proposal or prospectus

❏ Checking campus research policies if people will be subjects of your study

STAGE 2: GATHERING IDEAS AND INFORMATION

❏ Consulting bibliographies

❏ Locating information (in libraries, online, etc.)

❏ Determining/acquiring resources for the project

❏ Seeking materials through interlibrary loan

❏ Preparing questionnaires

❏ Preparing surveys

❏ Creating a plan for systematic observation of subjects

❏ Keeping track of information

❏ Establishing a database

❏ Contacting printers, Web consultants, research librarians

STAGE 3: WORKING WITH SOURCES

❑ Generating a working bibliography

❑ Evaluating sources

❑ Preparing an annotated bibliography

❑ Reading and positioning sources

❑ Annotating research materials

❑ Summarizing and paraphrasing sources

❑ Conducting interviews

❑ Distributing questionnaires or surveys

❑ Conducting studies or observations

STAGE 4: DEVELOPING THE PROJECT

❑ Refining your claim

❑ Organizing your project

❑ Finding a professional template

❑ Designing or drafting your project

❑ Submitting a draft or prototype

❑ Getting feedback on your project

❑ Responding to feedback

❑ Documenting your project

❑ Revising/editing your final project

❑ Testing your final project

❑ Submitting your project

2c Assess your strengths and weaknesses

Once you have a comprehensive idea of what your research project will require from you (or your team), plot those responsibilities against your timeline and decide how much effort to devote to each stage. If you know you are a competent researcher but a slow writer, you might allot extra time to drafting a research paper. Similarly, if you are a novice at interviews, you may want to schedule more interviews than absolutely necessary, figuring that the earlier ones might not be entirely successful. (See also Chapter 9, "Keeping Track of Information.")

This is the point to acknowledge any personal limitations. For example, if you have no experience with document design or managing graphics, you should rethink the wisdom of creating a project heavy on illustrations. Or perhaps you'd like to prepare a paper comparing great American novels, but you realize that you aren't a particularly fast reader. A paper about great American short stories might be more successful.

You also have to measure your resources. What kinds of materials can you find in your local community? Do you have the tools and money to produce exactly what you want? Do the members of your team have the experience to do the kind of project you envision? Adjust your plan accordingly. And expect to make many more such adjustments throughout the project.

Sometimes circumstances outside your project will change the timeline too. So anticipate minor calamities: interlibrary loan operating more slowly than you expected, fewer respondents replying to your survey than predicted, campus computer access growing more difficult at the end of the term.

2d Map out your project

Once you have established your hard points, listed the steps and stages of your project, and assessed your capabilities, you are in a position to sketch out your project in a calendar or timeline.

You can create a calendar simply by listing the due dates of a project and leaving sufficient space between them for the activities necessary to meet those deadlines. Then estimate the time necessary and/or available for each step in the project. Here's a calendar for a project with three major due dates and a variety of support activities, for each of which you would have to supply an appropriate completion date.

Calendar: Research Project

_____ Choosing a topic and defining the project

_____ Creating a management plan

_____ Determining campus resources

_____ Drafting the proposal

Topic Proposal: Due September 7

_____ Generating a working bibliography

_____ Gathering and evaluating materials

_____ Summarizing and paraphrasing sources

_____ Organizing/designing the project

_____ Drafting the project

First Draft: Due October 7

_____ Getting and responding to feedback on the draft

_____ Refining and rewriting the project

_____ Documenting the project

_____ Preparing the final materials

Final Draft: Due November 7

Your initial calendar should not be much more detailed: you'll waste time if you try to account for every movement in what is usually an unpredictable process.

You can also mark off your research project on an actual calendar—the kind that provides a box for listing each day's appointments and activities. With such a calendar, you can get a clear sense of the time available to do your work, perhaps coordinating it with your other commitments. Again, begin by marking down the firm due dates. Then look at the time available to complete the entire job, counting the actual days if it helps. If you are given only a completion date, estimate the halfway point of your project, and then decide what you must accomplish by that point—perhaps a complete first draft or a working Web site design. Whatever type of calendar you create, allow some slack toward the end to make up for time you will almost certainly lose earlier in the project.

A third type of calendar for your project is a timeline. Here the trick is to imagine a line moving steadily forward while various activities move through stages that may be overlapping or even circular. You can design a timeline that illustrates this process by mapping ongoing responsibilities below the more linear due dates. Following is an example.

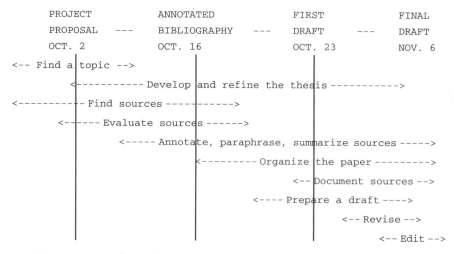

```
    PROJECT             ANNOTATED              FIRST               FINAL
    PROPOSAL    ---     BIBLIOGRAPHY   ---     DRAFT       ---     DRAFT
    OCT. 2              OCT. 16                OCT. 23             NOV. 6
<-- Find a topic -->
        <---------- Develop and refine the thesis ----------->
<--------- Find sources ----------->
    <------ Evaluate sources ------>
            <----- Annotate, paraphrase, summarize sources ----->
                <--------- Organize the paper --------->
                        <-- Document sources -->
                    <---- Prepare a draft ---->
                            <-- Revise -->
                                <-- Edit -->
```

Whatever form of calendar you create for your paper or project, allow yourself considerable flexibility. Sometimes your carefully considered plan will have to be reshaped when things don't go quite as you expect. Always remember that the point of having a schedule is to produce a product. All is not lost if you have to change a schedule to fit altered circumstances. Few projects ever meet all their initial goals.

2e Work as a team

You may be expected or invited to work as part of a team for some college projects. If so, use the occasion to learn how to work productively to achieve a common goal. You'll quickly discover that careful management is an important part of any collaborative effort. Here is some advice for organizing a group effort.

Decide how to make decisions. In most cases, you will want a process that is flexible enough to encourage input from every member of the team but also responsive enough to make timely decisions. A team might choose a project leader by consensus or election to keep its work on task and on schedule, or the team might create a more democratic mechanism for decision making—perhaps by meeting regularly during the project (even by email) and reaching a consensus through discussions or voting. In any case, it is crucial that people on a team agree on how to make decisions and then respect that process.

Make sure someone has an overview of the process. Whether a project has a leader or not, someone must keep track of what each person is doing. Even groups as small as three or four people can lose sight of project goals, resources, or timelines and waste time by duplicating efforts. That's why teams need a person to coordinate information within a group and to speak for the group to outsiders. A team working on a brochure, for example, should have one person explaining its needs to printers or clients; a team developing a research paper should direct its questions to an instructor through only one member. This knowledgeable individual might also have authority to allocate resources and adjust schedules to bring a project in on time.

Talk to each other. Members of a team need to talk with each other throughout a project so that they get a feel for each other's ideas, concepts, or goals. As much as possible, teams should practice "simultaneous engineering"—that is, a team should be aware of the impact their choices might have on each component of a project, especially in the early stages. For example, the "content" people on a Web project might want the site they are planning to be interactive, but they shouldn't count on offering online forums until they've discussed the idea with the people handling the design.

Assess the strengths of team members. When you work collaboratively, you can take advantage of what team members know individually and also compensate for their weaknesses. But you also want each member of the team to learn something from the entire research project. So in a collaborative effort in college, every member of the team should be exposed to almost every part of the project.

Still, people should work chiefly on those parts of a project for which they have skill, talent, and experience. They can be assigned their major responsibilities either by a project leader or by group consensus. But a team has to be sure people don't volunteer for responsibilities they can't handle. A little diplomacy and honesty early in a project can save a lot of heartache later.

Be frank about sharing responsibilities. Quite often, students working collaboratively on a project may be asked to assess each other's work. So it is important that team members understand their assignments and those of their colleagues—and expect to be held responsible for them. If you can't pull your weight on a project, let your colleagues know immediately so they can make adjustments. Perhaps you can take on a job you can handle better. The worst tactic is to string your team members along, leading them to expect work you can't or won't produce.

2f Prepare a research proposal or prospectus

For many research assignments, you may be asked to prepare a document outlining your topic, plans, resources, and qualifications for the project. By outlining your ideas early, you enable an instructor or supervisor to give you the advice or suggestions you need to keep a project on track.

We can't offer you a single form to cover all the possible types of projects you might explore. The prospectus for a minor project might fit on a single page; that for a senior thesis (or a dissertation) might run many pages. Any prospectus, however, will likely include many of the following elements.

❑ **A topic or topic area.** Identify your topic area and, if required, provide a rationale for selecting this subject.

❑ **A hypothesis or research question.** State your hypothesis or question. If required, discuss the hypothesis in some detail and establish its significance, relevance, or appropriateness.

❑ **Background information or review of literature.** Identify the background reading and research that provides preliminary grounds for your research. Or, for major projects, provide a full review of the professional work already done in your area of research, summarizing the articles and other scholarly materials that provide the context for your research.

❑ **A review of necessary sources and archival materials.** Identify the kinds of materials you expect to review for this project: books, articles, newspapers, documents, manuscripts, recordings, videos, artworks, databases, Web sites, email lists, and so on. You might also be asked to assess the availability of these materials and identify where and how you expect to gain access to them.

❑ **A description of your research methodology.** Outline the procedures you will follow in your research, and justify your choice of methodology. For many types of research, this section will be the most demanding part of the prospectus. You have to convince an instructor or supervisor that your approach will treat your subject adequately and provide valid and repeatable results. For example, if you intend to do a survey, you need to explain how you will generate and test your survey questions, how you will tally and validate responses to them, how you will select your respondents to assure a valid and adequate sample, and so on.

❑ **A description of your qualifications to undertake the project.** Show that you or members of your research team either possess or can acquire the knowledge and skills needed to carry out a project. You might point to courses you have taken (say, in statistics), expertise you have (perhaps in languages), or skills you can purchase (for example, the expertise of a printer or a Web designer).

❑ **An assessment of the ethics of your project if it might involve experiments on other people.** Most universities have strict guidelines for research with human subjects. Your instructor will likely make you aware of these rules, especially in fields in which human research is common, such as psychology and the social sciences.

❑ **An assessment of resources and/or costs.** Identify any special equipment, library resources, or other materials you expect to need for the project. Outline any travel that the work may entail. Provide a detailed estimate of costs for equipment, salaries, printing, and so on. In major research projects, the budget may be a separate part of the prospectus.

❏ **A schedule or timeline.** Estimate the stages of your project and provide firm dates for each item that must be submitted.

As you might guess, you won't be able to prepare a prospectus until you have selected and narrowed your preliminary topic and purpose. This process is described in Chapters 3 through 5.

GETTING INVOLVED

1. Compare a time when you were part of a well-run organization or project to an occasion when you were involved with a poorly organized enterprise. How would you account for the differences?

2. Observe the dynamics of leadership within one or two of the small groups to which you belong. How are decisions made? By whom? How well are those decisions respected? How does the group deal with dissent?

MANAGING YOUR PROJECT

1. Examine your entire project carefully and then break it down into four or five major stages. Those stages will vary, depending on the project. But you might imagine steps such as the following.

FOR A PAPER	FOR A WEB PROJECT
Finding/focusing on a topic	Determining purpose
Locating information	Determining basic site design
Reading and assessing sources	Assigning and developing pages
Producing a first draft	Establishing links
Getting feedback	Getting feedback and testing
Revising and editing	Fine-tuning the design

Then look at your stages in terms of the time available for completion, and establish a firm timeline for completing the paper. Be sure that the calendar leaves ample time for feedback from colleagues. The more time you allow for revision and fine tuning, the better your final project will be. That's because major projects often require a lot of work at the end: creating a Works Cited page, gathering notes, testing a design for "bugs," getting clean and handsome copies, and so on. Don't wait until the last minute.

2. Because organizing information will play a major role in your research process, skip ahead to Chapter 9, "Keeping Track of Information," to review procedures for recording and storing data. Use this review to guide your estimates of the time you'll need to complete a successful project.

3. Consider assembling a team for a collaborative research effort. In a group, you may want to discuss questions such as the following.

- What research and writing skills might your project require?
- What qualities would you look for in your colleagues?
- How will you organize your team?
- How will decisions be made?
- Who—if anyone—will be in charge?
- How will you communicate and coordinate your efforts?
- How will you schedule the work, and how will you deal with deviations from the schedule?
- How will you assess your work and share the credit?

Finding a Topic

Why is it that in a world of 4 billion people, virtually unlimited channels of information, thousands of years of history, hundreds of resource opportunities, and new controversies in most professions every day, a surprising proportion of students in the United States given the power to research any topic will choose capital punishment, abortion, marijuana/hemp, euthanasia, or school prayer? A cynic might suggest that it's because an enterprising writer can lift a project on these topics just about anywhere—from a sorority file, a big brother, a term paper company, a Web site. Change the name, alter the date, and add a recent source or two, and the work is done. Little effort is expended . . . and nothing learned.

A more charitable view might be that writers want topics that are both decently controversial and comfortably familiar because they then can be sure to find both an angle on the subject and plenty of respectable sources. Most people *do* have opinions about matters such as capital punishment or abortion and can rehash arguments they have heard from authorities they've been listening to all their lives. In other words, such topics are the intellectual equivalent of the Dairy Queen—filling, familiar, and always just around the corner. Once again, little is ventured to produce such a project and little gained. The effort is forgotten as soon as it is completed.

Expect more from a subject and yourself. And have more confidence in your ability and that of your colleagues to make discoveries about fresh issues and problems closer to you and your community—whether that community is a tiny college seminar on medieval history, a crowded lecture section on American literature since 1820, a film society considering the appeal of silent classics, or a neighborhood watch group looking for proven techniques to reduce vandalism.

A good subject alone doesn't make a research project successful. But you'll find that the energy that comes from discovering a topic that means something to you and your colleagues will make all the difference in the world. Finding a topic to write about begins with your own questions and ideas, usually prompted by class discussions and readings. But beyond that, you must place these ideas in the world outside the classroom by participating in conversations and discussions, face-to-face or online, and through outside reading, watching television, browsing through electronic newsgroups or the World Wide Web, and thinking about your topic.

3a Find a topic in your world

Many college research projects are open-ended—that is, your topic will be connected in some way to the general subject of the course, but the specific focus will be up to you. You're expected to explore topics related to course themes—typically, subjects such as gender, multiculturalism, the environment, religion, and education. In a history class, you might write about an era or movement or conflict (the Gilded Age, the Civil War); in a philosophy course, a movement (Thomism, Existentialism); in government, a theme or concept (balance of power); in the natural sciences, an experiment; in the social sciences, a field project. Within these broad areas, however, you still have much room to choose specific topics.

When it's appropriate, you should try to connect the assignment to your own experiences and to issues of consequence in the local, regional, or national communities. For example, you may be uneasy after watching a *Crossfire* debate on higher education. Do the participants' views reflect what you know about college? Are the facts and assumptions you have heard accurate, the claims consequential? A serious project might grow from such a query. Similarly, a history assignment on the civil rights movement could lead you to inquire about local concerns: Was your school or community ever segregated? How did your city or town react to civil rights initiatives or legislation? Do contemporary concerns for women or gay rights have roots in this earlier political movement?

We suggest placing issues in local, even individual, contexts—not just to make them more personally challenging, but also because you're more likely to do original research when your project explores real turf, not abstract territories. A generic paper on capital punishment will likely just rehash arguments a century old, but investigating a local death penalty case might produce significant insights.

Don't, however, expect a cogent topic to drop from the sky like the tortoise that brained Aeschylus (in legend, at least). Open yourself up to the world by reading critically everything you can get your hands on—local papers, university journals, a campus literary magazine, minutes of influential committees, fliers distributed by offbeat groups, online discussion forums. Watch TV this way too, especially the news channels (CNN, MSNBC, Fox News) and that most valuable and unfiltered political source, C-SPAN. Surf the Net, checking out political, cultural, and social sites of interest to you—or, maybe, those that offend you. (You're more likely to be moved to action by encountering something you don't like.) And talk with people, face-to-face or via electronic forums.

3b Connect your topic to a wider community

From the start, you should invite others to join the exploration of your topic. Look for campus events, clubs, or forums that might be related to the subject. Check the local papers for information about lectures, film groups, or community meetings where you might meet people interested in your work. And when you find such people, network with them to find more people and organizations invested in your subject.

If you are in a course with access to a local electronic network or chat room, invite classmates to join you in a session to discuss research ideas. As you try to explain your topic to others, you'll grasp it better yourself: its features will stand in sharper relief when viewed side by side with projects your colleagues are planning. You can also explore subjects via a class listserv (if your instructor sets one up) or through conventional email exchanges with instructors and colleagues.

Consider, too, how the project you are planning might be framed for a real audience, preferably one that includes many more people than yourself and an instructor. Take your assignment public. For example, the best medium for exploring the costs of local environmental cleanups might be a Web site; your paper describing local reading projects might have more impact redesigned as a feature story in a campus publication or as a multimedia presentation for recruiting literacy volunteers. Not all research efforts, of course, can be shaped this way. But even the most conventional paper can be written for more than just a grade.

3c Browse the library in your topic area

Look for a subject about which you can honestly say, "I want to learn much more about it." The enthusiasm you bring to a project will be evident in the work you eventually produce. Of course, not all subjects hold the same potential. Avoid stale controversies that have been on the national or local news without resolution for a long time—don't be one of a half dozen students submitting projects on an unresolveable campus concern with parking or football tickets. You'll find plenty of material on such subjects, but it is unlikely you'll add much to the existing debate.

Get closer to your subject by spending a few hours browsing in your library or on the World Wide Web.

Efficient sources for a preliminary exploration of academic topics are encyclopedias, beginning with any that deal specifically with your subject. The more specialized the encyclopedia, the better its coverage of a subject area is going to be. Library reference rooms have dozens of specialized encyclopedias covering many fields, and many libraries also offer electronic access to them. Ask reference librarians for their help.

CHECKLIST

Your browsing and background reading should

- Confirm whether you are, in fact, interested in your topic.
- Survey your subject so you can identify key issues and begin narrowing the scope of your project, if appropriate.
- Determine whether sufficient reliable resources exist to support your project in the time available.

Browse printed and electronic sources to find intriguing subjects that spark your enthusiasm. Then try to determine whether library and online resources are sufficient to support your project. Finding an intriguing topic will help guarantee your enthusiasm for a long-term project.

If no specialized encyclopedia is available or if the volume you select proves too technical, use one of the general encyclopedias, available in print or electronically.

BOUND	ELECTRONIC
The Encyclopaedia Britannica	*Britannica Online*
Encyclopedia Americana	*Encarta*
Collier's Encyclopedia	*Grolier Multimedia Encyclopedia*
Columbia Encyclopedia	*Academic American Encyclopedia*

To get a feel for your topic area, examine books or journals in the field. What are the major issues? Who is affected by them? Who is writing on the topic? You can learn more than you might expect from quick but purposeful browsing.

CHECKLIST
Specialized Encyclopedias

DOING A PAPER ON . . . ?	BEGIN BY CHECKING . . .
American history	*Encyclopedia of American History*
Anthropology	*International Encyclopedia of the Social Sciences*
Art	*Encyclopedia of World Art*
Astronomy	*Encyclopedia of Astronomy*
Communication	*International Encyclopedia of Communication*
Computers	*Encyclopedia of Computer Science*
Crime	*Encyclopedia of Crime and Justice*
Economics	*Encyclopedia of American Economic History*
Environment	*Encyclopedia of the Environment*
Ethics in life sciences	*Encyclopedia of Bioethics*
Film	*International Encyclopedia of Film*

Health, medicine	*Health and Medical Horizons*
History	*Dictionary of American History*
Law	*The Guide to American Law*
Literature	*Cassell's Encyclopedia of World Literature*
Multiculturalism	*Encyclopedia of Multiculturalism*
Music	*The New Grove Dictionary of American Music*
Philosophy	*Encyclopedia of Philosophy*
Political science	*Encyclopedia of American Political History*
Politics	*Oxford Companion to Politics of the World*
Psychology, psychiatry	*International Encyclopedia of Psychiatry, Psychology, Psychoanalysis and Neurology; Encyclopedia of Psychology*
Religion	*The Encyclopedia of Religion; Encyclopedia Judaica; New Catholic Encyclopedia*
Science	*McGraw-Hill Encyclopedia of Science and Technology*
Social sciences	*Encyclopedia of the Social Sciences*

3d Browse the Internet

Check out your subject by examining various online electronic resources such as Web sites or discussion groups. You can explore Web sites to see what others have posted on your subject, using search engines (see Chapter 7) to find the best locations in this vast environment. The quality of materials varies enormously (see Chapter 11). Still, a well-constructed Web site can perhaps provide a helpful overview of a subject as well as links to other sources. Many libraries also offer access to databases and other reference sources through the World Wide Web (see Section 6g).

Like Web sites, Internet discussion groups can help you understand the dimensions of a subject—what it involves and what the issues are. Internet discussion groups include both *asynchronous* communications, such as email, listservs, newsgroups, or HyperNews forums, and real-time *synchronous* communications, such as MUDs and MOOs, or chat rooms. In an asynchronous discussion, participants read messages that have been posted earlier and leave messages of their own for others to read at their convenience. In a real-time discussion, the participants are online at the same time, reading and responding immediately to each other, as they might in an actual conversation.

Email, listservs, and newsgroups. Many people use the Internet to communicate on a wide variety of topics. For instance, Internet discussion lists enable people with common interests to share information via email exchanges. Naturally, electronic mail, listservs, and Internet newsgroups can all be sources of material for a research project, and you might begin a discussion to help you discover what to explore. They can also be good places to ask questions or to find out about other potential sources. However, before using information obtained from email or listserv messages, make sure you get permission, and always give proper credit. (See Chapter 15.)

Some email lists and newsgroups are informal or classroom discussion lists. Others, such as *ClariNet,* are fee-for-subscription services that offer up-to-the-hour news reporting. Newsgroups come in all shapes and sizes, from raunchy or eccentric *alt.whatever* groups to moderated groups offering expert information on a wide variety of topics. Here is a sampling.

alt.algebra.help

alt.dorks

humanities.classics

info.academic-freedom

rec.animals.wildlife

rec.folk-dancing

soc.history.ancient

talk.environment

For example, if your subject is related to religion in the United States, you would find dozens of postings under *alt.religion, soc.religion,* or *talk.religion.* You can find discussions of current news events on the newsgroup *alt.current-events.usa.* Not all such sources will be equally helpful, but remember that you aren't seeking research material at this stage but deciding whether an issue merits more scrutiny.

You can find listservs and newsgroups with search engines such as *Tile.Net* or *Liszt* or search through newsgroups using *Deja.com.* Some listservs, newsgroups, and email programs such as *HyperNews* can be read on the WWW using a browser, or you may be able to read them in your Internet email editor. (See Chapter 6.)

Make sure you follow proper *netiquette* (the etiquette of the Net); although many listserv and newsgroup discussions are open forums, discussion lists often focus on specific topics, and list members do not want students or others posting queries. It is usually best to "lurk" for a while, read the FAQs (frequently asked questions) or other information about the list, and get a sense of the conversation before asking questions.

Telnet sites. Telnet is an application that allows you to log on to a remote computer and access its files and programs. Most telnet sites will require you to have an account on their server, with a log-in name and password. You may use telnet protocols to log on to your school computer from home. Once connected, you can work on that computer just as if you had accessed it directly. Many libraries allow telnet access to their catalogs, and most MOOs and MUDs (real-time synchronous communication sites on the Internet) use telnet protocols. Telnet sites, like most Internet sites, can also be accessed using a WWW browser and the address form telnet://address (for example, telnet://damoo.csun.edu:8888). There are various client programs available for telnet applications as well. Some may already be installed on your host computer, and others are available for free downloading on the Internet.

MOOs and MUDs are similar to the chat rooms with which you may already be familiar. In addition to holding scholarly conferences and meetings in MOOs, many teachers meet with students online. The format can range from informal classroom discussions to very formal scholarly conference presentations.

Internet Relay Chat (IRC). Internet Relay Chat (IRC) is probably one of the most popular and best-known forms of synchronous communication, or real-time conferencing. Recent technological developments and the proliferation of multimedia computers have brought developments in IRC client programs as well, including programs such as *Internet Chat* and *CUSeeMe* that support real-time audio or video. IRC is similar to the very popular and easy-to-use chat rooms found on many commercial sites, with separate channels available for various topics. You may also set up your own channels and moderate discussions.

Like MOOs and MUDs, IRC channels are sites to meet with people from around the world and discuss various topics in real time. You can conduct online interviews in these spaces with a wide variety of people, conduct surveys or ethnographic studies, or meet with group members to discuss your findings. Different "channels" in the IRC network represent distinct communities, or topics. Before logging a conversation or using information in your research, however, make sure you ask permission, and make sure to accurately cite your sources.

GETTING INVOLVED

1. Browse the World Wide Web to locate term paper sites such as *School Sucks* at http://www.schoolsucks.com. Examine the sites critically to get a sense of the types of subjects covered. Do the papers offered in such places look like serious research projects? Why or why not?

2. Working in a group, spend a day comparing the news coverage from several different news sources. You might assign one person to each different news outlet. Before beginning your research, agree on what you will compare. For example, you might decide to compare the stories covered and the time devoted to each by the various network news shows and news stations: ABC, CBS, NBC, CNN, Fox, and so on. Or you might compare the front-page stories in half a dozen different newspapers (or on their Web sites). Or you might analyze the coverage of one story given by various different media.

3. Spend at least half an hour examining the layout and holdings of the reference collection in your local or college library. Take time to gain a sense of the whole collection so that you know what kind of information you can find there when you get deeper into your research. Find out how to use the various pieces of equipment, from terminals for searching databases to microfilm readers. Be sure to locate the map room, the microfiche collection, and any special collections.

4. In the reference room of the library, locate and browse the various specialized encyclopedias in the collection. Compare these specialized volumes to more

general encyclopedias such as *Collier's* or *The Encyclopaedia Britannica.* When would you be better off using a specialized encyclopedia (if available) to find a topic? When might you benefit most from a general encyclopedia?

MANAGING YOUR PROJECT

1. What issues or problems concern your campus most at the present time? Can any of these issues be connected to a research project you might do for a particular course? Do any of these issues have a history you might explore in a class project or research paper? Could you do library work or fieldwork that might illuminate the issue or topic or add an important voice to an ongoing conversation?

2. What connections might you make between the project you are considering for a course and your local community? Could you do a project that draws on the resources of people around you or that involves local people or institutions? With which groups or institutions do you most identify? How might a group or institution benefit from research you might do into archives, local or regional history, or current issues or controversies?

3. Investigate any special resources, collections, museums, institutions, or groups in your community that might help you in shaping a project.

4. If you have access to the World Wide Web, look at some newsgroups, listservs, or telnet sites that focus on your topic. For information on searching and evaluating such resources, see Chapters 7 and 11.

Establishing a Purpose

Have you ever gone to a multiplex theater not knowing which movie you would see? At such times, chances are you did at least have a *type* of film in mind, depending on your mood and companions—perhaps a horror flick, a disaster epic, a comedy, or maybe a "date" movie. This preference likely then guided you to a film worth your two hours and $6.

As you might suspect, there's an analogy here to choosing a research topic—though not a perfect one. Just as it helps to know what kind of film you want to see before deciding on a particular movie, it helps to understand the purposes your paper or project might serve as you choose a subject. There are probably as many ways of defining the purpose of a research project as there are types of movies. But to make your choice manageable, we'll focus on just five. Given a research topic which engages you, but which you don't yet know how to handle, consider examining it as

- ❏ a question of fact,
- ❏ a question of definition,
- ❏ a question of value,
- ❏ a question of causality, or
- ❏ a question of consequence.

These five approaches have their roots in classical rhetoric as a means of deciding the issues a lawyer might argue in a courtroom. We'll illustrate these strategies through an imaginary research project addressing a political situation at a college, examining the approaches one at a time. But you should understand that they will almost always overlap in the work you do, one question leading naturally to another.

For now, let's imagine that you and a group of friends want to use a writing course assignment to challenge a proposal to raise fees to build a new student union. Those student fees have been increasing steadily on your campus in recent years until they almost equal your tuition charges. Many students—especially people working to put themselves through school—are feeling the pinch. What can you do? Advocates of the "fee enhancement" have already begun to take their case to the student body, which will have to approve the increase in a campus-wide referendum. Proponents are promising better food services in the new student union building, more space for campus activities, a bowling alley, and a theater. You and your colleagues agree to collaborate on a campus information project to explore the details of this fee increase and, depending on your research, to present alternatives to anyone willing to listen.

Given this scenario, what exactly are the issues you might address, and how might you best approach them? The five perspectives mentioned above can give you some direction.

4a   Consider the topic as a question of fact

You can approach almost any subject by exploring basic factual questions—reporting what is already known about a subject or what remains to be discovered. You might find such information in existing books, articles, surveys, and reports, or you may have to generate it on your own. Queries of fact include some of the familiar journalist's questions: *who, what, where, when,* and *how.* In answering these questions, you could find the topic and purpose for a project.

For example, in researching reasons to raise fees for a new student union, you might explore the need for a new union building: what facts suggest that the current building is insufficient, too costly to maintain, or too ancient to renovate? To answer such questions, you might have to visit various offices and archives. At the Buildings and Maintenance Office, you might dig up figures on the actual size of the building in square feet or on annual maintenance costs. Then you'd have to determine whether both figures are out of proportion when compared to figures for similar facilities on other campuses. Gathering and correlating such facts would represent genuine research.

In crunching all these numbers, you'd likely recognize a need to present them to potential voters clearly. So part of your research team may have to work with media and document design issues. If you decide to reach students through handouts or brochures, you may need graphics and tables to state the financial case clearly. If facts suggest that the new building would be on a controversial site or will disrupt campus traffic flow, you might want to generate maps to establish your point.

So factual questions, such as the following, provide a great way to begin your exploration of a topic.

- ❑ What is known about this subject?
- ❑ What remains to be discovered?
- ❑ What might readers find new or surprising about your subject?
- ❑ Are important factual matters relating to your subject in dispute?

As a result of such queries, you may decide to frame your project as a report, a brochure, or an informational Web site. Or when your research shows that the facts are in dispute, you may write an argument choosing to favor one set of facts over another.

SUMMARY

Questions of Fact

You are dealing with factual matters when your research leads you to check and verify what is already known about a subject. In other words, there's information you can find, evaluate, and report. You'll likely begin your research with specific questions—but other questions will arise as you learn more about your topic.

Projects based on questions of fact . . .

- Tell readers something they don't know.
- Prove that something known *is* so.
- Discredit false information.
- Explain how something came to be.
- Enumerate the parts or elements of a situation.
- Explain how something occurred.

4b Consider the topic as a question of definition

You can examine almost any subject by studying the meaning of its key concepts. You might find the standard meaning of these crucial terms in dictionaries and encyclopedias. Or you might have to come up with definitions on your own—for example, by creating questionnaires to discover how the public at large understands the terms, concepts, or ideas.

In the public arena, many civic debates turn on questions of definition, often expressed through the difference between paired terms—citizen/alien, welfare/handout, white lie/perjury, expenditure/investment, contribution/bribe, censorship/obscenity, and so on. Within such controversies, you may find compelling material for extended research into the historical meaning of terms, their legal status, or their changing implications. Although this binary approach is often simplistic, it can offer you a useful starting point.

An issue such as a student fee increase may not raise obvious questions of definition. But certain terms might quickly become controversial if your research places them in the public sphere. For example, students favoring the fee increase to build a new student union might describe what they are proposing as a *revenue enhancement* or *building use charge*—a matter you might dispute by looking more closely at those terms. Or perhaps the proposal might lead your team to explore the implications of a key term on your campus, such as *priorities* or even *student union*. If private companies or commercial food chains will handle more and more services in the proposed union, you might explore whether the building really will remain a *student* union—and whether students should be asked to pay for it.

Questions of definition may lead either to reports or to arguments. Your research effort might, for example, provide an extended definition of some concept in which you both define an idea and furnish many examples and illustrations to help readers understand it. Or a research project based on issues of definition may become an argument when the terms of the definition are in dispute.

SUMMARY

Questions of Definition

You are dealing with matters of definition when you examine questions about the nature of things. You'll be trying to understand definitions, create them, or refute them. Or you may be trying to decide whether something fits the criteria of a definition already established. Your exploration may begin with general sources (dictionaries) but will likely branch out to include more specialized information.

Projects based on questions of definition . . .

- Explore the classes to which things belong.
- Enumerate their distinguishing features.
- Examine basic similarities.
- Point out fundamental differences.
- Move to include someone or something in a larger group.
- Move to exclude someone or something from a group.

4c   Consider the topic as a question of value

You can examine almost any subject by framing it as a question of value. In fact, almost every day, you make snap judgments about dozens of things—movies, food, music, athletes, politicians, automobiles. Such informal evaluations are not that different from the more studied judgments you might make in a full research project, evaluating the work of a contemporary poet or judging the merit of a new social program. In these more formal situations, you will need to support your evaluations with convincing evidence because you become more accountable when you go public with an opinion, whether it is in print or online.

Situations that call for judgments and evaluations are numerous. You may be asked to assess a person's work or achievements; to judge the quality of a performance, a product, or an idea; or to compare persons, objects, or ideas in order to rank them.

How might issues of quality shape your research into the wisdom of building a new student union? It's likely that you'll have to explore many different aspects of quality: the merit of the current building, the potential benefits of a new facility, the impact a new facility might have on the quality of campus life, perhaps even the worth of the proposal itself. The point of research in this area would be to go well beyond mere opinion. You would have to look for strong evidence to support any claims of value you might offer, getting that testimony from the opinions of experts, from public surveys and questionnaires, from detailed and systematic observation, and from reading articles and reports on the subject.

You'd have to think carefully how to present your findings. If you wanted to show all sides of the issue, you might write a feature article for the campus newspaper or create a Web site that offers a variety of opinions—using tables, charts, or graphics to display information. But most evaluations will probably end up as persuasive pieces, with researchers taking definite stands in completely developed arguments, using the evidence they have gathered to support their judgment.

SUMMARY
Questions of Value

You are exploring a question of value when you have to judge the merit of an idea, concept, policy, institution, public figure, or activity. You'll have to decide what the valid criteria for judgment are and then determine whether what you are evaluating meets those standards. In a few cases, particularly in the sciences, standards of performance or quality may be defined precisely. But in other arenas, criteria of evaluation may be controversial. You'll need to understand such controversies to make convincing judgments of your own.

Projects based on questions of evaluation . . .

- Assess strengths or weaknesses.
- Explain why something has or has not worked well.
- Advise others in a course of action.
- Improve something by understanding its strengths and weaknesses.
- Assess the competition.
- Praise or blame someone or something.

4d Consider the topic as a question of cause and effect

Examining why things happen the way they do is one of the most important jobs of researchers. When done appropriately, cause-and-effect analyses are among our culture's most powerful (and habitual) operations. If that sounds overstated, just consider how regularly our leaders and the news media trace effects back to causes in order to dole out praise and blame: in describing the success or failure of policy decisions, in tracing the causes for disasters, in tracking the environmental consequences of various actions, in attributing behavior to various societal influences.

You can find specific topics easily by thinking about cause-and-effect relationships. For example, you might design a project to explain what would happen to campus enrollment if student fees were raised to pay for a new student union building. Would fewer poor or minority students be able to attend? Would blue-collar students consider registering at another school? Or you might look at other effects of building a new structure. Who or what might be displaced by the new building? How would food service revenues be affected? How might campus life be altered?

Questions of cause and effect can lead to reports when the causal analysis is more factual than speculative. The more speculative your analysis, the more likely it will move in the direction of argument. But even such arguments can be informative when, for example, research suggests a variety of possible causes for a particular phenomenon.

SUMMARY

Questions of Cause and Effect

You are exploring a cause-and-effect question when you want to know why something happened. You can explore such questions from two directions, either by looking at an existing event or phenomenon and researching its causes or by examining a new force and speculating what its consequences might be. For example, you might explore the factors causing a national increase in single-parent families, or you might examine the future consequences of this change in family structure.

Projects based on cause-and-effect questions . . .

- Explain why something happened.
- Consider what might happen as a result of certain trends or movements.
- Challenge accepted explanations for certain phenomena.
- Challenge stereotypical thinking.
- Affirm the validity of certain explanations in the face of new challenges.
- Explore the relationships between various causes and effects.
- Probe the complexity of political and social relationships.
- Overturn superstitions or simplistic explanations for complex phenomena.
- Undermine or question complex explanations for simple phenomena.
- Raise questions about cultural assumptions by examining their implications.

4e Consider the topic as a question of consequence

You might approach any subject by making it the subject of a proposal for action. Proposals often begin with a problem, a gap, or an uncertainty. You might begin with evidence that a given situation—in school, at home, in the country—must change. So you have first to define the problem, appreciating its complexities. Then you have to think creatively about its implications. For example, were you to oppose that student union fee increase, you might have to offer alternatives to the new building. So you'd have to research options for providing enough space for people on campus to meet, relax, and interact. One approach to the problem might be to find out what other schools have done to meet the needs of students—short of building expensive unions. Then, of course, you'd have to consider the best way to convey your information: a detailed report available both in print and online might be an impressive strategy.

In thinking through the consequences of a proposal, remember that it's also important to analyze public or professional attitudes toward your subject. You'll often need to explain what's wrong with current thinking on a subject before you can persuade readers to consider your new proposals. And, of course, you'll have to defend your own proposal thoroughly—its consequences, its feasibility, its advantages. But examination of a subject in terms of the action it might produce is usually a fertile way of deciding what to write about.

Questions of consequence often lead to papers or projects that are exploratory. Such work asks people to consider possible alternatives to existing situations along with offering a particular solution. If your research leads you to recommend strongly a specific course of action, then you might write a formal proposal.

SUMMARY

Questions of Consequence

You are addressing a question of consequence when you study a problem (local or national) to determine why current solutions aren't working and to suggest alternatives. First, you will have to establish the facts of the current situation and examine different perspectives on the problem. Then you'll offer a solution of your own, backed by information about its costs, feasibility, and likelihood of acceptance.

Projects based on questions of consequence . . .

- Present solutions to problems.
- Offer alternatives to the status quo.
- Consider the advantages of change.
- Consider the consequences of change.
- Consider the costs of change.
- Ponder the likelihood of change.

GETTING INVOLVED

1. Examine a daily newspaper or newsmagazine and find examples of stories or features that respond to each of the five types of questions discussed in this chapter.

   Questions of fact
   Questions of definition
   Questions of value
   Questions of causality
   Questions of consequence

Also look for examples of articles in which different purposes are combined. Do you find that particular types of writing dominate in particular sections of the paper or magazine? Why?

2. None of the questions discussed in this chapter would lead toward a project designed to entertain or amuse. Would an academic research project likely have entertainment as a primary goal? Might it have entertainment as a subsidiary goal?

MANAGING YOUR PROJECT

1. Identify two general subjects that might be appropriate topics for a research paper, and explore each using the five approaches described in this chapter—as we did with the student union fee increase as a topic. You'll likely find that some perspectives work better with your subject than others.

2. List the most interesting questions or perspectives your topic generates (see Exercise 1). Then look for connections between the questions to see whether different questions might be pursued in the same paper.

3. Once you are able to connect your potential topic to a specific purpose, locate an example of research that resembles the project you have in mind. If you decide to create a factual Web site, look for a Web site that presents documentary evidence. If you expect to prepare a proposal document yourself, look for a proposal argument. When you locate an appealing model, note its features and decide which you might emulate and which may not fit your project.

Narrowing Your Topic

Once you have a general topic for a research project and a sense of purpose (see Chapters 3–4), you can begin to focus your topic, either by putting it into words or by sketching it out. Some writers narrow and focus their topics by posing a specific *research question* for which they do not yet have a satisfactory answer.

> **RESEARCH QUESTION**
> Why is criminal violence increasing among juveniles at a time when the overall crime rate is decreasing?

Other writers prefer to guide even their early research by constructing a *hypothesis*, a statement that makes a claim to be tested in the project.

> **HYPOTHESIS**
> Despite a drop in the overall crime rate, violence among juveniles is increasing because of the pernicious influence of television.

Either a research question or a preliminary hypothesis will help to focus your research. But at this stage you don't have to commit to a position. Until the evidence comes in, be open-minded and always willing to revise your claim.

5a Pose questions

To gain more perspective on a topic, ask specific questions about it. Use your preliminary reading and discussions to learn what the issues are in a field or topic area. In your reading or field research, be curious about matters such as the following.

- ❏ The focal points of chapter titles and section headings
- ❏ The names of important people or experts
- ❏ The names of events or institutions related to your subject
- ❏ Issues or questions that come up repeatedly
- ❏ Issues about which there is controversy
- ❏ Issues about which there is doubt and uncertainty

When narrowing a topic such as mountain biking, begin with a preliminary research question: Does mountain biking damage local environments? As you explore your topic (or plan your field research), be curious and skeptical. Don't assume that you can know from the outset what your results may be.

Consider, too, what the implications of an issue might be. Ask questions, and write down your observations. Above all, while reading and discussing your topic, maintain an attitude of healthy skepticism. Be curious and adventurous in the questions you pose as you consider a subject.

Topic—Mountain biking

Do mountain bikes really damage the ecology of local parks?

What right do bikers have to bring vehicles onto public land?

Why has mountain biking grown so popular?

Topic—Marine parks

Does the confinement of whales and dolphins at marine parks really constitute cruelty to animals?

Do marine mammals actually live longer in the wild than in more protected environments? If so, why?

Who profits from keeping marine mammals in captivity—scientists or businesspeople?

Topic—Voting

Has voter turnout for national elections really been much higher than it is now?

Who would benefit from increased voter turnout in national elections?

What reasons do people give for not voting?

You can turn some questions into tentative hypotheses by making them claims.

The confinement of whales and dolphins at marine parks constitutes cruelty to animals.

But notice that you couldn't make some questions into hypotheses without additional information. (For example, you might not know for sure whether voter turnout has, in fact, been higher in previous decades or who exactly would benefit from increased voter turnout.) Spend time just thinking about your subject, comparing what you've learned from your sources, and decide what you can offer readers.

In most cases, narrowing subjects early in the writing process can make subsequent searches of print and electronic resources more efficient. If you've narrowed a subject too much, you'll know it soon enough.

5b Consider the kind of research appropriate to your project

As we demonstrate in some detail in Chapter 4, different projects will serve different purposes and require different kinds of research. Your research techniques and sources will often depend on whether your preliminary question or hypothesis involves a question of *fact*, of *definition*, of *value*, of *cause*, or of *policy*.

CHART
Sources for Questions of Fact

- Reference works, encyclopedias, almanacs
- Books, both scholarly and popular
- Journal articles and magazines
- Newspapers and online news services
- Interviews with experts
- Fieldwork
- Institutional and government Web sites

EXAMPLES OF FACT-BASED QUERIES AND CLAIMS

QUERY   How do children raised in day-care environments compare emotionally or intellectually with children raised at home by parents?

CLAIM   Violence among teenagers is higher now than in any previous decade in modern American history.

CHART
Sources for Questions of Definition

- Dictionaries and encyclopedias
- Books, both scholarly and popular
- Journal articles and magazines
- Surveys of opinion
- Listservs and Usenet groups

EXAMPLES OF DEFINITION-BASED QUERIES AND CLAIMS

CLAIM   Limiting campaign contributions is an abridgment of free speech. (What is "free speech"?)

CLAIM   Solitary confinement in prisons constitutes a form of cruel and unusual punishment forbidden by the Constitution.

CHART
Sources for Questions of Value

- Scholarly and popular books
- Journal/technical articles
- Popular and special-interest magazines
- Newspaper editorials and columns
- Book reviews, film reviews, product reviews
- Listservs and Usenet groups
- Individual Web sites

EXAMPLES OF VALUE-BASED QUERIES AND CLAIMS

QUERY   Is the quality of American filmmaking in decline?

CLAIM   The human genome project poses ethical problems most people cannot yet fathom.

CLAIM   Diomedes, not Achilles, is the real hero of *The Iliad*.

CHART
Sources for Questions of Cause

- Scholarly books
- Journal/technical articles
- Popular and special-interest magazines
- Newspaper editorials and columns
- Scientific experiments and observations
- Surveys and questionnaires

EXAMPLES OF QUERIES AND CLAIMS BASED ON CAUSE

QUERY   Why is the quality of American filmmaking in decline?

CLAIM   Enforcing new EPA pollution standards will endanger the economy of regions that rely on mining.

CLAIM   Spending more time in elementary school on reading will produce students better prepared in all subject areas.

CHART
Sources for Questions of Policy

- Scholarly and popular books
- Journal articles and magazines
- Newspapers
- Interviews
- Surveys and field research
- Listservs and Usenet groups
- Issue-oriented Web sites

EXAMPLES OF POLICY-BASED QUERIES AND CLAIMS

QUERY   What can be done to improve math education in American secondary schools?

CLAIM   Science literacy in local high schools might be improved by creating adjunct teaching positions for practicing scientists.

5c Review the library catalog and Web directories

Library catalogs are designed to make information manageable and accessible to researchers. But catalogs can also be powerful tools for generating topic ideas because they break complex subjects into manageable parts. So to find topic suggestions, learn to browse a catalog strategically. For example, under a very broad category such as "English literature," you may find such divisions as "postcolonial authors" or "Oriental influences" or "Renaissance." Subheads such as these, in turn, may lead to narrower divisions still ("Renaissance playwrights," "Renaissance theaters") and, perhaps, to categories that pique your interest more. And remember that each card or screen in the catalog provides information on a particular source. So the catalog could also lead you toward your preliminary research materials. (For more information on using the library catalog, see Section 6b.)

You can do a similar survey of World Wide Web directories such as *Yahoo!* which outline their major subject areas. For example, *Yahoo!* offers indexes of such areas as "Arts and Humanities," "Business and Economy," "Computers and Internet," "Education," "Entertainment," "Government," "Health," and "News and Media." Under each of these categories are subcategories with links to online sites related to the topic, as well as even more subcategories. "Arts and Humanities," for example, offers subcategories for "Countries and Cultures," "Electronic Literature," "History of Books and Printing," "Storytelling," and so on. By noting which headings and subheadings in a directory have the most entries, you can get a rough sense of what areas or topics are most productive and controversial. (See Section 6e for more details.)

5d Talk to people

Explain what you intend to explore in your project, and let the questions and comments of colleagues guide you toward key issues. You'll be surprised how often a classmate will raise an issue you hadn't considered. Or other people may be able to broaden your appreciation for a subject. For example, if you are considering a research project about the long-term effects of childhood abuse, you might consider joining a newsgroup or IRC channel discussion to find firsthand accounts of the experience. Many such opportunities are available online, though you should approach them carefully and sensitively—using the information you find there mainly to stimulate your own thinking. After all, people may not want their lives to become part of your research project.

GETTING INVOLVED

1. Here's a list of generic topics likely to be shrugged off as dull by most readers. For two of them, come up with specific research questions that might spark interest. If necessary, do some library or online research.

domestic cats	common cold
France	calculus
cheating	attention deficit disorder
Vikings	First Amendment

2. Examine textbooks from several of your college courses to see whether you can discern from the tables of contents, chapter headings, or graphics what the crucial issues, controversies, or subjects of research might be within each field or discipline. Do some types of textbooks or subjects reveal the research interests of their fields more readily than others? Why might that be so?

MANAGING YOUR PROJECT

1. Put your preliminary topic in the form of a research question. This is the question your paper might eventually answer ("Is it likely that explorers will find water under the surface of Mars?"). Or it is the question that will guide a brochure or Web site you are designing ("What volunteer opportunities do students have for improving literacy in our community?").

2. Put your preliminary topic in the form of a hypothesis. This is the statement that your paper may eventually support ("Explorers are likely eventually to find water under the surface of Mars"). Or it is the statement that might provide a rationale for your brochure, Web site, or other project ("The community provides many opportunities for students to volunteer for literacy projects").

Located on the Mediterranean coast in Egypt, the Alexandrian library (297 BCE–CE 391) was a Greek institution founded by Ptolemy I, one of Alexander the Great's generals and later the ruler of Hellenic Egypt. The library's "books," a collection that peaked at approximately 500,000 items, consisted mainly of papyrus scrolls (these were made of strips from the papyrus reed's soft inner pith) that could be written on and rolled up for storage. The library's large holdings established Alexandria as the center for intellectual exchange and the development of Western knowledge in ancient times. The library endured a series of fires before it was destroyed completely in 645.

As you browse library sources to find research topics, you will be using techniques for finding information and classifying it that are based on systems developed in the Alexandrian library. That library was a place for scholars. They wore the clothing of the intelligentsia—the white Roman toga signified this privileged class. Women, for a time, also wore togas, and some even pursued scholarly activities, but their absence from this illustration speaks to their role in Alexandrian scholarship.

◎ DON'T MISS...

- **The library tour in Section 6a.** Explore your library and learn how to use its diverse collections and facilities.

- **The guide to online catalogs in Section 6b.** Don't be intimidated by computer catalogs: they are essential tools for research.

- **The guide to periodical indexes in Section 6d.** You'll need to consult these indexes for many types of research projects.

- **The list of Web search engines and directories in Section 6e.** Search engines are a key to locating information on the World Wide Web.

BOOKMARKS: Web Sites Worth Knowing

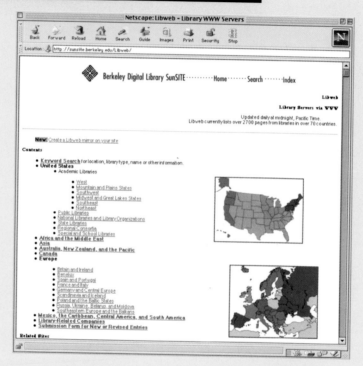

Libweb index of "Library Servers via WWW,"
http://sunsite.berkeley.edu/Libweb/

Even when you're looking for offline sources, the Internet can help you. Sites such as the *Libweb* index of library servers allow you to locate libraries that list their holdings on the Web. *Libweb* lists more than 2,500 libraries worldwide that have online, searchable catalogs. Once you identify a library and find what you need in its online catalog, you can request the material from your school library via interlibrary loan. If you don't have time for that, *Libweb* offers a keyword search feature that lets you locate libraries in your area. You can check the catalog online to make sure the library has what you need before you visit in person.

Additional Sites
CARL Corporation, "Access for All," http://www.carl.org
The WWW Virtual Library, http://vlib.org/Overview.html

PART

II

Gathering Ideas and Information

CHAPTER 6
Finding Information

CHAPTER 7
Doing Keyword Searches

CHAPTER 8
Conducting Field Research

CHAPTER 9
Keeping Track of Information

Doing research can be like detective work—a lot more glamorous to imagine than to do. The process of research requires both grit and daring. The grit is easy to appreciate since there is no getting around the time and energy required to track down or acquire accurate information. Even with the aid of computers, which speed up certain kinds of searches beyond the wildest dreams of earlier scholars, researchers today still must explore a wide range of materials, gather that information, and then keep track of it. If they don't emerge from library stacks as dusty as they used to, they're still likely rubbing their eyes.

But research takes daring too: researchers have to enjoy solving problems. When promising trails lead nowhere (as they often do), researchers need to locate new ones, often carving those paths themselves. They have to look for connections that might not be immediately obvious or find new ways to use what they have discovered. Like a clever detective, an experienced researcher looks for patterns in materials that others dismiss as hopelessly chaotic.

So it may help to think of a research project as a puzzle to be solved—a story in which you are playing Sherlock to everyone else's Watson.

6

Finding Information

Once you have a research question or hypothesis, your next goal for many projects will be to locate potential sources and to prepare a *working bibliography*, that is, a preliminary list of materials relevant to your topic (see Section 9b). Although it might be possible to go to your university library and simply browse the shelves until you find sources useful to a research project, the technique would be absurdly inefficient. Moreover, any books you might find on the shelf would likely represent only a small portion of the information actually available in the library. Obviously, you wouldn't rely on chance or serendipity to support serious research in a library. You would work systematically with bibliographies, indexes, library catalogs, and librarians to find the information you needed.

Systematic research is even more important today when you have to deal with an explosion of electronic sources, many of which were not designed with researchers and scholars in mind. For example, the very strength of the World Wide Web—its robust connection of millions of computers, files, and databases—is also its scholarly weakness. It presents a jumble of information, leaving users to screen nuggets of gold from mountains of slag. So it's essential that your searches be more efficient and knowledgeable than ever.

In this chapter, we explain some of the basic tools and resources you should use when sorting through these stacks of information. (For information about organizing your materials, see Chapter 17.) We urge you to be systematic and dogged in your work. Don't close off an investigation just because you haven't located materials you want. But don't be satisfied, either, if your initial searches produce more riches than you expect. The first cut is liable to be superficial or obvious. Always push deeper into the archives, libraries, and networks. Be curious and take risks.

6a Learn about your library

A first priority for any college student is to become familiar with the arrangement of campus libraries and research facilities. Don't be intimidated. Take a tour of these buildings, and be sure you can locate the following features.

❏ **Online catalog.** Most libraries now provide access to their collections via computer terminals that allow powerful electronic searches. Learn how to use these terminals. Find out whether remote access to the library catalog is available.

❏ **Card catalog.** Not all libraries have electronic catalogs. And even libraries with online terminals may not cover materials acquired before a specific date. The card catalog may provide your only access to these older materials. Find out whether that is the case, and know where the card catalog is located.

❏ **Reference room.** Large libraries often have a separate reference room staffed by librarians especially knowledgeable about finding information in many fields. Study this collection carefully, noting how materials are arranged and where heavily used items—from encyclopedias and almanacs to phone books and databases—are located. Note where the reference librarian is stationed.

❏ **Bibliographies and databases.** Most libraries house their most important bibliographies and data terminals in their reference collections. The bibliographies in various fields will often be large multivolume collections. Research databases will be arrayed around terminals, with their information accessed either online or via CD-ROM.

❏ **Microforms collections.** Many important materials, including documents, newspapers, and periodicals, are collected on rolls of film called *microfilm* or rectangular sheets of film called *microfiche*. Know where these collections are, how they are arranged, and how you can get to them. Learn to use microfilm readers, both the type that handles film and the type that reads cards.

❏ **Periodical collections.** You'll need to know both where current journals and periodicals are located and where bound or microfilmed materials are kept.

❏ **Newspapers.** As with periodicals, current newspapers are usually available in a reading room. But older newspapers will usually be available chiefly via microfilm, and then you will likely have access to only a limited number of major papers, depending on the size of your library collection. Online archives of newspapers are a recent innovation; you won't be able to search backward more than a few years.

❏ **Special collections.** Libraries often have rooms or sections for their rare or special items such as pictures and photographs, maps, government documents, and so on. Learn the location of any important collections in your library.

❏ **Audio/video collections.** Many libraries now have extensive holdings of audio/video materials as well as facilities for listening to or viewing CDs, tapes, and videodisks. Be sure you know where these collections are located, where and how they are cataloged, and how to use the playback equipment.

❏ **Circulation desk/library services.** Be sure you know not only where the circulation desk is but what other services the library offers you as a researcher. For instance, you can usually recall materials that are on loan if you need them for your project. In addition, most libraries are involved in interlibrary loan programs that enable you to acquire materials your library does not own. (Such orders take time, so don't wait until the last minute to make such a request.)

❑ **Directories.** Large libraries can be complicated facilities. Take advantage of any directories or pamphlets that a library offers to help you locate collections. Also note how the collections are arranged, where library call numbers are displayed, how the shelves themselves are arranged, and other aspects of the physical arrangement.

❑ **Photocopiers/computers/study areas.** Find out where in the library you can reliably copy information. In fact, it's smart to track down two or three copying locations since copiers get heavy use. Also check to see whether computer terminals or modem ports are available in the library and whether certain areas are set off for study and research.

❑ **Study carrels.** Many colleges and university libraries provide carrels in the library for people pursuing serious research. Find out whether you are eligible for such a carrel.

6b Use library catalogs efficiently

Once you can find your way around a research facility, begin your work by examining your subject in its catalog of materials. Most libraries now provide access to their materials via computer terminals, and some libraries can even be searched via the World Wide Web. But electronic catalogs sometimes cover only a library's more recent acquisitions. To do a thorough job, be prepared to move back and forth from computer terminal to card file during your research.

In traditional card catalogs, books and other materials could be located by author, title, and keyword. Electronic catalogs can be searched by the same categories, but more quickly and powerfully. Moreover, electronic catalogs may also indicate whether books have been checked out, lost, or recalled. If your library has an electronic catalog, learn its basic search techniques and commands. Some catalogs can search periodical indexes or online encyclopedias. On the facing page, for example, is the search menu screen for the online library catalog at the University of Texas at Austin at **http://dpweb1 .dp.utexas.edu/lib/utnetcat/keyword.html**. Notice that the screen supports a variety of keyword combinations and permits a user to specify the location, format, and language of the research material. Librarians find that most people use keyword searches to explore online catalogs. For much more about keyword searches, see Chapter 7. For a list of online library catalogs, you might examine the LIBCAT Web site at **http://www .metronet.lib.mn.us/lc/lca.html**.

An online catalog will also offer you practical information about any library holding. You'll usually be given a short entry first—typically the author, title, publishing information, date, and call number—with an option to select a fuller listing. The fuller listing will describe additional features of the book—whether the book is illustrated and whether it has an index or a bibliography, for example. Be sure to follow up on any new subject headings provided too: these are keywords for additional searches. For instance, if you were exploring hieroglyphics, a listing on that topic might also offer the keywords "Egyptian language—grammar" and "Egyptian language—writing." You probably wouldn't have thought of these keyword search terms on your own.

Netscape: UTNetCAT: Keyword Searches

| k | Forward | Home | Reload | Images | Open | Print | Find | Stop | N |

te: http://dpweb1.dp.utexas.edu/lib/utnetcat/keyword.html

Home Page | Net Search | Apple Computer | Apple Support | Apple Software

UT*Net*CAT *Keyword Search*

HE GENERAL LIBRARIES • THE UNIVERSITY OF TEXAS AT AUSTIN

yword searches retrieve records which include (or exclude, using **not**) the words you search. Use the Music Keyword rch page to search for music and recordings.

ELP: Author | Title | Subject | Mixed | Special Collections

Enter words for one or more keyword types:
tiple words of the same keyword type are connected by AND, unless you type OR or NOT.

Author	
AND ○ OR ○ NOT	
Title	
AND ○ OR ○ NOT	
Subject	
AND ○ OR ○ NOT	
Mixed	
AND ○ OR ○ NOT	
Music Publisher/Number	

tart KEYWORD Search | Clear | **OR...**

Select one or more optional search limiters:
he limiter term you want isn't shown, enter another. See complete lists in Help for each limiter.

ELP: Location | Format | Language | Place | Year

AND ○ NOT	ALL Locations at UT Austin	
AND ○ NOT	ALL Formats of Materials	
AND ○ NOT	ALL Languages of Materials	
AND ○ NOT	ALL Places of Publication	
AND ○ NOT	ALL Years of Publication	

tart KEYWORD Search | Clear

O TO: User's Guide | Help | Browse | Command | Reserves Lists

nd Comments

SUMMARY
Online Catalogs

For a book, online catalogs typically list . . .

- The call number and library location
- The author, title, publisher, and date of publication
- The number of pages and the book's physical size
- Whether the source is illustrated
- Whether the book contains a bibliography and index
- The subject headings under which the book is listed

The books you'll find as a result of catalog searches, whether by card or online, are essential research resources. They usually give more detailed and authoritative information than you'll find anywhere on the Internet yet—particularly when your topic deals with historical or academic subjects.

6c Locate suitable bibliographies

You will save time if you can locate an existing bibliography—preferably an annotated one—on your subject. *Bibliographies* are lists of books, articles, and other documentary materials that deal with particular subjects or subject areas.

CHART
Types of Bibliographies

- Complete bibliographies attempt to list all the major works in a given field or subject.
- Selective bibliographies usually list the best-known or most respected books in a subject area.
- Annotated bibliographies briefly describe the works they list and may evaluate them.
- Annual bibliographies catalog the works produced within a field or discipline in a given year.

To determine whether a bibliography has been compiled on your subject, first check in the reference room of your library. Chances are, however, that you won't find a bibliography precisely on your subject area; instead, you may have to use one of the more general bibliographies available for almost every field. The instructor of your course or the reference librarian should be able to suggest an appropriate volume or, more likely, a computerized index.

Although printed bibliographies are losing ground to up-to-date electronic indexes and databases, they are still available on many subjects. In addition, the bibliographies you'll find at the back of scholarly books, articles, and dissertations may prove invaluable. For one thing, they represent a selective look at a field, usually compiled by an expert, not by a search engine. Always check whether a scholarly work you are using includes a bibliography.

Only a few of the hundreds of bibliographic resources in specific disciplines are listed below.

CHECKLIST
Bibliographies

DOING A PROJECT ON . . . ?	CHECK THIS BIBLIOGRAPHY . . .
American history	*Bibliographies in American History*
Anthropology	*Anthropological Bibliographies: A Selected Guide*
Art	*Guide to the Literature of Art History*
Astronomy	*A Guide to the Literature of Astronomy; Astronomy and Astrophysics: A Bibliographic Guide*
Classics	*Greek and Roman Authors: A Checklist of Criticism*
Communications	*Communication: A Guide to Information Sources*
Engineering	*Science and Engineering Literature*
Literature	*MLA International Bibliography*
Mathematics	*Using the Mathematical Literature*
Music	*Music Reference and Research Materials*
Philosophy	*A Bibliography of Philosophical Bibliographies*
Physics	*Use of Physics Literature*
Psychology	*Harvard List of Books in Psychology*
Social work	*Social Work Education: A Bibliography*

6d Locate suitable indexes to search the periodical literature

Indexes list many useful items that cannot be recorded in a library catalog: journal articles, magazine pieces, and stories from newspapers, for instance. Such material is called the *periodical literature* on a subject. You shouldn't undertake any college-level research paper without surveying this rich body of information. For example, if you wished to explore the subject of school vouchers, you'd likely want information from magazines such as *Newsweek* and *US News and World Report* and newspapers such as *The New*

York Times and *The Washington Times.* To find such information, you would go to indexes, not traditional library catalogs.

In the past, all periodical indexes were printed works, and you may still need to rely on such helpful volumes to find older sources. For more current materials, however, you'll likely use electronic indexes. These powerful search tools may even be supplemented by databases (electronic storehouses of information) that provide not only the bibliographical facts on an article—who published it, where, and when—but even abstracts of the pieces. Some electronic resources furnish the full texts of news stories, magazine articles, literary works, and historical documents to print out or download to your computer (depending on copyright rules).

Ordinarily you can get access to indexes in your library reference room. Electronic tools may also be available via online library catalogs or Web sites. You owe it to yourself to learn how to use these resources, especially those designed for your academic major. Most indexes, printed or electronic, are relatively easy to manage—provided that you read the explanatory information that typically accompanies them.

Electronic indexes usually support title, author, or keyword searches (see Chapter 7), but they may also permit searching by other "fields"—that is, the categories by which data is entered. For example, a database may be searchable not only by author and title but also by publisher, place of publication, subject heading, accession number, government document number, and so on. Powerful indexes and databases such as *LEXIS-NEXIS* may require special commands and search techniques.

You may want to start periodical searches with general and multidisciplinary indexes such as the following.

> *ArticleFirst* (electronic)
>
> *CARL Uncover* (electronic)
>
> *Expanded Academic ASAP* (electronic)
>
> *Periodical Abstracts* (electronic)
>
> *Readers' Guide to Periodical Literature* (print)
>
> *Readers' Guide Abstracts* (electronic)

But all major academic fields have individual indexes for their periodical literature, most of them computerized. Because new indexes may be added to a library's collection at any time, check with your reference librarian about the best sources for any given subject and how to access them.

CHECKLIST
Indexes and Databases

Doing a project on . . . ?	Check this index . . .
Anthropology	*Anthropological Literature*
Architecture	*Avery Index*

Art	*Art Abstracts*
Biography	*Biography Index*
Biology	*Biological and Agricultural Abstracts; BIOSIS Previews*
Business	*Business Periodicals Index; ABI/Inform*
Chemistry	*CAS*
Computer science	*Computer Literature Index*
Current affairs	*LEXIS-NEXIS*
Economics	*PAIS (Public Affairs Information Service); EconLit*
Education	*Education Index; ERIC (Educational Resources Information Center)*
Engineering	*INSPEC*
Film	*Film Index International; Art Index*
History	*Historical Abstracts; America: History and Life*
Humanities	*Francis; Humanities Abstracts; Humanities Index*
Law	*LegalTrac*
Literature	*Essay and General Literature Index; MLA Bibliography; Contemporary Authors*
Mathematics	*MathSciNet*
Medicine	*MEDLINE*
Music	*Music Index; RILM Abstracts of Music*
Philosophy	*Philosopher's Index*
Psychology	*Psychological Abstracts; PsycLit; PsycINFO*
Public affairs	*PAIS*
Physics	*INSPEC*
Religion	*ATLA Religion Database*
Science	*General Science Index; General Science Abstracts*
Social sciences	*Social Science and Humanities Index; Social Sciences Index; Social Sciences Abstracts*
Technology	*Applied Science and Technology Abstracts*
Women	*Contemporary Women's Issues*

Here is some advice for searching an electronic index or database.

❏ You may be able to search some electronic databases remotely, from home or from terminals in open-use labs; other databases may be available only on certain library terminals or on CD-ROM. Many electronic indexes and databases may require you to enter your library or student ID number for access. Check with your reference librarian for details.

❑ Be sure you are logged on to the right index. A library terminal may provide access to several different databases or indexes. Find the one appropriate for your subject.

❑ Read the description of the index to find out how to access its information. Not all databases and indexes work the same way.

❑ When searching by keyword, check whether a list of subject headings is available. Match your search terms to those on the list before you begin. You'll save time.

❑ Try synonyms if your initial keyword search turns up too few items.

6e Check the World Wide Web

The World Wide Web is a hypertext pathway into the vast resources of the Internet. Web browser software such as Netscape *Navigator* or *Internet Explorer* presents information via "pages" that can contain text, graphics, and sound as well as hypertext links; the browsers also support email, Usenet newsgroups, and other forms of electronic communication. The Web can distribute just about any information that fits on a screen, including photo archives, artwork, maps, film clips, charts, and magazines. Web users move through different "sites" by selecting words or graphics linked to other related resources.

You must understand, however, that the Web is not a library. It has not been systematically designed to support research, so you cannot apply the same research techniques or assume that what you find there is reliable. What goes online is not routinely cataloged, edited, or reviewed, so the quality of information on the Web varies greatly and its organization can be chaotic. As a result, you must approach the Web with caution when you use it as a tool for research. You may quickly find superb and up-to-date information on your subject, or you may struggle to locate material that proves unreliable, malicious, biased, and wrong. In short, you need to appply critical skills to survey Web sites for information. (See Chapter 11 for much more advice about evaluating all types of sources.)

Once you have been introduced to the resources of the World Wide Web, you'll appreciate the need for search engines and directories—tools that help you cull particular information from the hundreds of millions of Web pages now online. Such guides, constantly refined and upgraded, are readily available—just click the "Search" button on your Web browser. But you have to use them properly. Among the best known are the following.

About.com	http://home.about.com/index.htm
AltaVista	http://www.altavista.digital.com/
AOL Netfind	http://www.aol.com/netfind
Ask Jeeves	http://www.askjeeves.com/

Excite	http://www.excite.com/
Google	http://www.google.com/
HotBot	http://www.hotbot.com/
InferenceFind	http://www.inference.com/
LookSmart	http://www.looksmart.com/
Lycos	http://www.lycos.com/
WebCrawler	http://webcrawler.com/
Yahoo!	http://www.yahoo.com/

Most search engine sites include online guides to both basic and advanced search techniques. Take a few minutes to read such "help" files to discover the remarkable and changing features of these highly competitive tools.

The basic tool of most search engines is the keyword search. For keyword search strategies, see Chapter 7.

Some Web directories such as *Yahoo!* also enable you to search the Web by categories. The *Yahoo!* opening screen presents a series of general categories that may narrow down to the topic you hope to explore. You begin with the first tier of categories.

Arts	News and Media
Business and Economy	Recreation and Sports
Computers and Internet	Reference
Education	Regional
Entertainment	Science
Government	Social Science
Health	Society and Culture

When you select a topic, subtopics appear. "Education," for example, divides into more than three dozen major subtopics and many minor ones; in effect, *Yahoo!* breaks the category down and offers additional topics for exploration. It also provides links for current news (in this case, relating to education), for education indexes, and for current online chats and programs. So *Yahoo!* is a tool that supports both research and the potential for interactive dialogue.

There are two points you should understand: (1) Web engines and directories all work a little differently and have different strengths and weaknesses, so you should explore your subject on more than one search engine to see what turns up. (2) Web search engines and directories may have huge databases with access to tens of millions of documents and Web pages, but there is no guarantee that any search engine will cover everything available on the Internet. Every engine is selective in how and what it covers. So explore your subject using more than one engine. Even searching on a different day can often return different results. Sites may be down temporarily, and new sites are constantly added and old ones deleted.

Commercial Web search engines aren't the only resource for finding information and links on the Web. Hundreds of reference sites have been created by libraries, universities, and government institutions with more scholarly intentions. Here are just a few places to look. (Be aware that Web addresses change frequently for many sources; check our Web site at http://www.awlonline.com/researchcentral for updates.)

Argus Clearinghouse	http://www.clearinghouse.net/
Books on the Internet	http://www.lib.utexas.edu/Libs/PCL/Etext.html
English Server (CMU)	http://eserver.org
Infomine	http://lib-www.ucr.edu/
InfoSurf	http://www.library.ucsb.edu/subj/resource.html
Internet Public Library	http://www.ipl.org/
Knowledge Source (SIRS)	http://www.sirs.com/tree/tree.htm
Library of Congress Subject Guide to Internet Resources	http://lcweb.loc.gov/global/subject.html
SunSite	http://sunsite.berkeley.edu/InternetIndex/
The Universal Library	http://www.ul.cs.cmu.edu/
Voice of the Shuttle	http://humanitas.ucsb.edu/

For more such search engines and directories, check out *Yahoo!'s Searching the Web* at http://www.yahoo.com/Computers_and_Internet/Internet/World_Wide_Web/Searching_the_Web. There are also many commercial software packages that can search the Net even while you sleep. Of course, no search engine or software can guarantee it will find sources that are authoritative and relevant to your topic. But you can make searches more productive and less daunting by deciding where you will search, specifying a time for the search, and deciding in what form you want to receive your information.

Decide where you will search. Many search engines allow you to limit a keyword search to a specific *domain* or document type on the Internet. These are filter options you may want to exercise, depending on your research project. For example, the WWW search engine *snap.com* allows you to make any of the following choices.

Search by domain (.com, .edu)

Search by media type (audio, image, Java)

Search by extension (.gif, .txt)

Search by country

Search by language

You could, of course, search the entire WWW to find information about a current event, but you might choose the image option instead if you are looking for visual texts related to your subject. Or if you wanted to explore what educators are saying about your subject, you'd obviously consider searching sites with an .edu domain. Perhaps you only want to search the top-level pages of Web sites to be sure your subject receives serious attention. You can select that option.

Search engines like *snap.com* even enable you to search by geographic locations. That means you could search, if you chose, only WWW materials on your subject from specific geographic areas (Europe, South America, Africa, etc.) or in specific languages.

Decide the time frame for your search. Many keyword searches can be limited to specific periods of time, ranging from years to just one day. Clearly, you can reduce the number of hits for a given keyword this way, making your work more efficient and timely.

But you can also use searches limited by time to discover who was thinking what, when. How often were terms such as *multiculturalism* or *partial-birth abortion* used five years ago? How often are they being used today? You could find out by using a time filter on a database such as *LEXIS-NEXIS*.

Decide how you want your information reported. With online library catalogs and electronic indexes, you can usually print out the information you want directly from the terminal screen or save the information to a disk. Sometimes you may have to select an individual item to get full bibliographic data.

With search engines on the WWW, you usually have options for reporting your hits—useful when the numbers of potential items are likely to be large. You can usually specify the number of hits the engine will report, from just a few to "all." Sometimes, too, you can have the reports on individual items in full or abstract form. Since you can easily get the full form if you need it, it often makes sense to start off asking just for the abstracts. The short listings fit on a screen more easily, too.

Finally, you may want to examine your results. Quite often the results will be reported with suggestions for additional searches or with a link marked "More like this." The search engine is suggesting other directions for your work.

6f Consult biographical resources

Often in preparing a research project, you'll need information about famous people, living and dead. Powerful sources are available to help you in the reference room. Good places to start are the *Biography Index: A Cumulative Index to Biographic Material in Books and Magazines; Bio-Base; LEXIS-NEXIS; Current Biography;* and *The McGraw-Hill Encyclopedia of World Biography.*

There are also various *Who's Who* volumes, covering living British, American, and world notables, as well as African Americans and women. Deceased figures may appear in *Who Was Who.* Probably the two most famous dictionaries of biography are the *Dictionary of National Biography* (British) and the *Dictionary of American Biography.*

On the World Wide Web, you might check out the database maintained by the A&E program *Biography* at http://www.biography.com. For the wisdom of famous people, see the Web version of the 1910 edition of *Bartlett's Familiar Quotations* at http://www.columbia.edu/acis/bartleby/bartlett or, for more recent remarks, *The Quotation Page* at http://www.starlingtech.com/quotes. To search for private individuals, you can use features such as *Yahoo!'s* "People Search" on the World Wide Web. It provides addresses and phone numbers with almost frightening ease.

CHECKLIST

Biographical Information

YOUR SUBJECT IS IN . . . ?	CHECK THIS SOURCE . . .
Art	*Index to Artistic Biography*
Education	*Biographical Dictionary of American Educators*
Music	*The New Grove Dictionary of Music and Musicians*
Politics	*Politics in America; Almanac of American Politics*
Psychology	*Biographical Dictionary of Psychology*
Religion	*Dictionary of American Religious Biography*
Science	*Dictionary of Scientific Biography*

YOUR SUBJECT IS . . . ?	CHECK THIS SOURCE . . .
African	*Dictionary of African Biography*
African American	*Dictionary of American Negro Biography*
Asian	*Encyclopedia of Asian History*
Australian	*Australian Dictionary of Biography*
Canadian	*Dictionary of Canadian Biography*
Female	*Index to Women; Notable American Women*
Mexican American	*Mexican American Biographies; Chicano Scholars and Writers: A Bibliographic Directory*

6g Consult guides to reference works

The reference room in most libraries is filled with helpful materials. But how do you know what the best books are for your needs? Ask your reference librarian whether guides to the literature for your topic are available, or check the reference section using the call number that you used to locate circulating books.

LIBRARY OF CONGRESS CLASSIFICATION SYSTEM

A	General Works
B	Philosophy, Psychology, Religion
C–F	History
G	Geography, Anthropology
H	Social Sciences, Business
J	Political Science
K	U.S. Law

L	Education
M	Music
N	Fine Arts
P	Language and Literature
Q	Mathematics, Science
R	Medicine
S	Agriculture
T	Technology, Engineering
U	Military Science
V	Naval Science
Z	Bibliography, Library Science

Also useful in some situations are printed or electronic indexes that list all books currently available (that is, books that are in print), their publishers, and their prices. Updated frequently, such indexes include *Books in Print* (print or electronic) and *Paperbound Books in Print.*

6h Locate statistics

Statistics about every imaginable topic are available in library reference rooms and online. Be sure to find up-to-date and reliable figures.

CHECKLIST
Statistics

TO FIND ...	CHECK THIS SOURCE ...
General statistics	*World Almanac; Current Index to Statistics* (electronic)
Statistics about the United States	*Historical Statistics of the United States; Statistical Abstract of the United States; Stat USA* (electronic); *GPO Access* (electronic)
World information	*The Statesman's Yearbook; National Intelligence Factbook; UN Demographic Yearbook; UNESCO Statistical Yearbook*
Business facts	*Handbook of Basic Economic Statistics; Survey of Current Business; Dow Jones–Irwin Business Almanac*
Public opinion polls	*Gallup Poll*
Census data	*Census 1990* (electronic)

Also consult resources such as *CyberTimes Navigator* at http://www.nytimes.com/
library/tech/reference/cynavi.html, *The Internet Public Library* at http://ipl.sils.umich
.edu/ref/RR/ or *On-line Reference Works* at http://www.cs.cmu.edu/references.html.
Even *The Old Farmer's Almanac* is on the Web at http://www. almanac.com. Commercial online services such as America Online or Prodigy may offer access to additional reference sources.

6i Check news sources

Sometimes you'll need information from newspapers, particularly when your subject is
current and your aim argumentative or persuasive. For information before about 1995,
you'll have to rely on printed papers or microfilm copies since electronic newspapers
and news services are a more recent phenomenon. If you know the date of a particular
event, however, you can usually locate the information you want. If your subject isn't
an event, you may have to trace it through an index. Only a few printed papers are fully
indexed. The one newspaper you are most likely to encounter in most American libraries is *The New York Times,* usually available on microfilm. *The New York Times Index* provides chronological summaries of articles on a given subject. A second U.S. paper with an index is *The Wall Street Journal.*

A useful reference tool for more recent events is *NewsBank,* an index available since
1982 in electronic format. It covers more than 400 newspapers from across the country,
keyed to a microfiche collection. *Facts on File* summarizes national and international
news weekly; *CQ Researcher* gives background information on major problems and controversies. To report on what editors are thinking, examine *Editorials on File,* a sampling of world and national opinion.

For very current events, you can search hundreds of newspapers and news services
online. Online news resources worth consulting include the following.

CNN Interactive	http://www.cnn.com
C-SPAN Online	http://www.c-span.org
Fox News	http://www.foxnews.com
London Times	http://www.the-times.co.uk/news/pages/Times/
MSNBC	http://www.msnbc.com/news
National Public Radio	http://www.npr.org
The New York Times	http://www.nytimes.com
Reuters	http://www.reuters.com/reutersnews/
USA Today News	http://www.usatoday.com
The Wall Street Journal	http://www.wsj.com
The Washington Times	http://www.washtime.com/

A directory such as *Yahoo!* at http://www.yahoo.com/News_and_Media/Newspapers
can point you to hundreds of online newspapers of every sort. You may have to register
to use some of these sites.

Another important online resource is the *ClariNet* news service, which you can find among the newsgroups on Web browsers. Some schools now offer a useful Web version of *LEXIS-NEXIS* that you may find helpful, especially with topics currently in the news.

6j Check book and film reviews

To locate reviews of books, see *Book Review Digest* (1905), *Book Review Index* (1965), or *Current Book Review Citations* (1976). *Book Review Digest* does not list as many reviews as the other two collections, but it summarizes those it does include—a useful feature. Many electronic periodical indexes also catalog book reviews, including *Academic Periodical Index* (1988) and *Readers' Guide to Periodical Literature* (1983).

For film reviews and criticism, see the printed volumes *Film Review Index* (1986) or *Film Criticism: An Index to Critics' Anthologies* (1975) as well as the electronic *Film Index International.*

6k Join in electronic conversations

Some online resources have no print equivalent: they represent ongoing discussions about ideas or work in progress. You will find such resources on the Internet's Usenet newsgroups and listserv discussion groups. You may have interactions in other electronic forums as well; in MOOs you can interact within imaginary environments, or with local networking software such as Daedalus *InterChange* you can join a class discussion held online.

CHECKLIST
Listservs

A listserv is a type of mail program that maintains lists of subscribers interested in discussing a specific topic. Users must subscribe in order to read or post messages.

Major characteristics: Lists are run on large computers; many subscribers are experts working in fields related to the list topic. Lists are often moderated to screen out irrelevant material or "noise." Old messages may be archived.

Use for: Excellent window on current issues. Good for listening in on the practitioners' conversations, discovering opinions, noting solutions to common problems, and learning about other available print or online resources.

Searching: When you subscribe, check the welcome message for instructions for searching the archives.

CHECKLIST
Usenet Newsgroups

A Usenet group works like a listserv except that you need not subscribe to the list either to read its messages or to participate in the discussion.

Major characteristics: Thousands of groups focus on topics from *A* to *Z.* There is wide variation in the expertise of contributors. Anyone may read or post messages. Just browsing the list of Usenet groups can suggest topic ideas.

Use for: Conversations about popular topics and about little-known, obscure subjects. Almost every political group, social interest, religion, activity, hobby, and fantasy has a Usenet group.

Searching: Check the welcome messages and the FAQs (frequently asked questions) for information on how to search. Many lists have archives of older discussions.

Usenet groups, listservs, and similar tools can furnish you with interactive and up-to-the-second information on a topic from many points of view. These electronic conversations may introduce you to experts on your subject from all over the world or to knowledgeable amateurs—or to people simply blowing steam. They offer you the chance to question people actually doing the research or living the experiences you are writing about. But you must be very careful when you take factual information from such environments: make it a habit to confirm any statistic, fact, or claim from such a source with information from a second and different type of authority—a book, an article, a reference work.

Some Web search engines now cover Usenet groups so that you can find and even join online conversations on your topic if such a discussion group exists. (To find older archived newsgroup materials, see *Deja.com* at **http://www.deja.com**.) Usenet groups can help you give a dialogic dimension to a project, placing your own work within an existing community of thought.

These interactive sources can provide a close-up view of your subject. But keep the bigger picture in mind too. Rely on more traditional resources—journals, books, encyclopedias—to keep the full subject in perspective and to balance other individual and idiosyncratic points of view you may find online.

61 Write or email professional organizations

Almost every subject, cause, concept, or idea is represented by a professional organization, society, bureau, office, or lobby. So it makes good sense to write or email an appropriate organization for information on your topic; ask for pamphlets, leaflets, reports, and so on. Many organizations offer detailed information on their Web sites. For mailing addresses of organizations, consult *The Encyclopedia of Associations,* published by Gale Research. Use a search engine to find Web sites.

Also remember that the U.S. government publishes huge amounts of information on just about every subject of public interest. Check the *U.S. Government Periodicals Index* or the *Monthly Catalog of U.S. Government Publications* for listings. Or use a Web site such as *Fedworld Information Network* at http://www.fedworld.gov to look for the material you need.

GETTING INVOLVED

1. Take a tour of your college library or research facility, especially if it is significantly larger than any library you have used before. Many larger libraries have brochures describing their resources and services. Some may offer tours, either self-guided or led by library staff.

2. Use the resources of your library to prepare a brief report about the week of your birth. Use newspapers, magazines, books, and any other resources to find information to help convey what the week was like. Don't limit your account just to news events. Find out what you can about the popular culture of the time—check the ads, movie reviews, sports pages, even the comics.

3. Working in a group, use the resources of the reference room to prepare a fact sheet or pamphlet on your city, town, or college or on a prominent local institution. Imagine that the brochure might be distributed in a packet given to newcomers. Decide first what information might be useful (for example, population data, the average cost of a three-bedroom home, average temperatures) and then find it.

4. Check out the Web directory *Yahoo!* and examine the way it categorizes information. Choose several subjects and then see how long it takes you to find information using only the listings of subjects. (In other words, don't use the keyword search function.)

5. In class, come up with a list of five or ten barely famous people. (These should be individuals of some accomplishment who are not household names.) Then assign teams to find out basic biographical facts about the lives of these individuals—everything from their places of birth and birth dates to the names of their children.

MANAGING YOUR PROJECT

1. Explore your subject in your library's catalog. Begin by looking specifically for books on your subject.

2. Try to locate a bibliography particularly suited to your subject. The more spe-

cific the bibliography, the better. But don't ignore the general bibliographies available in many fields.

3. Make a list of the indexes that you must consult for your project. Then spend a few minutes learning to use these tools. A little time spent reading about how these indexes work may save you a great deal of time later.

4. Explore your topic on the Web using a directory such as *Yahoo!* Do the categories in the directory point you to topic areas you hadn't considered?

5. Explore your topic on the Web using a search engine. But first come up with keywords that will help to both identify and narrow your subject. (For help, see Chapter 7.)

The Phoenician alphabet was introduced to Greece in the ninth or tenth century BCE. But it wasn't until the late eighth century BCE that Greek books, in the form of scrolls, became common. The production of books depended on a ready supply of papyrus (a trade good from Egypt) and on scribes who laboriously wrote the texts by hand. (Several scribes are pictured here in this nineteenth-century wood engraving.) To write, the Greeks used a thick reed pen, a knife for sharpening the pens, pumice for smoothing the papyrus, and a sponge for erasing. The scribes seem not to have employed the sponge frequently, to judge from the many mistakes in their texts. Likely, the scribes used their sponges to "erase" entire texts in order to reuse the papyrus for a new work.

Many of the Greek scribes worked in the library at Alexandria (see tabbed divider 1, p. 41) where they were paid by the line and according to the quality of their script. Some scribes likely worked on cataloging the scrolls by subject, a way of classifying information. Today, the principle behind that original Alexandrian catalog is still evident in the online catalogs we search routinely.

◎ DON'T MISS . . .

- **The explanation of keyword and Boolean searches in Chapter 7.** You need to understand how keyword searches operate to use them effectively. Boolean searches enable you to focus your research on the Web and reduce the number of useless "hits."

- **The discussion of field research in Chapter 8.** Not all research involves finding out what other people have said. Sometimes you will have to conduct your own surveys or interviews.

- **Important suggestions in Chapter 9 to help you keep track of what you find.** Whether you use note cards or electronic databases, you will want to organize your search materials.

BOOKMARKS: Web Sites Worth Knowing

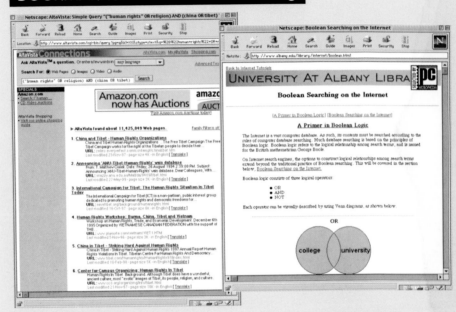

"Boolean Searching on the Internet,"
http://www.albany.edu/library/internet/boolean.html

For information on how to get the most out of search engines on the Web, try the simply designed but powerful guide "Boolean Searching on the Internet" (shown at right). It's an easy-to-follow tutorial that demonstrates how to use Boolean operators to find precisely what you're looking for on the Web. Each Internet search engine uses Boolean operators in slightly different ways, and this site makes the differences between the search engines easy to understand and remember. The screen shot on the left shows how you can use Boolean logic to narrow a search with *AltaVista*.

Additional Sites
Search Engine Watch, "News, Tips and More About Search Engines,"
    http://www.searchenginewatch.com/
The Spider's Apprentice, "Tips on Searching the Web," http://www.monash.com/spidap.html
The RSCC Online Writing Lab, "Tips for Interviewers,"
    http://www2.rscc.cc.tn.us/~jordan_jj/OWL/Interview2.html
The Purdue University Writing Lab, "Note-take Effectively,"
    http://owl.english:purdue.edu/Files/132/5c-notes.html

Doing Keyword Searches

You need to know how to perform efficient keyword searches to explore many basic research resources, such as online library catalogs, electronic indexes, and the Internet. A keyword search is simply a scan of an electronic text or database that locates a given word or phrase in the text of the file or in a list of keywords designated by the author or publisher. When you use the "find" feature of a word processor, you are performing a simple keyword search. Increase the power of this technique and apply it to much larger databases and you have a *search engine,* one of the fastest-developing of contemporary research tools. Such engines can seek not only the word(s) you've specified but related terms and phrases as well.

Perhaps the best advice we can give you for performing a keyword search is to read the instructions for the tool you are using, whether an electronic catalog, a search engine, or a directory. (A search engine searches Web pages on its own; a directory is a database of Web pages compiled by people.) Keyword searches are all similar in some respects, but the rules and "filters" that control any given system will differ. Your ability to focus a search and get the best results depends on knowing how to direct that search. You'll be surprised by the sophistication of some search engines, particularly those on the World Wide Web (see Section 6e), which seem, at times, to anticipate your needs. But you can waste time if you ignore the information waiting beneath "Help," "Simple Search," or "Advanced Search" buttons on the screen.

One other tip: Be sure to type keywords carefully, especially proper nouns. A misspelled search term can prevent you from finding available information.

7a Understand how a simple keyword search works

A keyword search identifies the files in a catalog or database that contain the keyword(s) you have typed into a box or line on the screen. A librarian or instructor may be helpful in guiding you toward appropriate keywords for your searches.

Or you can use research tools themselves creatively to find powerful keywords. For example, when searching a library catalog, always look for cross listings for your particular subject—that is, other terms under which your subject is entered. Follow up on

When doing keyword searches on electronic databases, be ingenious and persistent. Some preliminary reading on your topic may suggest helpful synonyms for your search term. Learn to use Boolean searches too. An effective Boolean search may reduce the number of worthless hits you receive in your search.

those suggestions. So, for example, if your project on Civil War ironclad ships leads you to search with the term "Monitor" (the name of a famous Union ship), a particular catalog entry might include cross listings such as these: "Civil War"; "Merrimac"; "U.S. Navy, history"; "Ericsson, John." You could then probe the catalog using each of these new terms.

You will have to be ingenious and dogged at times in choosing keywords for Web searches. For example, if you need to know whether alcohol is legally considered a drug, you could begin with general keywords such as "alcohol" or "drugs." But you'd be swamped by the number of responses—and you might never find the particular information you needed. Here is where a little preliminary reading might pay off (see Section 3c). If you learn that drugs are regulated by the Federal Drug Administration, you could try searching with that term or, even better, its familiar acronym: FDA. Once you locate the FDA's official site on the Web, you could then search it for "alcohol" to find the information you were seeking. "FDA" might not have been the first term to come to mind when you started your exploration, but it is a logical keyword, given the information you were seeking.

So the keywords you choose—whether names, places, titles, concepts, or people—will shape your search. A comparatively small database, such as an online library catalog, may ask you to indicate whether a word you are searching is a title (t), author (a), subject (s), or some other type of term the system recognizes. In such cases, typing a title (*Master and Commander*), the name of an author (Patrick O'Brian), or a narrow subject keyword (Napoleonic wars) will often produce manageable numbers of items to examine and read.

t (title)	*Master and Commander*	8 items
a (author)	Patrick O'Brian	26 items
s (subject)	Napoleonic wars	25 items

You could easily look at all the items that appeared either on the computer screen or the printout resulting from this simple search. So a simple keyword search may be adequate when the database you are exploring is small or the term you are searching is distinctive.

However, as we have suggested, a simple search of the same items on the World Wide Web, a huge database, might overwhelm you.

Master and Commander	1,230,000 items
Patrick O'Brian	910,000 items
Napoleonic wars	227,000 items

Similarly, even typing a narrowed subject listing into an online library catalog may provide too many items for you to read and research.

Naval history	1,800 items

In these situations, you need more sophisticated search techniques. One such technique is called Boolean searching.

7b Understand the principles of Boolean searching

When you do a Boolean search, you are actually doing two or more searches simultaneously and studying the point where those searches overlap. Most search engines in online catalogs, databases, and Web browsers use some form of Boolean searching. You control a Boolean search through a set of specific terms or symbols.

For example, by linking keywords with the term AND, you can search for more than one term at a time, identifying only those items in which the separate terms intersect. It may help to visualize these items in terms of sets.

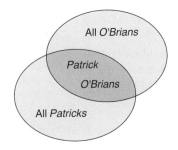

You initiate a Boolean search in different ways. One way is to insert AND between terms you wish to search.

Patrick AND O'Brian

miniature AND schnauzer AND training

Washington AND Jefferson AND Constitution

Another is to select an appropriate command from the search engine, such as *HotBot*'s "all the words" option. Asking the engine to search for only those items in which all the words you've specified occur usually reduces the information glut, but sometimes not enough to make the results manageable.

Master and Commander	from 1,230,000 to 34,000 items
Patrick O'Brian	from 910,000 to 65,700 items
Napoleonic wars	from 227,000 to 3,400 items

You can, of course, further refine a Boolean search simply by increasing the number of search terms—the more specific the better. Consider what happens when you add "Great Britain" to an earlier online library catalog search, "naval history."

Great Britain naval history   from 1,800 to 450 items

Or look at what happens when we specify O'Brian's profession, using *HotBot's* "all the words" filter on the WWW.

Novelist Patrick O'Brian   642 items

At this point, the logic of the *Hotbot* search engine is also helping us, trying to figure out which of the more than 600 items might be most helpful. As it turns out, the resulting search still produces no first-rate material. But that's not unusual in Web searches. You have to keep plugging away.

Other Boolean commands allow you to direct database searches in different ways.

OR   Using OR between keywords directs the search engine to find any examples of either keyword. Using OR might widen a search, but it would also allow you to locate all documents that cover related concepts.

> dog OR puppy
> Congress OR Senate

NOT   Using NOT between terms permits you to specify sites with one term but not another. This may be useful when you want to exclude certain meanings of a term irrelevant to your search.

> Indians NOT Cleveland
> apple NOT computer
> republican NOT party

( )   Putting items in parentheses allows for additional fine tuning of a search. In the first example below, you could locate documents that mentioned either Senator Gramm or Senator Hutchison but not Senator Kennedy or Senator Hatch.

> Senator AND (Gramm OR Hutchison)
> church NOT (Mormon OR Catholic)
> pickup NOT (Ford OR Dodge)

Some search engines use + and − signs to select the same functions.

+   Putting + (a plus sign) immediately before an item, without a space, indicates that the word following it *must* be in the document being sought. Let's say, for example, you are looking on the WWW for definitions of terms. You might format the requests this way.

> +wetlands +definition
> +"sports car" +"definition of"

−   Putting − (a minus sign) immediately before an item, without a space, indicates that the word following it *must not* be in the document being sought. Let's say you wanted to search for documents about Richard Nixon that didn't discuss Watergate or China. You could format the request this way.

+Nixon −Watergate −China

7c Refine your electronic search

To narrow a WWW search even more, you can search for a specific and distinctive phrase either by placing it between quotation marks or selecting the "exact phrase" option on a search screen. This technique is essential for Web research. Type "novels of Patrick O'Brian" into the search engine *AltaVista,* and it hunts its vast database for only those sites where that phrase occurs in its entirety. The narrowing is dramatic.

novels of Patrick O'Brian   17 items

And this time, those items include a Patrick O'Brian Web page, a newsletter, and, best of all, a list of other O'Brian links that leads to a newsletter index and a mailing list for online conversation about O'Brian's maritime novels.

You can use exact phrase searches creatively in many different ways. If you can't recall who is responsible for a particular expression or quotation, for example, "defining deviancy down," you can make it the subject of an exact phrase search on the WWW. Do so in the Web directory *Yahoo!* and you'll quickly find the expression attributed to Senator Daniel Patrick Moynihan, in the very first item located by a search of that directory.

You can also combine exact word searches with various Boolean commands to find precisely what you need if you can identify appropriate keywords.

"Ten Commandments" AND ("Charlton Heston" OR "Yul Brynner")

"pickup truck" NOT (Ford OR Dodge)

Some databases allow you to refine searches further by language or by publication type. The potential of such searches is limited only by your imagination and the speed of your modem or online connection.

As with mathematical equations, there is a distinct order of operations in Boolean searching: Boolean operations are evaluated from the left to the right, with operations in parentheses evaluated first. Make sure you read the directions for the particular software or search engine you are using, and experiment with it until you feel confident.

7d Evaluate your electronic search

With search engines and directories, you can get results quickly and determine whether (or how) new material illuminates your chosen subject: did you receive the results you expected or something quite different? Don't be satisfied with your initial searches, even when they supply ample information. Another combination of keywords or a different search path might provide still better material.

Each time you search and get an unexpected response, ask yourself why. Ideas may be hidden under synonyms of the word you searched. If the first try doesn't work, look for clues in the results you receive (or don't receive). Check spellings and try synonyms. Don't give up.

7e Keep a record of your search

Probably the most important research strategy of all is keeping track of your work—not only the potential sources you locate but also the search terms you have used. This way, you will be able to locate information again if necessary later in the research process, by using the same search strings.

Many WWW sources can be found quite simply by guessing. Often the domain name of a source includes the name of a familiar company or organization. For example, *CNN Interactive* can be found at http://www.cnn.com; the White House home page is at http://www.whitehouse.gov.

Sometimes you can find different information about your subject just by moving "up" the directory tree of a Web site address. For example, the Electronic Frontiers Foundation site offers links that provide an overview on the issue of intellectual property—a matter of concern to many writers today. Here is the address of that site.

> http://www.eff.org/pub/Intellectual_property/HTML/
> ip-overview.html

But you can find more specific information about copyright issues simply by trimming the original address to the following.

> http://www.eff.org/pub/Intellectual_property

And moving up the tree still further takes you to the main page for the organization as well as to links for related topics such as free speech and privacy.

> http://www.eff.org

So you can mine an electronic address to see what it has to offer. That's why it helps to understand something about the *domain names* of electronic addresses (see Section 12a).

Keeping track of any sources you find along the way in a project can also help you if your topic later develops in directions you had not anticipated. In the WWW browser Netscape *Navigator,* you can use your "Bookmarks" file to store the addresses of potentially useful sites you have visited. In Microsoft's *Internet Explorer,* you can store addresses in your "Favorites" file. Or use the "copy" and "paste" features available in most software applications to save information accurately, either printing it out (with all relevant bibliographical information) or saving files to a disk. If you have access to a database program, you may want to use it to compile your list of sources. And don't overlook the value of handwritten note cards that allow you to shuffle and organize your sources to fit your project.

For more about keeping track of your sources, see Chapter 9.

GETTING INVOLVED

1. Try out your local library's electronic catalog. What kinds of searches does it permit? What different kinds of library materials will it search? What limits can you place on searches?

2. Choose a database you expect to consult often in your college career, and locate the documentation that explains how to use it. Explore the database, using this search information until you feel confident enough to explain its functions to another user.

3. Compare two different Web search engines. First read all you can about the search engines. The home page of a site will usually offer you links to various options, including documentation on how to use the site, search options available, and suggestions for how to use the engine. Compare the features of the site.

   Then choose some keywords related to a subject that interests you and type them into the two search engines. Compare the kinds of results you get: the number of hits, how the hits are reported, how the hits are classified, the quality of the hits. Report your findings to classmates and compare your conclusions with theirs.

MANAGING YOUR PROJECT

1. Describe your project to your reference librarian, asking him or her to suggest appropriate *descriptors* for your subject (terms by which your subject might be described in catalogs and databases).

2. Begin the exploration of your subject in the library catalog. In every preliminary item you find, check for other subject listings under which your topic is cataloged. Use these new terms as keywords for additional searches.

3. Consider different combinations of keywords that might help you narrow your search. Or vary the forms of words by which you are searching.

   alcohol → alcoholism → alcoholic
   democracy → democratic
   "moon shot" → "moon landing" → "Apollo 11"
   "House of Representatives → "US House" → Congress
   "Lyndon B. Johnson" → LBJ → "President Johnson"

4. Explore your subject with at least two different Web search engines or directories. Keep track of the tools you use and the search terms you try. Use the tools to narrow your search as necessary. Be sure to note what it is you are searching: complete Web sites, just the headings of Web pages, newsgroups, recent postings, and so on.

5. Begin to assemble your preliminary bibliography. Create note cards for printed sources you consider valuable. Also create note cards for important online material. Immediately print out or download any useful material from newsgroups or listservs; this material might not be available next time you look for it. Keep track of all bibliographical data, including the date of access for electronic items. (The date of access is simply the day on which you examined an electronic source.)

6. Create a special "Bookmarks" or "Favorites" file for pages and sites from the World Wide Web you expect to visit again. You can organize this file in various ways, grouping related items and even annotating them.

Conducting Field Research

Although much college research occurs in the library or online, some of your projects may lead you to seek information on your own through interviews, surveys, and close observation. Such *fieldwork* is particularly common in disciplines such as psychology, anthropology, and education; if you are pursuing degrees in these areas, you'll likely learn formal techniques for field research. But informal fieldwork can be useful in other, less rigid research situations provided that you describe your procedures accurately and properly qualify your conclusions. Here we'll look briefly at conducting interviews, using questionnaires, and making observations.

8a Conduct interviews

Sometimes people are the best sources of information. If you can discuss your subject with an expert, you'll add credibility, authenticity, and immediacy to a research report. If you are writing a paper about an aspect of medical care, talk to a medical professional. When exploring the financial dilemmas of community theaters, try to interview

Successful field research relies on communication with the appropriate subjects and authorities. The best interviews are face-to-face dialogues, but email, newsgroups, and listservs also provide valuable opportunities for conversation with research subjects and experts.

a local producer or theater manager. If writing about problems in the building industry, find a builder or banker with thirty minutes to spare.

Of course, it is now possible to consult with knowledgeable people via email, newsgroups, or listservs (see Section 6k). Although online chat tends to be less formal than face-to-face conversation, such queries still require appropriate preparation and courtesy. For a directory of experts willing to consult via email, check out *Pitsco's Ask an Expert* at http://www.askanexpert.com/ or *Find/SVP* at http://www.findsvp.com.

CHECKLIST
Conducting a One-on-One Interview

- Write or telephone your subject for an appointment, making clear why you want the interview.
- Confirm your appointment the day before, and be on time for your appointment.
- Be prepared for the meeting. Learn all you can about your subject's professional background, education, work history, and publications.
- Have a list of questions and possible follow-ups ready in your notebook. Establish the basic facts: *who? what? where? when? how? why?* Then, when appropriate, pose questions that require more than one-word answers.
- Focus your queries on your research question: don't wander from the subject.
- Take careful notes, especially if you intend to quote your source.
- Double-check direct quotations, and be sure your source is willing to be cited "on the record."
- If you plan to tape or log the interview, get your subject's approval first.
- Promise to send your subject a copy of your completed project.
- Send a thank-you note to an authority who has been especially helpful.

8b Conduct surveys

Research projects that focus on your local community may require surveys of public opinion and attitudes not available from other sources. So you may have to supply the information yourself by creating questionnaires and conducting studies. Yet polling is demanding, and even creating a useful questionnaire requires ingenuity. You'll have to work hard to produce research results that readers will respect. Still, the principles behind effective polls and surveys are not inscrutable.

To begin with, you should have a clear idea about the information you are seeking. In other words, you distribute questionnaires not to see what turns up but as a way of answering research questions you have already formulated: Do people on my do[rm] floor feel personally secure in their rooms? Would people in my neighborhood sup[port] the presence of a halfway house for juvenile offenders? Are people willing to pay add[i]tional taxes for improved public transportation?

You have to formulate good questions, whether you are simply gathering factual information or sampling public opinion. Asking the right question isn't easy. You don't want to skew the answers you get by posing vague, leading, or biased questions, such as the following.

VAGUE What do you think about dorm security?

REVISED What are your concerns (if any) about personal security in Aurelius Hall?

LEADING Are you in favor of the city's building a halfway house for juvenile criminals right in the middle of our peaceful Enfield neighborhood?

REVISED Do you favor the city's plan to build a halfway house for former juvenile offenders in the Enfield neighborhood?

BIASED Would you support yet another tax increase to fund a scheme for light rail in the city?

REVISED Would you support a 1-cent increase in the current sales tax to fund a light rail system for the city?

To make responses easy to tabulate, you will often want to provide readers with a range of options for answering your questions.

```
How do you feel about the following statements?

Respond using the appropriate number.

1  I disagree totally.

2  I disagree somewhat.

3  I neither agree nor disagree.

4  I agree somewhat.

5  I agree totally.


Our bus system serves the whole community.    _____

Our bus system operates efficiently.          _____

Our bus system runs on time.                   _____

Bus fares are too high.                         _____

A sales tax increase for buses makes sense.    _____
```

In addition to exploring your specific issues, you may want to gather demographic data on the people you are surveying; this information may be useful later in interpreting your findings. You must be able to protect the privacy of the people you survey and offer reasonable assurances that any information they volunteer will not be used against them in any way. But personal data can reveal surprising patterns, particularly when you are asking questions about political and social topics.

About you. Knowing a little about respondents to this survey will make interpretation of the data more significant. Please answer the following questions as best you can. Leave off any information you would rather not offer.

1. What is your gender?

    _____ M   _____ F

2. What is your marital status?

    _____ Married

    _____ Single, divorced/separated/widowed

    _____ Single, never married

3. What is your age?

    _____

4. What is your race or ethnicity?

    _____ Asian

    _____ Black/African American

    _____ Hispanic

    _____ White

    _____ Other

5. What is the highest level of your education?

    _____ elementary school or less

    _____ some high school

    _____ high school graduate

    _____ some college

    _____ college graduate

    _____ postgraduate or professional school

    _____ other

Try to anticipate the questions your own queries might raise in a respondent's mind. For example, the list of educational achievement might be puzzling to someone who went to a technical or trade school out of high school. The category of "other" often helps in doubtful cases.

Be sure you survey enough people from your target group so that readers will find your sample adequate. You ordinarily need to choose people at random for your survey, and yet those polled should represent a cross section of the whole population. Getting the right mix can be tricky. Surveying just your friends, just people who agree with you, or only people like yourself will almost certainly produce inadequate research.

You may have to provide an incentive to get people to cooperate with your survey. In most cases, this means suggesting that their responses may help to solve a problem or serve others in some way. J. D. Powers, the company famous for surveying new-car owners, sends a crisp dollar bill with its survey to thank potential respondents. You may not be able to go that far, but you do need to consider whether you can offer some incentive for a response, particularly when your survey is lengthy (as the J. D. Powers survey is).

Finally, you'll have to tabulate your findings accurately, present the results in a fashion that makes sense to readers, let readers know the techniques you used to gather your information, and, most important of all, report the limits of your study. Those limits provide the qualifications for any conclusions you draw. Don't overstate the results.

CHECKLIST
Conducting a Survey

- Understand the purpose of your survey or questionnaire clearly before you create it. What information do you want to gather?
- Prepare clear, fair, and unbiased questions. Test your questions on others to be sure participants in your actual survey will understand them.
- Consider the type of responses you need from respondents. Should they respond to a scale? to a list of options you provide? Should they fill in blanks?
- Consider how much space might be adequate for responses and how much space might be too much.
- Create questionnaires that are easy to read, easy to fill out, and easy to tabulate.
- Create questionnaires that are convenient to return. If necessary, provide properly addressed envelopes and return postage.
- Give respondents appropriate assurances about the confidentiality of their responses and then abide by your commitment.
- Keep track of all your sampling procedures so you can report them accurately in your research.

8c Make systematic observations

Some of the best field research you can do may come simply from careful study of a phenomenon. The techniques of observation you use for a college research project may not be so rigorous as those of professional ethnographers who make a science of such studies, but you do need to take the process seriously. On their own, people are notoriously unreliable in recounting what they have seen; their observations are often colored

Field researchers, such as the ones pictured here examining materials in a Kenyan mine pit, make use of appropriate technologies, observe carefully, and take their study seriously. Your own field research may add depth and reliability to your project.

by their prior expectations, experiences, and assumptions. (Not surprisingly, the sworn testimonies of eyewitnesses to events are often conflicting.) So in making research observations—whether about the behavior of sports fans at a football game or the interactions between infants and staff at a day-care center—you want to employ techniques that counteract your biases as much as possible and ensure the reliability of your claims.

In recording your observations, you might begin with a double-column spiral notebook to separate your actual observations of a phenomenon from immediate reactions to it. Your written notes should be quite detailed about matters such as time, place, duration of the study, conditions of the observation, and so on. You may have to summarize such information later.

Of course, you need not rely on notebooks alone for your records. To assure an accurate account of what you are studying, use any appropriate technology: photography, tape recording, video recording, transcription of online conversations, and so on. Naturally, you will need to have permission to gather this type of information. If you make multiple observations over a period of time, follow the same procedures each time and note any changes that might affect your results. For example, a group of students conducting a traffic count of the patrons entering a major campus facility would want to perform the counts on typical campus days—not during spring break or on days when the weather is unusually bad.

CHECKLIST

Making Observations

- Understand the purpose of your observation. What information do you hope to gather? In what forms can that data be gathered and reported?

- Study any literature on your subject and become familiar with the issues or subjects you are studying. What background information do you need to have on your subject(s) to make informed and perceptive observations?

- Plan the method of your observation. How can you gather the information you need? How can you minimize your own impact on the situation you are observing? Will it be necessary for you to obtain permission from an institutional review board or another regulatory authority?

- Practice techniques of observation. Determine what methods work best.
- Work with others to confirm the reliability of your observations. Cross-check your field notes with those of fellow researchers.

GETTING INVOLVED

1. Carefully watch a news or entertainment interview on television—videotaping it if possible. Then study the session closely and try to work backward to determine what the interviewer would have had to find out in order to ask the questions he or she did. What research did the interviewer (or support staff) do? How much did the interviewer rely on common knowledge? What questions did the interviewer pose that you would have been unable to ask without more background information?

2. Write a one-page news release about one of your classmates and his or her accomplishments, background, or career objectives, using information you accumulate from a brief interview. For this interview, prepare a list of questions to help you find out as much as possible about an aspect of your classmate's life. (Your subject may decline to answer any question without explanation, so frame your questions with a sense of your audience.) After you have drafted your press release, show it to your classmate for a critique. Revise the press release on the basis of your classmate's comments.

3. Recall a time recently when you have been either surveyed orally (probably over the telephone) or asked to respond to a questionnaire prepared to discover public opinion. Why and how do you think you were selected for the survey? How much might the questioners have known about you demographically, and what demographic questions were posed? For example, were you asked about your age, income, gender, or employment? How many questions were posed? Were the questions balanced or open-ended—or did you feel you were being directed toward any particular conclusion? Could you tell from the survey or questionnaire what the people sponsoring the project were trying to establish?

4. Choose a local activity, behavior, or phenomenon to observe closely enough to record some data and draw conclusions. Pick a relatively simple subject: How many students use a library database in a two-hour period? What techniques do students use to secure their bicycles near the university library? What types of vehicles do faculty members tend to drive? Study the phenomenon or question for a very limited time, taking careful note of the questions or problems

that arise as you do your systematic observation. Then, in a report to class-mates, explain the complications that you encountered in your study and what modifications you might have to make if you were to design a larger, more de-tailed, and more systematic study.

MANAGING YOUR PROJECT

1. Decide how or whether your subject would benefit from interviews with ex-perts or other people involved in your topic. What might you learn from these interviews that you might not discover in printed or electronic sources?

2. Does your topic need information from a survey or questionnaire? Even if it seems that a formal survey is unnecessary, might your project benefit from the results of an informal survey of opinion that provides an opening for your work? For example, a survey might reveal apprehensions or general ignorance about your subject. You could introduce your subject by reporting the results of your survey.

3. Does your subject require systematic observation of any kind? If so, briefly sketch out your methodology for the observation and share the report with your instructor or colleagues. Get feedback on the techniques you will use to be sure they are valid and reliable.

9

Keeping Track of Information

These days, organizing your research materials may be as important as collecting them. Not only might you soon acquire stacks of note cards, bibliography cards, and photocopies, but you may also amass notes from interviews, data from surveys or experiments, printouts from Web sites and listservs, lists of electronic addresses, disks of images in various formats, MOO transcripts, audio and video files, and software copies of your own work, perhaps in several versions. Somehow, you'll have to bring all this information together and make sense of it.

So even before you begin your research, you need a strategy to record, classify, and protect information as you gather it. The basic principle is simple: Keep track of everything. With printed sources, be especially careful to record page numbers and dates. For electronic sources, be sure to record both electronic addresses and dates of access for online materials.

9a Classify the materials you might be gathering

By classifying your research resources, you can decide how and where to record them. If you'll be relying chiefly on print items, you can rely on a system of note cards, photocopies, and bibliography cards to manage much of the project. But even then you may want to include charts, graphs, and illustrations in the paper, some of them created on software, some downloaded from electronic sources. Or you may choose to use an electronic software package to keep track of your research. So you will likely add a computer disk to your research portfolio—two in fact, one as a backup because disks do get lost or go bad.

If you're working with electronic sources, you may still need note cards for bibliographical references, including electronic addresses. You'll also need to keep a folder for printouts, a disk for electronic files, maybe even a Zip disk for a large Web project.

Other types of work may require different resources and strategies. If your project involves interviews, you'll need notebooks for recording responses of subjects. If you tape-record these conversations, you may need to prepare transcripts to share the conversations with your readers. For projects that generate factual information, you may have to learn how to construct a database to study your findings, using existing database software. Such software will help you see your results from many different angles and then present it efficiently through charts and graphs.

Consider, too, where to keep all the stuff you accumulate while working on a project. A rugged, closable folder with ample pockets and safe storage for papers and disks is a good investment. Be sure it bears your name and a local phone number in case you lose it. Also put your name and phone number on all computer disks without exception; sooner or later, you'll leave an important disk in a machine at a computer facility.

It also helps to organize your computer information intelligently: keep your data in one location on your hard disk, name your files in a logical way, and update files consistently so that you are always working with the latest version of a document. That's especially important if several people will be involved in revising and editing the final product.

9b Prepare a working bibliography

It doesn't matter whether you are using print or electronic sources or whether your project will culminate in a paper, a Web site, or a brochure. You need to know where your information came from, and the best way to keep track is to record bibliographical data as you move through your sources, developing a working bibliography.

There still may be no simpler way to create the bibliography and track your sources than to keep an accurate set of 3-by-5-inch bibliography cards, one source per card. Note cards will prove invaluable when you assemble the Works Cited or References pages required in any standard academic paper. Each bibliography card should contain all the information you may need to find a source again later or to record when you accessed an electronic source such as a newsgroup or Web site. For printed sources, be sure to include a library call number or a location (current periodicals, for example, may not have call numbers). Typical bibliography cards might look like this.

```
TL
410
V36
1999
PCL Stacks

van der Plas, Rob. The Mountain Bike Book:

     Choosing, Riding, and Maintaining the

     Off-Road Bicycle. 3rd ed. San Francisco:

     Bicycle, 1993.
```

```
CNN Interactive. "Shuttle Atlantis makes

    repair call to Mir." 17 May 1997.

    http://www.cnn.com/TECH/9705/16/

    shuttle/index.html (19 May 1997).
```

The bibliographical information you need will depend on the type of source you are using. This will vary considerably for books, articles, newspapers, and electronic sources. For the exact information required, check the MLA, APA, CMS, CBE, and COS Form Directories (pp. 242, 281, 312, 327, and 212). When using a Web page, always record the full Web address and make a note of the date you accessed the site.

In some cases, writers skip bibliography cards because they can print out a list of potential sources from online library catalogs, electronic databases, and Web search engines (such as *AltaVista* or *Excite*—see pp. 52–53). This strategy can be risky because the information on a Web search page printout is usually insufficient for preparing a Works Cited page or References list. Such printouts can also be misplaced easily among the many papers a research project typically generates. So if you rely on such printouts for bibliographical information, keep the lists in one place and know what's on them.

A better alternative to note cards might be an electronic program that keeps track of your notes and sources. Database software of this kind is often easy to use and quite powerful, though you may need a laptop computer to take it into the library.

9c Make photocopies and prepare note cards for printed sources

Photocopy or print out passages from sources you know you will quote from directly and extensively. While a case can be made for taking all notes on cards, the fact is most researchers—faculty and students—now routinely either photocopy or download their major sources when they can. In such cases, be sure your copies are complete and legible (especially the page numbers). If you are copying from a book or magazine, also take a moment to duplicate the title page and publication/editorial staff material. You'll be glad you did later.

In all cases, attach basic bibliographical information directly to photocopies and printouts so you know their source, making sure each document is keyed to a full bibliography card. That way, you'll later be able to connect information to its source. (If you

You will want to photocopy important sources, especially any material you anticipate quoting. You can also take notes directly on the photocopied text. Be sure to photocopy the title page of a source because it will have bibliographic information you'll need later.

are extraordinarily organized, you might even color-code information from key sources by topic.) Use highlighter pens to mark those passages in photocopies and printouts you expect to refer to later, and keep all these materials in a folder. Never highlight original material or write in library books.

Even when you rely heavily on copied material, you may still need to record some information on index cards. While 3-by-5-inch cards are fine for bibliographic entries, larger ones work better for notes. Be sure each note card for a source includes the author's last name or a short title so that you can connect the notes with the right bibliography card. For example, a note card recording information from Rob van der Plas's *The Mountain Bike Book* might be headed simply "van der Plas, *Mountain*," since you have a bibliography card with fuller information on the book (see p. 82).

Don't crowd too much information on a single note card; it's more efficient to record only one major point, quotation, or statistic on each. That way, you will be able to arrange cards into an outline of your article, with data exactly where you need it. For the same reason, write on only one side of a note card. Information on the flip side of a card is easily ignored.

CHECKLIST
Information for Note Cards

- Author's last name and a shortened version of the source's title (for accurate reference to the corresponding bibliography card)
- A heading to identify the nature of the information on the card
- The actual data or information, correctly summarized, paraphrased, or quoted
- Page numbers or the correct URL for locating the source, as well as the date of access for online sources

9d Print or download electronic sources

How you record data from an electronic source will depend on how you expect to use it. If the electronic source is simply providing information, you may want to treat it like a printed source, recording data on note cards or printing out the source itself. Print-outs may be essential from sources whose information changes from day to day—such as Web sites, newsgroups, chat sessions, or any online conversations. Some of this material may be archived electronically, but it is usually much safer to print out material you will cite later, carefully recording all necessary bibliographical information on the sheets. Also be sure to record when you made the printout since most documentation for electronic material will require a date of access.

It is possible to copy many electronic sources directly to disk, and copyright considerations usually allow you to make copies for personal use. Do back up all such copies, keeping them, for example, on both a floppy disk and your hard drive. Be especially careful that you know where all downloaded images come from and who owns their copyrights. As you do with printed sources, you have to document and credit all copyrighted pictures, photographs, or images borrowed from the WWW, whether you use them in a paper or in an electronic project. In addition, if your project is to be published on the WWW or distributed outside the classroom, you may need to acquire permission from the copyright owner to use the material. (See Chapter 15.)

When your project will be completely electronic—a Web site, for example—you'll be working with some sources differently. For instance, rather than recording information from other Web sites, you'll likely link directly to them or make electronic copies of images you intend to use in your project. But remember that when you borrow information or images from other sources that can't be reached online via a link, you must provide traditional documentation.

A particularly efficient way to organize information gathered mainly from the WWW is to use your browser's "Bookmarks" or "Favorites" feature. Bookmarking a site simply adds it to a menu list so that you can return to it again easily. But Web browsers also enable you to organize such bookmarked items and even (in some cases) to annotate them. When you begin a project, you may want to create a folder for it on the bookmark menu and move all Web sites relevant to your search into the designated slot, annotating each entry to remind you of its relevance to your research. Note, too, that you can save your list of bookmarks to a disk and thus transport them from machine to machine.

GETTING INVOLVED

1. Do a campus survey of electronic and computer resources. Find out such basic facts as these.

   - From where, when, and how can you gain access to your college library catalog? Can you search the catalog via the WWW?
   - Does the library catalog indicate whether books or other materials are checked out? What is your library's policy on recalling books?

- What hours are campus computer facilities open? Will these facilities be readily available at crunch times—for example, when papers and projects are due at midterm or near the end of the term?
- What access do you have to printers and copiers? Again, will these facilities be available during crunch periods?
- What restrictions might you face in using lab facilities or software? For example, before committing yourself to a complex multimedia project, be sure you will have access to equipment you need.

2. Investigate your library's interlibrary loan policies. Find out how you can acquire materials your own library might not have, how long it might take to acquire materials, and what costs you might have to pay.

MANAGING YOUR PROJECT

1. Plan your research strategy. Begin by considering how you will keep track of your bibliography information—the data you will list for each source on a Works Cited or References page. Typically this information will include author, title, publication information, volume numbers, dates, page numbers, and date of access (for electronic items). Consider using note cards or a bibliography or note-taking program to record this information. Set up a routine for listing all the sources you examine, even those you might not use at all. As a project grows, you'll appreciate having a record of all the sources you've looked at so you don't waste time inspecting some materials twice.

2. Set up a procedure for taking notes from your sources. If you are using note cards, it is important to link the note cards for individual sources to your bibliography cards. You can do this in a variety of ways, but make sure the link is always clear. If you are keeping track of information via a computer program such as *TakeNote*, the software will make the linkage between notes and bibliographic information for you.

3. Back up or copy your most important materials. Always consider the possibility that some part of your project might get lost or erased. Would you be able to recover the information?

Even before online technologies, instructors teaching research spent time explaining how to make appropriate use of sources. But they could be reasonably confident that much (though not all) of what students found in libraries had been vetted by professionals to underwrite its suitability for academic research. To one degree or another, books, journals, newspapers, and magazines had been tweaked by editors, sanctioned by publishers, and selected by librarians. Researchers might still find plenty of junk on the shelves or choose materials utterly wrong for their projects. But at least they began their work in the ballpark.

Today, there's no ballpark. In electronic environments, anyone can publish, and it seems almost everyone does. The new sources—Web sites, listservs, newsgroups, chat rooms—are raising constructive questions about who controls information and why. So everything instructors said formerly about reading critically now counts double.

We cover such matters carefully and offer a relatively new technique we call *positioning*. *Positioning* is simply a conscious effort to describe where a source is coming from—what its biases might be, who is behind it, who supports it, and within what contexts it is operating. The point of positioning is to help you and your audience read more self-consciously, aware that no "text" exists in isolation. The more you know about what you are reading, the more intelligently and powerfully you can use a source.

PART

III

Working with Sources

10

Choosing Appropriate Sources

Experience teaches us to trust some people more than others. The same is true of research resources. No matter what your project is, you want supporting materials that will seem authoritative to people reviewing your work.

For many subjects, traditional research resources—books, articles, and newspapers—now form just the tip of an iceberg. You may also have to consider pamphlets, microfilm, maps, field data, transcripts of interviews, CD-ROMs, databases, Web sites, videos, listservs, email, and more. Moreover, many judgments about the credibility of research materials that used to fall on publishers and librarians now fall squarely on your shoulders. That's because some electronic sources come to you almost directly from their authors today, unreviewed and unrefereed. Yet the complications caused by online sources only highlight responsibilities that writers have always shouldered. Before you use any source, you have to determine its strengths, limits, and appropriateness.

10a Consider the relevance of your sources

These days, search tools such as electronic catalogs and indexes may point you to thousands of potential resources. When you find yourself with an embarrassment of riches, first try narrowing the scope of your project even more than you did initially (see Chapter 5). Or scan the titles in your preliminary bibliography. You'll usually be able to cut a large number of obviously irrelevant items. For example, if you did a keyword search in your library catalog on "Washington" for a project on the first U.S. President, you'd immediately cut any entries on George Washington University or Washington, D.C.

Note, too, that some catalogs, indexes, and search engines provide summaries or abstracts of the works they contain. Such summaries may suggest whether a full article or site deserves your attention. But recognize the limits of these brief descriptions: you may have to examine the source itself to appreciate its value.

Many scholarly sources—especially in the social and natural sciences—routinely include abstracts of lengthier research studies. Such abstracts usually convey a clearer

Early in a project, take some time to assess the variety of library resources available to you. Establish their reliability, strengths, limitations, and appropriateness to your project. In some cases, you may want to draw on a special library collection, such as maps or government documents.

sense of the content than the brief descriptions of a piece you might find in a database or search index listing. Some instructors may even allow you to cite an abstract itself in your paper if you cannot locate the actual article summarized in it. So abstracts can be valuable tools for narrowing a list of potential sources.

However, there is no magic formula for determining how relevant a source is to your topic—other than exercising critical judgment. You must decide what the material in question adds to your project—crucial information? supportive commentary? an alternative perspective? Indeed, if a source makes points you had not previously considered or if it convincingly challenges your own views, ethics dictate that you acknowledge it in your work.

After you've cut obviously irrelevant materials from your preliminary bibliography, you have more important decisions to make. One of those judgments is deciding what types of sources are most appropriate to your project.

10b Consider the purpose of a source

The value of a source will depend both on its trustworthiness and on the uses you intend to make of it. For example, if you were writing a report on the official positions taken by the two major political parties in a distant presidential election, you'd probably depend on scholarly books and articles published by reputable writers and on newspaper accounts archived in the library. But if you were developing a project about a current political campaign, you might examine less scholarly materials and read the views expressed in current campaign literature, recent magazines, and even Web sites and Usenet groups. You could also conduct interviews or cite polls. These sources might lack the authority and perspective of scholarly books or even official party materials, but they could still provide an excellent survey of political attitudes.

Ultimately, you have to decide what research materials suit your topic best and then be prepared to defend their relevance, especially when readers are apt to resist them—as they might when you quote from personal home pages or Usenet discussions.

But even if sources can't be described as simply "good" or "bad" without considering their purposes, they do have characteristics you must weigh when working on particular projects. We've summarized some of those features in a table below, but our guidelines should be taken with caution, understanding that any single source might differ from our characterizations. One suggestion: in researching a subject, the best sources for you are likely to be those just a step or two above your current level of knowledge—you want to push yourself to learn more without exceeding your depth.

10c   Examine scholarly books and reference works

Scholarly books are among the most carefully researched, reviewed, and edited sources you can find, though they are rarely current because they take time to prepare. Scholarly books make claims intended to advance knowledge; scholarly references summarize what is reliably known. Their authors are authorities, and their assertions are fully documented; sources used are summarized in a bibliography. Such books, thoroughly in-

ASSESSING SOURCES

Source	Purpose	Authors	Audience/ Language
Scholarly books	Advance or report new knowledge	Experts	Academic/ Technical
Scholarly articles	Advance or report new knowledge	Experts	Academic/ Technical
Serious books and articles	Report or summarize information	Experts or professional writers	Educated public/ Formal
Popular magazines	Report or summarize information	Professional writers or journalists	General public/ Informal
Newspapers, news services	Report current information	Journalists	Popular/ Informal
Sponsored Web sites	Varies from report information to advertise	Varies, usually Web expert	Varies/ Usually informal
Individual Web sites	Varies	Expert to novice	Varies/ Casual to slang
Interviews	Consult with experts	Experts	Varies/ Technical to colloquial
Listservs	Discuss specific subjects	Experts to interested amateurs	Varies/ Technical to colloquial
Usenet newsgroups	Discuss specific subjects	Open to everyone	Varies/ Technical to obscene

dexed, are usually written for scholarly or professional audiences and, consequently, may use technical language. They are often published by university presses.

10d Examine scholarly articles

Scholarly articles (print or online) are a major means by which researchers report their original findings and make their arguments. Like scholarly books, these articles are carefully refereed, reviewed, and edited for readers familiar with a given field and technical vocabulary. They scrupulously follow the conventions of professional organizations (MLA, APA, CBE) when it comes to reporting information and documenting sources.

Publisher or Medium	Reviewed/ Documented?	Current/ Stable?	Dialogic/ Interactive?
University press	Yes/ Yes	No/ Yes	No/ No
Scholarly or professional journal	Yes/ Yes	Usually no/ Yes	No/ No (unless online)
Commercial publishers	Yes/ No	Depends on subject/ Yes	No/ No (unless online)
Commercial publishers	Yes/ No	Yes/ Yes	No/ No (unless online)
Commercial press or online	Yes/ No	Yes/ Yes	No/ No (unless online)
Online WWW	Sometimes/ Links to other sites	Regularly updated/ Sometimes	Sometimes/ Often
Online WWW	Usually no/ Links to other sites	Varies/ Varies	Sometimes/ Sometimes
Notes, recordings, email	No/ No	Yes/ No	Yes/ Yes
Online email	No/ No	Yes/ Sometimes	Yes/ Yes
Online email	No/ No	Yes/ No	Yes/ Yes

They appear in professional journals such as *Journal of Counseling Psychology, Memory and Cognition,* and *Critical Inquiry* and on the Web sites of professional organizations or online journals. Though challenging, scholarly articles are essential sources for much college writing, especially for work in one's major.

10e Examine serious trade books and serious periodicals

These are written for well-educated but nonexpert readers, people who wish to acquire more than general knowledge about a subject. Serious periodicals and books often report information derived from scholarly works. Claims are made carefully with sources identified, but such books and essays may not be fully documented. Serious works usually try to avoid the technical language of scholarly pieces. Works in this category are excellent sources for much college writing, particularly for papers written outside your own field of expertise. Serious periodicals include *Scientific American, The New Republic, National Review, The New Yorker,* and *The Humanist.* Many of these publications are available online as well as in print editions.

10f Examine popular magazines and books

Works of this kind (print or online) tend to be less demanding and shorter than serious or scholarly materials because they serve more general audiences. Quite often, popular books and magazines base their claims on other, more technical sources, but these sources may not be specifically identified, documented, or linked. Some popular magazines are designed expressly for people with specific interests, everything from skiing Colorado to repairing old furniture. In these areas, they may claim a kind of expertise unavailable in other sources. Popular sources may also report events, trends, and political currents more quickly than other materials. So you can base a college project on popular sources when your subject is derived from current events or popular culture. Some familiar popular magazines include *Time, Psychology Today, Natural History,* and *Smithsonian.* Some magazines such as *Slate* have been specifically created for online environments; others may be available in both print and electronic versions.

Don't forget that newspapers and news organizations can be valuable sources. Newspapers (print and online) and Web news sources such as *CNN Interactive* and *MSNBC* provide up-to-date and generally reliable information about current events, popular culture, and political opinion. Most newspapers and news organizations have political biases that you should consider in examining their treatment of stories and issues. Libraries often have microfilm collections and indexes of older, influential newspapers such as *The New York Times* or *The Washington Post.* Newspapers that now publish part of their daily reportage online have the advantage of being easily searchable.

10g Examine sponsored Web sites

Material on the World Wide Web varies enormously in quality because anyone with access to a computer and server can post pages there. Many sites, however, are sponsored by well-known institutions, organizations, and companies and, as a result, share in the credibility of their supporting groups. Thus, Web sites posted by the U.S. government or by colleges and universities usually contain reliable information, though caution must always be exercised. (A college site, for example, might include unedited and unofficial pages posted by faculty, staff, or students.) Sites for major companies, too, may provide interesting material or links for a project, but you'll want to consider the commercial intention of most such ventures. Web search engines often provide rankings (*Lycos Top 5%*, *Magellan Internet Guide*, *Excite Reviews*) of sponsored Web sites.

10h Examine individual Web sites and home pages

Web sites maintained by individuals vary enormously in quality of information, design, and currency. The vitality of the Web is due, in no small part, to the vigorous participation of people from around the globe sharing their expertise and interests. It would be folly to ignore the research potential in the millions of Web pages that individuals have created on every subject imaginable. Yet use great caution when relying on information from sources about which you likely know so little. Unlike traditional books or articles, individual Web sites are rarely refereed or reviewed by third parties who might take some responsibility for their accuracy. They may be updated irregularly or designed haphazardly, presenting information in formats difficult to read or access. Such sites may be invaluable for recording opinions and ideas; for factual claims, you may want to confirm any hard facts offered in an individual Web site with information from other sources.

10i Consider interviews and email

Interviews with authorities are important sources of information. But the information you receive in these circumstances, both the answers you receive and the questions you ask, must be accurately recorded. You must also remember that an expert speaking or writing to you may be less precise and less accountable than the same person offering information in print.

10j Consider listservs and Usenet groups

A *listserv* is a program working online that allows a group of people who subscribe to the list to have extended email conversations. Listservs enable people with specific interests to share their ideas and research. If you join a group germane to your subject, you can quickly learn a great deal about the nature of current interests and debate. But listservs have all the advantages and disadvantages of any extended conversation—participants may vary widely in what they know; facts and figures may be reported unreliably; the credentials of participants may not be well known.

A Usenet group works like a listserv except that you need not subscribe to the list either to read its messages or to participate in the discussion. Anyone with access to the Internet can participate in any of the thousands of Usenet groups. As you might guess, these groups are often more valuable for what they reveal about the range and depth of feeling on a subject than for any information you may find there. You'll find reasons to cite Usenet discussions in some projects, but use these materials with caution since you have no reliable way of confirming their credibility.

GETTING INVOLVED

1. Use a Web search engine to find any online occurrences of your own name. If any hits come up, examine these citations to determine what you could discover about yourself before following the links to pages where your name is mentioned. How useful are these items in describing or identifying the places where you are named? (If you aren't on the Web, search for someone else you know—especially if he or she uses the Web often or has a Web site.)

2. On what types of sources might you rely if you were looking for information on the following subjects?

   - the most recent World Series
   - the Persian Gulf War
   - the Oscars
   - the human genome project
   - current trends in popular music
   - solvency of the Social Security system
   - cultivation of aloe plants

3. Browse several Web sites sponsored by the federal government. Locate them using *Yahoo!* at **http://www.yahoo.com/Government/U_S_Government/**. How authoritative do these sites seem? What types of information are available? Do you detect political biases in any sites? For presentation in class, write a brief assessment of the site you regard as most useful to a researcher.

4. Browse several corporate sites. You can locate them using *Yahoo!* at **http://www.yahoo.com/Business/Companies/**. How authoritative and thorough do these sites seem? What types of information are available? What limitations and biases do you detect on any of the sites? For presentation in class, write a brief assessment of the site you regard as most useful to a researcher.

5. Browse a half dozen or more personal Web sites or home pages. You can locate them using *Yahoo!* at **http://www.yahoo.com/Society_and_Culture/People/ Personal_Home_Pages/**. What types of information might a researcher find on such sites? What are their strengths and weaknesses? In class, be prepared to describe any site you find potentially useful to a researcher.

MANAGING YOUR PROJECT

1. In creating a preliminary bibliography, begin by cutting obviously irrelevant materials—those that are off the subject, too old to be reliable for your subject, too far below or above your level of expertise, and so on.

2. Check that your bibliography includes a variety of sources. Unless your project requires it, don't rely on a single type of source or just a single author.

3. Resist the temptation to do all your research online. For many subjects, the most reliable and thorough sources will still be books and printed articles. Because of the care with which printed materials are written, organized, and indexed, they may be just as easy to use as many online sources.

Initially, Oxford University (pictured here in an English manuscript illumination from 1453) did not have a library. Officially recognized by the Pope in 1214, Oxford University began collecting books in 1253. In 1380, New College became the first Oxford college to have its own library, and others followed suit. Despite the library's growing collection and reputation, zealots of the Reformation decimated the collection during the reign of King Edward VI in 1550. The Oxford University library reopened as the Bodleian Library in 1602, with a large donation from Sir Thomas Bodley. This library is noted today for its manuscript collection, Shakespeareana, and English books.

The collection at the Bodleian Library grows considerably each year because the library receives free copies of all books published in Great Britain. The Bodleian Library Web site at www.bodley.ox.au.uk provides information on the library's special collections; this is an excellent place to locate primary sources. You might also want to search OLIS, the Oxford libraries online catalog. Of course, be sure to evaluate these and all other sources carefully.

◎ DON'T MISS . . .

- **The discussion in Section 11c of the timeliness and stability of sources.** You'll want to know exactly how electronic sources differ from printed sources.

- **The exploration of biases in sources raised in Section 11d.** As a researcher, you must weigh the special interests served by even the most "objective" sources.

- **The warning in Section 11f about advertising that appears in many online sources and services.** You'll need to consider whether this commercial activity affects the reliability of a source.

BOOKMARKS: Web Sites Worth Knowing

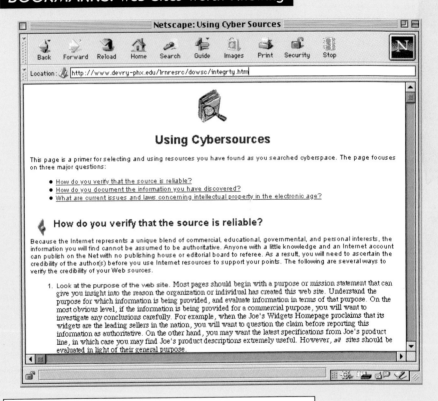

"Using Cybersources,"
http://www.devry-phx.edu/lrnresrc/dowsc/integrty.htm

How do you know the Web site you're looking at is reliable? One place to start is the "Using Cybersources" page, which offers easy-to-follow guidelines for determining whether a source is acceptable for academic research. It also provides links to other sites with additional guidelines.

Additional Sites

"Critically Analyzing Information," http://www.library.cornell.edu/okuref/research/skill26.htm
The Good, the Bad, and the Ugly: or, Why It's a Good Idea to Evaluate Web Sources,
    http://lib.nmsu.edu/staff/susabeck/eval.html
UCLA College Library Instruction, "Thinking Critically About World Wide Web Resources,"
    http://www.library.ucla.edu/libraries/college/instruct/web/critical.htm

Evaluating Sources

During your research, you'll likely encounter various points of view on your topic, some of which will differ from your own. Don't be surprised or dismayed. Even cold facts and figures can be interpreted differently. (Is a glass half empty or half full?) Because of differing perspectives, it is important to appreciate all the factors shaping your sources.

In this chapter, we present guidelines to help you evaluate sources in terms of their authority and perspectives. But be sure to rely on your own critical judgment too. If a source leaves you feeling uneasy about its claims, consider that your readers may feel the same way about it. You don't want to build a case on shaky evidence.

11a Consider the authority and reputation of a source

Reputable books or reference tools will be cited in the literature you accumulate on a project; you'll soon recognize the names of important scholars and key works, too. If you haven't acquired them in your own collection of data, go back to the library and pick them up. Do the same with electronic sources; Web sites on a topic usually provide links to other, similar materials. Inevitably, the most useful sites will appear often. Track them down.

There are also growing numbers of review tools for online materials. You might consult, for example, *WebCrawler*'s *Best of the Net* or the Gale *CyberHound's Guide*.

11b Consider the credentials of experts, authors, or sponsoring agencies

This advice might not seem too useful at first when you are exploring a new subject. But you'll quickly pick up names as you read about any subject—people mentioned frequently as experts or authorities. (You may hear your instructors mention writers who deal with your topic.) When scanning a lengthy printout of potential sources, look for these familiar authors. But don't be drawn in by celebrity alone—particularly when the names of famous people are attached to subjects about which they may have no special expertise.

With Web sites, listservs, and other online materials, you may find yourself in a quandary about the credentials of your "authors." For example, you may have no more to go on than the word and email addresses of people involved in Usenet group discussions. When you report factual information from such sources, you will usually want to confirm it through second, more familiar sources. (Reporting opinion is a different matter.) On personal Web sites, check the credentials writers claim for themselves, and then try to verify them. If Web authors offer email addresses on their sites, you can follow up their claims with a one-on-one exchange, asking for the sources used to support the claims on their pages. Be open-minded but skeptical.

You can be more confident about electronic information when the sponsoring agency of the source is one you would trust in a printed environment. Acquiring information online from *Reuters News Service* or *USA Today* is almost equivalent to seeing the same information in print. That means you should, of course, remain sensitive to issues that apply to any type of source: questions of fairness, bias, completeness, and so on.

11c Consider the timeliness and stability of a source

Timeliness is relative.

With books and articles, the date of publication is important. In general, you want your projects supported by the most current and reputable information in a field. But your instructors and librarians may point you to classic pieces, too, that have shaped thinking in your topic area. For many college papers, you should have a mix of sources, some from the past, some quite recent. While books and articles may sometimes be difficult to acquire, a complex infrastructure of library collections and catalogs assures the relative stability of the material. Important books and journals don't usually disappear.

Timeliness is a somewhat different matter in much newer electronic environments, complicated by the unstable nature of many online sources. No conventions currently govern the millions of Web pages, so not every site you visit will provide dates for its original posting or its most recent update. You'll want to check for both since the Web is full of outdated sites, posted and largely forgotten by their authors. Currency is less a factor in listservs, Usenet groups, and other email postings because the turnover of material is very rapid, changing from day to day. But that also means that something you read today may be gone tomorrow—or sooner. Obviously, you need to print out or download relevant postings from such sources or check to see whether the source you are using archives its materials.

Web sites pose similar problems. Some sponsored sites enable you to search their archives for past stories or postings. But those archives may not be complete or may not go back many years: we are a long way from having electronic sources that are as stable, comprehensive, and dependable over the long run as printed books and articles. The stability of electronic sources is a matter to ponder deeply, especially when you are considering a long-term research project. However, you cannot simply ignore important information online merely because it may not be permanent.

11d Consider the biases of a source

You'll especially need to consider political, social, and religious leanings when you are dealing with controversial subjects. In deciding which items on a lengthy list to read or what people to interview or survey, it may help to select opinions from across the spectrum. Otherwise you may write a whole paper unaware that some important perspectives are being ignored.

It is important to understand that almost all sources have points of view that shape the information they contain (and determine what they exclude). Sometimes those biases are apparent. You do not have to read much to realize, for example, that the editorial page of *The New York Times* tends to be liberal in its politics and that of *The Wall Street Journal* conservative. It may be harder to detect similar biases in scholarly journals, popular magazines, or news services on the Web, but be assured that they are there. If you are in doubt about the broad-mindedness of the sources you have selected, consult with instructors or librarians—being aware that they, too, have points of view and may try to influence your selection.

11e Consider how well a source presents key information

The design of a source is probably of greater concern with Web sites than with printed books and articles, for which the conventions were established years ago. Still evolving as an information tool, the Web brings together the complex resources of print, visual, and audio media, sometimes brilliantly, sometimes garishly. A well-designed Web site identifies its purpose clearly, arranges information logically, uses graphics to enhance its mission, gives access to its materials without exhausting the capacity of its users' technology, furnishes relevant and selective links to other responsible resources, and provides basic bibliographical information: the identity and email address of the author or sponsor, the date of the posting, the date of the most recent update, and so on. Standards for Web documentation, of course, are still developing. You cannot automatically discount a site that does not include this information since an author's authority is not dependent on his or her knowledge of technology and the constraints of electronic publishing, but you will need to consider what the lack of documentation may mean to your own research.

11f Consider commercial intrusions into a source

Books today rarely have much advertising, and we are accustomed to dealing with ads in print magazines. But commercial intrusion into Web sites is growing enough to warrant concern when assessing resources. Sponsored Web sites—especially search engines—are often so thick with commercial appeals that they can be difficult to use. Moreover, your search itself may bring up specific advertising messages in an effort to direct you to a sponsor's material. No library catalog ever exerted this kind of pressure.

Sponsored sites may also reflect the commercial connections of their owners, especially when news organizations are, in fact, owned by larger companies with entertainment or other commercial interests. What appears—or doesn't appear—on a site may be determined by who is paying for the message. You shouldn't automatically discount commercially sponsored sites such as these, but do consider how advertising may affect the information you find, as well as what effect using information from these sources will have on your reader's evaluation of your own credibility.

11g   Consult librarians and instructors

Librarians and instructors can help you in assessing the quality or appropriateness of a source. They often have the expertise to cut right through a lengthy list of references to suggest the three or four you should not miss. Those leads will often enable you to make subsequent judgments on your own.

Librarians and instructors may even correct biases in your own research strategies, directing you to sources you might have avoided or considered suspect. They may suggest solutions, too, to problems you are having with experiments, interviews, statistical sampling, and so on.

GETTING INVOLVED

1. In the periodical room of your local library, look for journals or magazines targeted to specific groups of people—either ethnic, religious, social, economic, or political. Where or how are the biases of the periodical made evident? Be sure to consider such factors as the advertisements, layout, images, and language of the magazines.

2. Most search engines display advertisements. Open a search engine on your Web browser and explore the advertisements you see. What types of products are highlighted? What effects might this advertising have on a visitor to the Web site? In what ways might a reader on the Web be influenced by these and similar ads?

MANAGING YOUR PROJECT

1. As you recall your preliminary reading and scan your preliminary bibliography, do certain names stand out—people of authority on your subject whose names are cited often? Find out all you can about these authors. Be sure they are cited for the right reasons, and check what they have to say about your topic.

2. For each source, answer any of the following questions that apply.

   • Is the source appropriately timely? Would a more recent source be more up to date or less reflective?

   • Is this a source a reader will be able to follow up reliably? If not, can you still afford to use it? Does it serve some purpose that might not require following up?

- What are the biases of this source? How should you adjust your reading of the source to account for the bias? How will you describe the bias to readers?
- How does the source present its information? Does the author cite sources and provide evidence for all assertions? Is the presentation clear and well organized? Can you reliably find what you need?

12

Reviewing and Positioning Sources

As you gather or create materials for a project, review them critically in terms of your research question or hypothesis (see Chapter 5). To incorporate any material into your research effort, you must understand its impact on your work: Does source material or data you generate yourself advance your argument or undermine it? fill a hole in your background information or raise new questions? suggest novel perspectives or reinforce existing ones? change your opinion or validate it? Approach all research materials actively and intensely, reading or responding to them slowly, thinking deeply about their implications and ideas. This critical activity might—perhaps *should*—lead you to refine your initial thinking (see Chapter 16) and to do even more reading and research.

12a Review data and resources critically

Skimming materials may make sense when you are browsing a subject early in the research process. But most of your subsequent research will require reading of the *critical* variety. Critical work involves interrogating your sources and methods, asking questions that help you understand the context, claims, and authority of each piece of information you find or generate.

- ❏ Are my findings valid and repeatable?
- ❏ Was I careful not to skew my methods to generate data favorable to my thesis or hypothesis?
- ❏ Was I careful to incorporate a variety of perspectives into my research or reading?

You should ask very specific questions about any facts and figures you encounter in your sources.

- ❏ Do the authors have firsthand knowledge or experience of their subject matter?

102

❏ Are all critical claims adequately documented?

❏ Are my sources in conflict about important basic claims? If so, what might explain those conflicts?

❏ Do my sources appeal to logic, or do they make unwarranted appeals to emotions?

❏ If facts and figures are presented, where did they come from?

❏ Are figures the result of government or university studies?

❏ Are the figures presented in a biased way? Could the figures be used to support different arguments?

❏ Are the samples in surveys used complete and representative?

❏ Can controversial facts and figures be verified by other sources?

Be sure to check whether a source ends with a bibliography or a set of notes. A bibliography not only will point you toward additional information but may also indicate how thorough an author has been in covering a subject.

❏ Are the references used authoritative?

❏ Does the author include references to works that might disagree with his or her point of view?

❏ Are the facts and figures presented in the work from reliable and diverse sources?

You can learn a lot about a source by asking such questions.

Sometimes you can find clues to the authority of a source outside the work itself. For printed sources, the title page or book jacket gives important information: a university press such as Columbia University Press or Oxford University Press will probably wield more authority than a trade press targeted toward a popular market (see Section 10b). However, no single press or place of publication is ideal for all subjects. Authorities on extreme sports or haute couture are more likely to write for monthly magazines than for Harvard University Press. Even a comic book might be an authoritative source for a project on popular culture.

Establishing the authority of online sources may be more of a challenge. Virtually anyone with the necessary technological skills can become a "published" author on the World Wide Web without the benefit of comments from editors, corrections from fact checkers, advice from reviewers, or support from publishers. For better or worse, much online material goes unscreened from authors to readers.

However, the World Wide Web does offer a kind of "book jacket"—the *domain name*. The domain name, which is usually the first part of the Internet address (called the *uniform resource locator,* or *URL*), can provide some important clues to the location of the author (and, hence, perhaps to his or her authority). The URL itself breaks down into specific parts: the type of protocol used to access the resource, the domain name where the file resides, any directories and/or subdirectories, and the file name and type. URLs may lack some or all of these parts. When citing sources, however, it is important that you include the entire URL as shown in your browser.

Protocol	Domain	Directory	Subdirectories	File	File Type
http://	www.cas.usf.edu	english	walker	mla	.html
http://	www.m-w.com				
http://	www.columbia.edu	acis	documentation/ghttp	search-info	.html

Generally, the domain name or Internet address identifies where the information resides. For example, a document at http://www.cas.usf.edu resides on the World Wide Web server (*www*) for the College of Arts and Sciences (*cas*) at the University of South Florida (*usf*), an educational institution (*edu*). The last part of the domain name gives important information about the type of site. These are some common designations.

.com   Commercial site

.edu   Educational site

.gov   Government site

.org   Organization (usually a nonprofit) site

12b Position your research materials

Even after you've decided that source material or data are appropriate and reliable (see Section 12a), you should "position" them within your project to identify their perspectives and biases. Positioning a source helps you use sources with your eyes wide open, conscious of the contexts that can shape and influence information.

Sources, after all, do reflect different generational, political, social, and economic biases and attitudes. Differences of gender, religion, or worldview may shape the materials you gather in ways that bear on your research. Even the methods used in creating the source material will influence how you present them: Was a survey scientific? Was a study sponsored by a group with a stake in its outcome? Does a document you cite represent a person's carefully considered judgment, or is it a paid endorsement, a political creed, or even a parody? You need to know before you go public with it.

The answers to such questions will help you define how to use sources responsibly. You owe it to readers to be honest with information and to share what you learn about your sources when that information affects your conclusions. You might even have to investigate your sources to be sure they are reliable. If an expert providing statistics in support of nationalized health care is a scholar at a liberal think tank, you and your readers should know; if a columnist you quote in supporting a flat tax proposal is wealthy enough to benefit significantly from the policy change, that's relevant information.

Following are examples of attempts to position two short articles, both of which appear in the two chapters immediately following (pp. 110 and 115). Your own efforts to position a source might be much less formal than these: positioning is not so much a written assignment as a mental exercise you should perform with all your research materials and methods. Still, the examples may help you to formulate the kinds of questions you need to ask in order to appreciate what a source is and does.

EXAMPLE 1   Editorial titled "Leave the People Home" by Alex Roland

POSITIONING   "Leave the People Home" is an editorial that appeared in USA Today on July 7, 1997, following the successful landing on Mars of a research robot. The piece, written by Alex Roland, appears as a rebuttal to the paper's official editorial position endorsing exploration of Mars by human explorers. Owned by Gannett, USA Today is a daily newspaper available throughout the country, with a predominantly liberal editorial page. It routinely publishes counterpoints to its editorials. USA Today notes that Alex Roland, "chair of the history department at Duke University, teaches technology history and is a former NASA historian." Roland's academic credentials and work with the American space agency appear to give him authority to write on this subject. The editorial was accessed online on July 7, 1997, for a Web project exploring the pros and cons of a human mission to Mars.

EXAMPLE 2   Online Magazine article titled "The Nikes Jumped Over the Moon" by Robert Shrum

POSITIONING   This short article analyzes a television spot titled "Cow," produced for Nike shoes by Jim Riswold, Alice Chevalier, and John Jay of the Wieden & Kennedy advertising agency. Shrum's analysis appeared in the online journal Slate on December 13, 1996, as part of the "Varnish Remover" series. Slate is a magazine created by Microsoft founder Bill Gates and edited by liberal political commentator Michael Kinsley, former editor of The New Republic. Slate describes Robert Shrum as "a leading Democratic political consultant." One might expect the review of Nike's ad to reflect the similar political interests and

```
concerns of the author and the magazine. The
analysis, available at http://www.slate.com/Ad/
96-12-13/Ad.asp, was accessed on July 5, 1997,
for a project investigating Nike's involvement
in contemporary social causes.
```

CHECKLIST
Positioning Your Source

- What are the background and interests of the author(s)?
- What are the interests and biases of the publisher?
- How much authority does the source claim?
- Are the assertions of authority justified?
- Does the source or method purport to be objective and/or scientific?
- Does the source present itself as subjective and/or personal?
- Whose interests does the source or method represent?
- Whose interests does the source or method seem to ignore?
- What do readers need to know about the source or method?

GETTING INVOLVED

1. Locate a recent newspaper article or column that cites a number of facts or statistics. Then play fact checker: underline or highlight the specific facts in the piece, and use your skills as a researcher to verify the facts or numbers as best you can. Use the resources of a library reference room and the World Wide Web (if necessary). How accurate are the claims that the article or columnist makes? Were the facts presented clearly and in their full context? Or did the piece you studied use information selectively or present it unfairly? Especially good pieces for this exercise are newspaper and magazine columns that address contentious political issues.

2. Following are several Web addresses. Study them thoroughly and then describe what you can learn about the site from the address alone. What type of site might it be? Is it likely to be authoritative? How regularly will it be updated and maintained? How long is it likely to be around?

   http://www.nytimes.com/
   http://www.whitehouse.gov/WH/html/briefroom.html
   http://www.media.daimlerchrysler.com/index_e.htm
   http://etext.lib.virginia.edu/

When you've completed your speculation, look at the actual sites and compare your expectations with the reality of the sites.

MANAGING YOUR PROJECT

1. After you have assembled a working bibliography (see Section 9b), use the checklist in this chapter to position your major sources, describing them as best you can. Observe that positioning a source is different from evaluating it. When you position a source, you are describing the research context of the materials: Who is offering the material? What are their points of view and biases? What baggage do the sources carry?

2. After positioning your sources, check that they are sufficiently diverse. You want your source material to suggest the breadth and depth of your reading. If all your sources reflect the same perspectives, come from the same publishers, and show similar biases, you may need to expand your preliminary bibliography.

3. If your project relies on materials you generated yourself, position your own methods of inquiry. For example, if you are relying on a survey, what are the strengths and weaknesses of that approach? If you are designing a scientific experiment, what are its underlying assumptions? If you decide to interview subjects rather than gather factual data on an issue, what is the rationale for that approach, and how might it affect the information you are gathering? (That is, what kind of information might an interview reveal that a survey will not—and vice versa?)

4. Position yourself within your project. What assumptions and biases do you bring to the material? Do you favor a scientific methodology in your work, or do you prefer a more humanistic approach to your subject? Is your work influenced by a particular social, ethnic, religious, sexual, or political orientation? What experiences or training directed you toward this inquiry? To help you position yourself, think about how someone outside the project might view you.

5. Assess what you have learned from positioning your sources and methods. If you've done a thorough job locating your sources, you may discover that the mainstream research in a field reflects selected interests or points of view. Or certain ideas or voices may be ignored while others receive unexpected emphasis. Consider why this may be so. Are the possible reasons institutional, political, cultural, economic? Ponder this information and use it as you see fit in your own treatment of the research materials.

13

Annotating Research Materials

When you have positioned printed and online sources, you can begin mining them for information. One way to do that is to *annotate* the material you've gathered—that is, to attach comments, questions, and reactions to it. The point of such annotation is to identify ideas and information worth returning to and, more important, to engage in a dialogue with the authors and sources you are reading.

Annotation is obviously not an option when you are reading library books and materials; in these cases, you'll have to record your reactions in notes, summaries, and paraphrases (see Chapter 14). But much research material today is photocopied, downloaded, or read online—and these media support different forms of annotation.

13a Highlight key information

Many researchers working with photocopied material use highlighting pens to tag important passages. But often the highlighting is both too frequent and too random to be of much use. If you underscore every passage that strikes you as interesting, you may end up with pages glowing pointlessly with color. Use color chiefly to help you locate material you intend to use later. Consider these strategies for marking a printed text.

❑ Highlight sentences you expect to quote directly. These possible quotations should be *very* limited in number. Don't highlight material that is generally interesting or even, in some respects, important—give attention to such information in your notes or through marginal comments.

❑ Highlight important dates, facts, or figures that you might have difficulty locating later. Such highlighting can be smart when you're dealing with especially dense passages of prose.

❏ Highlight any sentences that might be considered a thesis or an important summary of the piece. Such sentences should be relatively rare. Don't highlight the topic sentences of paragraphs; you'll brighten too much material if you do.

❏ Highlight any key names or sources you might wish to consult later.

❏ Never mark a text that is not your own property.

13b Use marginal comments to start a dialogue with your sources

A marginal comment is a more powerful tool for critical reading than a quick highlight. To make a comment, you have to respond to a text actively—not just point out what someone has said. That's why you should make it a habit to read with pencil in hand, either annotating the text itself or immediately taking notes on cards.

Ask pointed questions as you read. Record your reaction to the materials you are reading, note connections you see to other material, and jot down any ideas that pop into your head. Each section you highlight should also probably be accompanied by a marginal comment that explains the importance of the passage or gives your reaction to it.

You can use the annotation features of word-processing programs to record your reactions to files you download from your computer. But once again, your comments are the essential element. These annotations can later be incorporated into the paper or project itself if they are thoughtful and entirely in your own words.

Even pages from the World Wide Web can be marked with comments and, in some cases, annotated as part of an ongoing, online discussion. For instance, you can use *Netscape Navigator's* "Bookmarks" feature to gather together all Web sites or pages relevant to your project, arranging the items in folders that reflect its overall structure, one folder per major section or theme. It is even possible to annotate each bookmark to remind yourself why the site or page is important.

Of course, you can and probably should take conventional notes on all important sources, online or off.

On the following page is an example of a source that has been annotated in its margins. (To see this source positioned, turn back to page 105.)

"The Nikes Jumped Over the Moon"

by Robert Shrum

Cow is an animated fairy tale that targets the subteen who still responds to the child within. But it is just as likely to engage the old folks of the athletic shoe market—Gen-Xers and the thirtysomethings. (As far as Nike is concerned, anyone past these demographics is a retired consumer.)

Naturally, we never see a real shoe in this animated spot—that would break its tone. It opens, instead, with a cow grazing in a bucolic field. Out of shape and shoeless, this one is an eater, not an exerciser. Reponding to the whistles and taunts of Old Man Moon, she attempts to re-enact the fairy tale and "jump over the moon." Leaping, then falling ("Ooh," says the moon), she lies splayed on the feeding ground.

The fallen creature now responds to the strains of "Destination Moon" on the soundtrack: "Come and take a trip in my rocket ship." And what is the rocket? A Nike "swoosh" logo appears in a thought balloon over the animal's head. The brand doesn't have to be mentioned: In the age of the advertised image where television often seems more real than real-life, the Nike swoosh is ubiquitous. The cow squeezes into the barn, then races outside wearing Nikes. "We'll travel fast and light," the song goes—as the animal soars over Old Man Moon, punching him so hard that he sees stars.

Cow's message isn't that Nikes are a substitute for working out. Rather, the spot tells you that if you wear the shoes and just do the rest, you'll soar, whether your moon be the NBA, a three-mile jogging path, or a playground. The high-jumping bovine also reinforces Nike's core identification with basketball and the Bulls' Michael Jordan. And, because the spot uses an animal, excluding all references to race, gender, or a particular sport, soccer kids in Beverly Hills are as likely to embrace it—and the product—as hoop shooters in Harlem.

The spot ends with the Nike slogan that is now as familiar as the swoosh. Evoking freedom, a safe rebellion, Just Do It is the life-affirming bookend to Nancy Reagan's Just Say No. *Cow* recruits the next generation of Nike wearers by building a bridge between young people's innate sense of play and the next stage—competition. Shoes signify more than sports these days. They stand for self-image. If young people do it now, Nike knows they'll keep doing it later. The fairy tale goes on: Buy the shoes, and jump the moon. And it doesn't matter if it's all bull.

Handwritten margin notes:

Tone here suggests Shrum is suspicious of Nike?

Shrum describes the Nike ad.

"Image is everything"

Shrum's thesis—or a summary of the Nike ad?

Did Nike eliminate race/class issues deliberately? Or is Shrum reading into the ad something not there?

Has Shrum proved that the shoes = self image?

Confirms my original suspicions about Shrum & Nike.

GETTING INVOLVED

1. Take a close look at newspaper or magazine articles (or Web sites) that use "pull quotes"—sentences or phrases drawn from the article that are highlighted in a box or in another way to attract a reader's attention. In some ways, pull quotes work the same way as highlighting does when you are reading a serious source carefully, looking for the words or phrases that best represent what an author has said. But look at pull quotes carefully. Do they always represent the full content of a piece accurately, or do they often focus on the more sensational aspects of a piece?

2. Look for a book or another printed source that uses running annotations as part of its basic structure. (If necessary, ask a librarian for help.) Some textbooks and computer manuals are designed this way, as are many editions of the Bible. Marginal commentary (or glosses) was also common in older books and manuscripts. If you find an example of a "glossed" text, examine how the running comments function. Do they highlight what is in the text? What other functions does the commentary have?

3. Pop-up videos are, in effect, music videos with commentary. Do these added highlights and remarks add to (or detract from) your experience of the videos? To what other sorts of materials might the pop-up feature add interest?

MANAGING YOUR PROJECT

1. If you prefer highlighter pens for marking sources, pay attention to the suggestions in this chapter for limiting your comments. Highlight only those passages or bits of information you need to find quickly or cannot afford to lose when you later assemble your project or write your paper.

2. Annotate in the margins of photocopied material carefully. Making the comments should help you practice reading texts actively. Record your responses, whether you agree with your sources or find yourself doubting what you read. In fact, you may want to read both ways: as what scholar Peter Elbow describes as "believing and doubting."

3. Review your note-taking process carefully at this stage. Are the methods you are employing working? Are you keeping track of your sources and also your comments on them? Modify any procedures not working now before you get deeper into your project.

Summarizing and Paraphrasing Sources

To some researchers, summaries and paraphrases of source materials may seem like holdovers from a time when photocopiers and computers weren't widely available. In that ancient era, you *had* to take detailed notes because you couldn't count on having the necessary books and articles on your desk when you did a project. But why bother today taking detailed notes when you can just mark up copies of actual sources (see Chapter 13) or download the texts and images you want?

The answer is simple. In summarizing or paraphrasing research materials, you get to know them much better. You're far more likely to understand sources when you have read them carefully enough to put their claims into your own words; you're more likely to appreciate or question evidence when your own fingers trace out an assertion, fact, or statistic. Further, in moving from reading to writing, you also demonstrate just how well you understand key concepts in research materials.

So, as you can see, summarizing and paraphrasing are far more active processes than scribbling comments in margins or sweeping photocopied texts with highlighter pens—although both techniques may help you in summarizing and paraphrasing. (For how to highlight and comment on texts effectively, see Chapter 13.)

Make it a habit to either summarize or paraphrase all your major sources.

14a Decide whether to summarize or paraphrase a source

Your choice of summary or paraphrase will be determined by both the source and the use you intend to make of it.

A *summary* captures the gist of a source or some portion of it, boiling it down to a few words or sentences. Summaries tend to be short, extracting only what is immediately relevant from a source. Summarize those materials that support your thesis but do not provide an extended argument or idea you need to share in detail with readers.

When summarizing a source, identify its key facts or ideas and put them in your own words. When an article is quite long, you might look for topic ideas in each major section. If you have a photocopy of the source, highlight any sentences that state or emphasize its key themes. Then assemble these ideas into a short, coherent statement about the whole piece, one detailed enough to stand on its own and make sense several weeks after you examine the material. The summary should be entirely in your own words (for advice about avoiding plagiarism, see Chapter 15).

A *paraphrase* usually reviews a complete source in much greater detail than does a summary. When paraphrasing a work, you report its key information or restate its core arguments point by point *in your own words.* You will typically want to paraphrase any materials that provide detailed facts or ideas your readers will need. Predictably, paraphrases run much longer than summaries.

Prepare a paraphrase by working through the original source more systematically than you would with a summary. An effective paraphrase will meet the following conditions.

❑ The paraphrase reflects the structure of the original piece.

❑ The paraphrase reflects the ideas of the original author, not your ruminations on them.

❑ Each important fact or direct quotation is accompanied by a specific page number from the source when that is possible.

❑ The material you record is relevant to your theme. Don't waste time paraphrasing those parts of the source of no use to your project.

❑ The material is entirely in your own words—except for clearly marked quotations.

Practically speaking, making the distinction between summaries and paraphrases is often less important than simply taking the notes you need for a project. In gathering this information, you'll often find yourself switching between summary and paraphrase, depending on what you are reading. Now let's look at a source first summarized and then paraphrased.

14b   Summarize sources to highlight key concepts

On page 115 is the complete text of an editorial that originally appeared in *USA Today* on July 7, 1997, shortly after the successful landing on Mars of a research robot called *Pathfinder* and an onslaught of problems on the Russian space station *Mir.* Written by Alex Roland, chair of the history department at Duke University, the piece rebutted *USA Today*'s editorial position in favor of human exploration of Mars.

To prepare the editorial for either a summary or a paraphrase, you might first highlight and annotate the information most relevant to your project (in this case, focused on the research question "Should humans explore Mars?").

To prepare a summary, you would assemble the key claim and supporting elements into a very concise restatement of the overall argument. The summary should make sense on its own—a complete statement you might use later in your project itself.

But don't be surprised if you go through several versions of that sentence before you come up with one that satisfies you.

EFFECTIVE SUMMARY

> Alex Roland, chair of history at Duke University and a former historian at NASA, argues in USA Today (7 July 1997) that using automated unmanned spacecraft to explore planets such as Mars makes better sense than sending people on such missions because humans in space increase costs and risks and reduce the potential for long-term productive science.

How can something as simple as a summary go wrong? There are a number of ways. You might, for example, make the summary too succinct and leave out crucial details. Such a summary scribbled on a note card might be useless when, days later, you try to make sense of it.

INEFFECTIVE SUMMARY

> He argues that using people increases costs and reduces the science. International space station, 1997. Better reason to send after? Budget and technology.

Or your summary might fail because it misses the central point of a piece by focusing on details not relevant to the argument. Useful in a different context, these facts are misleading if they don't capture the substance of what the author wrote.

INACCURATE SUMMARY

> Alex Roland, chair of history at Duke University and a former historian at NASA, argues in USA Today (7 July 1997) that the Pathfinder mission to Mars was very inexpensive and that, very soon, we will be launching an international space station.

Yet another danger is that you might use the actual words of the original author in your summary. If these unacknowledged borrowings make their way into your project itself without both quotation marks and documentation, you would be guilty of plagiarism (see Chapter 15). In the example following, language taken directly and inappropriately from Roland's editorial is boldfaced.

PLAGIARIZED SUMMARY

> Alex Roland, chair of history at Duke University and a former historian at NASA, argues in USA Today (7 July 1997) that **all the really useful things done in space have been achieved with automated spacecraft controlled by people on**

> Earth. Machines can reach more places, stay
> longer, and take more risks than people.

You can appreciate how tempting it might be to slip these words from this "plagiarized summary" into the body of a paper, forgetting that you didn't write them yourself. To avoid plagiarism, the safest practice is *always* to use your own words in summaries.

"Leave the People Home"
by Alex Roland

The debacle currently unfolding aboard the *Mir* space station argues against sending people to Mars any time soon. To think about a manned Mars mission now is like planning your next cruise during an abandon-ship exercise.

The problem is putting people in space. All the really useful things done in space have been achieved with automated spacecraft controlled by people on Earth. The record is long and impressive—scientific probes to the planets and beyond, communications satellites, weather satellites, reconnaissance satellites, the global positioning system.

Two bad things happen when humans come aboard. First, cost increases by an order of magnitude, mostly to pay for life-support equipment and safety precautions. Second, the spacecraft becomes a lifeboat. Whatever mission it was intended to conduct—research, exploration, commerce—takes second place to saving the crew and returning them to Earth. The people, supposedly a means to some end, become the end themselves.

The *Pathfinder* spacecraft, due to touch down on Mars July 4th, is a case in point. At a tiny fraction of what a manned mission would cost (indeed, at a small fraction of the cost of a single shuttle mission), this resourceful spacecraft, and the roving *Sojourner* vehicle it carries, will do more and better research than astronauts could do. Machines can reach more places, stay longer, and take more risks.

But machines, you say, are not as dramatic, not as interesting as people. It is not the practicality of a manned Mars mission that appeals, but the romance. Sending people to Mars is a feel-good mission that speaks to the basic human longing to explore.

Well, our next feel-good mission is already booked. Later this year, components of the international space station are scheduled to rocket into orbit. In 1999, three years before construction is complete, people will begin to inhabit it permanently. If it proves useful, more durable and safer than *Mir,* there will be plenty of time and a better argument for sending people to Mars.

For now, however, we have all we can do to find a reason, a budget, and a technology to keep people in orbit.

Handwritten margin notes:
- Find out what was happening on Mir. └ check newspaper indexes?
- True? Look for opposite view.
- Connect to Apollo 13 moonshot?
- } Crucial point
- Robots work harder than people? ↓ possible quotation
- Yes. We can't ignore why people explore.
- 1997 (by "this year")

14c   Paraphrase sources to record important ideas and their supporting details

A paraphrase of "Leave the People Home" (page 115) would be appreciably longer than a summary because a researcher would expect to use the information differently, probably referring to the source in much greater detail. Here's one possible paraphrase of the editorial.

EFFECTIVE PARAPHRASE

> Recent problems on the Russian space station Mir, Alex Roland argues in a USA Today editorial (7 July 1997), make it clear why a human mission to Mars may not be a good idea: people in space cause problems that robots don't. Automated spacecraft perform almost all the really important work in space (communications, weather satellites, global positioning). Spacecraft that carry astronauts must also take along everything that keeps them alive, adding tremendously to the weight and complexity of missions. When something goes wrong, the whole project is jeopardized by the need to preserve the lives of astronauts. The Mars Pathfinder expedition, in contrast, was accomplished far more cheaply than even a routine space shuttle launch and yet can do more science over the long term than a human expedition because it isn't as vulnerable. We may like the adventure and romance that come along with human space exploration, and we'll have that experience with the international space station to be launched in 1999. But humans in space are an expensive and possibly unnecessary luxury.

You'll notice that this parphrase covers all the major points in the editorial in the same order as the ideas originally occurred. It also borrows none of the author's language. With proper documentation, any part of the paraphrase could become part of a final research project without the need for quotation marks (see Sections 19a–19b).

How can paraphrases go wrong? One way is to confuse the claims in a source with your own opinions. A paraphrase should accurately reflect the thinking of the original author, so reserve your comments and asides for annotations or other, separate notes. Consider how the following paraphrase might misreport the views of Alex Roland if the researcher later forgets that the boldfaced comments in the example are, in fact, personal notes and annotations.

INACCURATE
PARAPHRASE

> Recent problems on the Russian space station
> Mir, Alex Roland argues in a USA Today editorial
> (7 July 1997), make it clear why a human mission
> to Mars may not be a good idea: people in space
> cause problems that robots don't. **You could**
> **argue, though, that people can fix problems**
> **robots can't: one reason Mir has been in space**
> **so long is that cosmonauts can repair the**
> **station**. True, automated spacecraft perform
> almost all the really important work in space
> (communications, weather satellites, global
> positioning)--**if you ignore the more complicated**
> **experiments performed by astronauts. No robot**
> **could have fixed the Hubble Space Telescope, for**
> **example.** Spacecraft that carry astronauts must
> also take along everything that keeps them
> alive, adding tremendously to the weight and
> complexity of missions . . . .

You get the point. The reactions to the editorial are valid, but they don't represent an accurate paraphrase of the original article.

A paraphrase also should not reorganize or improve on the structure or argument of the original piece. For example, the following paraphrase doesn't actually add material to Roland's editorial, but it rearranges the information radically.

INACCURATE
PARAPHRASE

> Americans may like the adventure and romance
> that comes along with human space exploration,
> and we'll have that experience again soon with
> the international space station to be launched
> in 1999. But humans in space are an expensive
> and possibly unnecessary luxury, argues Alex
> Roland in a USA Today editorial (7 July 1997).
> Spacecraft that carry astronauts must also take
> along everything that keeps them alive, adding
> tremendously to the weight and complexity of
> missions. When something goes wrong, the whole

project is jeopardized by the need to preserve
the lives of astronauts. That's the lesson we
should have learned from recent problems on the
Russian space station <u>Mir</u>. The Mars <u>Pathfinder</u>
expedition, in contrast, was accomplished far
more cheaply than even a routine space shuttle
launch and yet can do more science over the long
term than a human expedition because it isn't as
vulnerable. So a human mission to Mars may not
be a good idea: people in space cause problems
that robots don't. Automated spacecraft perform
almost all the really important work in space
(communications, weather satellites, global
positioning).

The most dangerous and academically dishonest sort of paraphrase is one in which a researcher borrows the ideas, structure, and details of a source wholesale, changing a few words here and there in order to claim originality later. This sort of paraphrase would be plagiarism even if the material were documented in the research project. Writers can't just change a few words in their sources and claim the resulting material as their own work.

PLAGIARIZED
PARAPHRASE

The catastrophe now unfolding aboard the <u>Mir</u>
space station argues against launching people to
Mars any time soon. To consider a manned Mars
mission now is like planning your next flight
during a midair crisis.

The difficulty is sending people into outer
space.

Most of the really useful things achieved
in space have been done with automated
spaceships controlled by technicians on Earth.
The record is quite impressive--scientific
probes to the planets and beyond, communications
satellites, weather satellites, reconnaissance
satellites, the global positioning system . . . .

You'll see the fault very readily if you compare these plagiarized paragraphs with the opening paragraphs in Roland's original editorial.

14d Connect your research materials

Your work with sources doesn't end once you have finished paraphrasing or summarizing them. You must now consider them thoughtfully in relationship to each other. Indeed, if you think of your project as a lively conversation, you'll want to be sure that no single voice dominates the conversation in your project or goes unchallenged. That means that you shouldn't compose any major part of your work without drawing on a variety of sources. And every part of the project should reflect the depth of your research and reading.

In some projects, you'll want to cite sources that reinforce each other, especially when you're trying to build a persuasive case. In other situations, you may find authoritative sources that differ significantly; then you have to decide which to endorse or, perhaps, leave that choice to readers. When sources have pronounced biases (political or otherwise), be sure to read them "against" pieces with alternative views to keep your own perspectives broad. And when you borrow material from online discussion groups, always find more conventional sources to confirm specific facts, figures, or claims you find there.

Following is an exemplary paragraph from an undergraduate research paper by Andres Romay on the rising homicide rate among juveniles. It makes its case by synthesizing five different sources—as indicated by the parenthetical notes. The sources furnish the information, but Andres Romay provides the logic that leads from data to conclusion.

```
     A second factor contributing to the increasing rate of

homicides committed by juveniles is easier access to firearms

among adolescents. According to the Justice Information

Center, between 1984 and 1994, guns became much more available

to teens than in earlier decades ("Partnership").

Additionally, there was a 156 percent increase in weapons

offenses for juveniles within the same decade (Butts).

Approximately one in every eight suburban youth and two in

every five inner-city youth carried a gun at some time

(Osofsky 3-4). Since juveniles have had this increased access

to guns, juvenile killings with firearms have quadrupled (Gest

36). Instead of teens settling their disputes by fistfighting

or stabbing, they now resort to shooting. Since gunshots are

more likely to be fatal than other kinds of injuries, it is

easy to see why the rate of homicides would increase as guns

become more available. A pilot program in Boston launched in

1984 to reduce the availability of guns to adolescents through

stiffer penalties and advanced systems of gun tracing has,
```

```
predictably, reduced the number of juvenile killings in the
city (Kennedy). Clearly, the availability of guns has a causal
relationship to the juvenile homicide rate.
```

GETTING INVOLVED

1. In the library, browse the collection of recent magazines and journals to find one or two that provide formal abstracts: you may have to choose a scholarly journal to find this feature. Read over the abstracts in these journals, and then decide whether you'd classify such an abstract as a summary or a paraphrase. How useful are these abstracts? In what ways might you use them in preparing your own research project?

2. While in the magazine section of your library, look for two or three magazines that annotate their tables of contents, briefly explaining the substance of their main articles and features. Then compare several of these brief summaries to the articles in the magazines. Would you describe these table of contents blurbs as accurate summaries, or do they (occasionally, at least) serve any other functions—such as enticing readers into the magazine itself? Where else do you find similar kinds of brief—and enticing—summaries?

3. In class, working in groups of five or six, choose a substantive article from the campus newspaper. Have each member of the group prepare a summary of the piece—no more than 150 words. Then compare and contrast the summaries. What—if anything—did every member of the group include in the summary? Over what matters was there considerable variance?

MANAGING YOUR PROJECT

1. Survey your working bibliography and decide which sources you expect will require full paraphrases, which ones will be handled adequately through summaries, and which ones may require a combination of approaches.

2. Decide how you want to keep track of your notes—whether summaries or paraphrases. You'll likely decide that 3-by-5-inch index cards are not large enough for full paraphrases—though the smaller cards may serve well for keeping track of preliminary bibliography items. Be sure to preserve a tight connection between your bibliography cards and the actual notes you take.

3. Explore the features of note-taking programs such as *TakeNote* if you have access to one. Such programs handle the logistics well, linking notes and bibliographical information effortlessly. Such programs may encourage you to take more thorough notes than you do usually and may help you see more connections between your materials.

In 1455, Johann Gutenberg (1397–1468) produced the Gutenberg Bible, the first book printed with movable type. Before Gutenberg's invention, all books had been either handwritten by scribes or made from woodcuts. Not surprisingly, such works were difficult to produce, costly, and rare. Movable type made book production much easier. In creating his Bible, Gutenberg imitated manuscript form. He used Gothic script and vellum pages—neither numbered nor titled—and each page of the book was meticulously hand-illuminated. The Bible is set in 42-line columns of Latin text in three volumes. No one knows for sure how many of the Bibles Gutenberg printed, but today 40 copies are known to exist. A page from one of the Bibles appears in the illustration above.

Gutenberg's movable-type printing press remained the standard for book production until the nineteenth century. The development of printing and book distribution inevitably led to new conventions in research and publishing. Laws and guidelines were eventually established to protect the "intellectual property" of authors while giving scholars a way to use and credit sources. All writers share ideas and should honestly credit their sources, whether they are cited in the text, in a bibliography, or on an acknowledgments page.

◎ DON'T MISS . . .

- **The material on collaboration in Section 15b.** You may be encouraged to work collaboratively on some college research projects.

- **The discussion of intellectual property rights in Section 15c.** As a researcher, you'll want to know what intellectual property is and how the concept may affect your work.

- **The distinction between summaries and paraphrases of source material explained in Section 15e.** Be sure to review this material before you start taking notes.

BOOKMARKS: Web Sites Worth Knowing

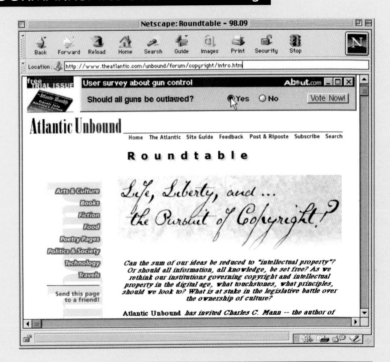

"Atlantic Unbound Roundtable: Life, Liberty, and the Pursuit of Copyright?"
http://www.theatlantic.com/unbound/forum/copyright/intro.htm

In the future, will you have to pay for each time you read a book, see a video, or visit a Web site? *Atlantic Unbound's* discussion of copyright provides a fascinating insight into the complex issues surrounding the future of intellectual property. Four experts participated in three rounds of discussion on the site in September 1998. The conversation, along with the comments of readers, can be read in its entirety on *The Atlantic's* Web site.

Additional Sites
"10 Big Myths About Copyright Explained," http://www.templetons.com/brad/copymyths.html
"Academic Integrity," http://www.csudh.edu/srr/newpage4.htm
Centre for Research Ethics, http://www.cre.gu.se/
Writer's Roost Online Writing Resources, "Academic Integrity,"
    http://www.ukans.edu~writing/docs/integrity.html

Understanding Academic Responsibility and Intellectual Property

College writers often bridle when they hear terms like *plagiarism* and *collusion,* knowing that being accused of either offense can undermine one's integrity or ruin a career. Worse, many students worry so much about inadvertently violating the seemingly arcane rules that surround academic sources that they avoid research entirely when they can. That's a shame because research ought to be regarded as an exciting journey, not as an obstacle course full of traps. You'll enjoy research a lot more if you can learn to regard the principle of academic responsibility as an ally, protecting your work and that of others.

Simply crediting the sources you use in a research project is often not enough, however, especially if you borrow materials from electronic environments such as the World Wide Web. You can be meticulous and thorough in your citations and still be in violation of copyright law. Legislators and other interested parties are now debating how copyright legislation should change to reflect the changing nature of the publication and communication of ideas. But some of the proposals threaten our ability to use sources at all. It is therefore important that we follow guidelines for use of electronic sources based on common sense, ethics, and the unique nature of electronic publications.

15a Understand the ethics of research

You should summarize, paraphrase, quote, and document research materials carefully, not to avoid charges of plagiarism but because you have an ethical responsibility to represent the ideas of other writers accurately, to back up your own claims, and to assist readers in checking your research.

Readers and writers alike depend on the integrity of their sources. The elaborate networks of information we have built can be trusted only if researchers themselves are trustworthy. Moreover, as collaborative and electronic projects make authorship more complex, we need to depend more than ever on the good faith of researchers and writers. Most students do understand that it is wrong to buy a paper, to let someone heavily edit a paper, or to submit someone else's work as their own. But many students do not realize that taking notes carelessly or documenting sources inadequately may also raise doubts about the integrity of a paper. Representing the words, ideas, or creations you found in a source as your own, intentionally or not, constitutes *plagiarism*, and instructors take this seriously. Luckily, plagiarism is easily avoided if you take good notes and follow the guidelines discussed in this section.

15b Understand the special nature of collaborative projects

Whether working with writers in your own classroom or with students in other locations across a network, you'll find that in truly collaborative projects, it can be tough to remember who wrote what. And that's good. So long as everyone understands the ground rules, joint authorship is not a problem. But legitimate questions do arise.

❏ Must we write the whole project together?

❏ Can we break the project into separately authored sections?

❏ Can one person research a section, another write it, and a third edit and proofread it?

❏ What do we do if someone is not pulling his or her weight?

❏ Do we all get the same grade?

The time to ask such questions is at the beginning of a collaborative project. First, determine what your instructor's guidelines are. Then sit down with the members of your group and hammer out the rules.

The authorship and source problems of collaborative projects done on paper pale when compared with the intellectual property issues raised by electronic projects. Hypertext authors may link words and images from dozens of authors and artists and various sources and media. Every part of the resulting collage might be borrowed, but the arrangement of the parts will be unique. Who then should be credited as the *author* of the hypertext? Conventional documentation formats may not be adequate to handle the unique problems of electronic environments.

15c Understand intellectual property rights

Patents, trademarks, and copyrights are all ways of protecting original creations and ideas. When we create an original machine or process, we patent it, which means we own the rights to produce the invention: we can sell (or rent) those rights to others, and we can receive compensation for such use. When we create an original work of words or art, online or in print, the same premises apply, only the concept is called *copyright* instead of *patent.* We still own the rights to reproduce our work; we can sell (or rent) those rights to others; and we have the right to receive compensation or recognition for such use.

Copyrighted material may be included in other works, such as research projects, without prior permission or payment of royalties, under the doctrine known as *fair use.*

> The fair use of a copyrighted work, including such use by reproduction in copies or phonorecords or by any other means specified [. . .], for purposes such as criticism, comment, news reporting, teaching (including multiple copies for classroom use), scholarship, or research, is not an infringement of copyright. (17 U.S.C. Sec. 107)

Whether or not a given use is protected by this definition is based on the following considerations.

1. The purpose and character of the use, including whether such use is of a commercial nature or is for nonprofit educational purposes;
2. The nature of the copyrighted work;
3. The amount and substantiality of the portion used in relation to the copyrighted work as a whole; and
4. The effect of the use upon the potential market for or value of the copyrighted work. (17 U.S.C. Sec. 107)

Usually, fair use involves no more than 10 percent of a work (a poem, paper, or other document) and giving proper credit to the author or creator (see Chapter 19). Violations of fair use can bring on legal penalties and charges of plagiarism.

15d To avoid plagiarism, acknowledge all direct and indirect borrowings from sources

Suppose that in preparing a research paper on mountain biking, you come across the following passage from *The Mountain Bike Book* by Rob van der Plas.

> In fact, access and right-of-way are the two intangibles in trail cycling these days. The sport is getting too popular fast, and in defense, or out of fear, authorities have banned cyclists from many potentially suitable areas.
>
> You will probably use forest service or fire roads intended for hikers most of the time. Don't stray off these trails, since this may cause damage, both to the environment and to our reputation. As long as you stay on the trails and do it with a modicum of consideration for others, you have nothing to fear and should not risk being banned from them by public agencies.
>
> In many areas a distinction is made between single-track trails and wider ones. Single tracks are often considered off-limits to mountain bikers, although in most cases they are perfectly suitable and there are not enough hikers and other trail users to worry about potential conflicts. In fact, single trails naturally limit the biker's speed to an acceptable level.

If you decide to quote all or part of this selection in your essay, you must use quotation marks (or indention) to indicate that you are borrowing the writer's exact words. You must also identify the author, work, publisher, date, and location of the passage. In MLA documentation style (see Chapter 23), the parenthetical note and corresponding Works Cited entry would look like this.

```
As Rob van der Plas reminds bikers, they need only use common

sense in riding public trails: "As long as you stay on the trails

and do it with a modicum of consideration for others, you have

nothing to fear and should not risk being banned from them by

public agencies" (106).
```

```
Works Cited
van der Plas, Rob. The Mountain Bike Book: Choosing, Riding, and

    Maintaining the Off-Road Bicycle. 3rd ed. San Francisco:

    Bicycle, 1993.
```

You must use *both* quotation marks and the parenthetical note when you quote directly. Quotation marks alone would not tell your readers what your source was. A note alone would acknowledge that you are using a source, but it would not explain that the words in a given portion of your paper are not your own. For the same reason, providing complete references in hypertexts is still necessary, even though you may link a quotation to the original. Online sources may move or disappear, and readers often print out or save hypertexts to disks, making links inoperable.

You may need to use the selection above in indirect ways, borrowing the information in van der Plas's paragraphs but not his words or arrangement of ideas. Here are two acceptable summaries of the passage on mountain biking that report its facts appropriately and originally. Notice that both versions include a parenthetical note acknowledging van der Plas's *The Mountain Bike Book* as the source of information.

```
Rob van der Plas asserts that mountain bikers need not fear

limitations on their right-of-way if they ride trails responsibly

(106).
```

```
Though using so-called single-track trails might put mountain

bikers in conflict with the hikers, such tracks are often empty

and underutilized (van der Plas 106).
```

Without documentation, both versions above might be considered plagiarized even though only van der Plas's ideas—and not his actual words—are borrowed. You must acknowledge ideas and information you take from your sources unless you are dealing with common knowledge (see Section 19b) even though the exact words you use to express the ideas may be your own.

15e Summarize and paraphrase carefully

A proper summary or paraphrase of a source should be entirely in your own words (see Chapter 14). Some writers mistakenly believe that they can avoid a charge of plagiarism by rearranging or changing a few words in a selection; they are wrong. The following passage would be considered plagiarism—with or without a parenthetical note—because it simply takes the source's basic words and ideas and varies them slightly.

PLAGIARIZED

```
In trail cycling today, access and right-of-way are the two
intangibles. The sport of mountain biking is getting too popular
too quickly, so defensive authorities have banned cyclists from
many potentially suitable areas out of fear.

    Mountain bikers typically use forest service or fire roads
and trails intended for hikers most of the time. They shouldn't
stray off these trails, since this may cause damage, both to the
environment and to the reputation of cyclists. As long as mountain
bikers remain on the trails and do it with a modicum of
consideration for others, they need not fear and should not risk
being restricted from them by public agencies.
```

15f Understand the special nature of the electronic classroom

Even though governments around the world (including our own) have yet to decide what the laws will be regarding copyrights, fair use, and electronic sources, some guidelines for handling electronic materials have developed, based on current laws. You need to understand these guidelines and principles.

❑ **Follow guidelines already established for published (i.e., print) sources, if possible.** For print, generally the rule of thumb has been that quoting 10 percent or less of a work constitutes fair use. For online sources, you should continue to abide by this same guideline. For print papers that will be used only in the classroom, you may not need actually to obtain permission; however, you should be aware of the steps necessary to do so and should try to locate the information required. For work to be distributed outside the classroom, however (for instance, to be published on the World Wide Web), it is imperative that you at least make an attempt to acquire permission.

❑ **Point to (or link to) text files, images, audio, or video files in online projects rather than downloading them, if possible.** Some sites offer graphic images to users at no charge and may specifically request that users download them. Requests such as these should be honored. However, graphics and other files should not be downloaded without permission. Users may instead point to images and other types of files rather than downloading them. Of course, courtesy suggests that users request permission even to link to an image or file, since this link may add to traffic on the file server where the image is stored.

❑ **Always cite sources carefully, giving as much information as possible to allow the reader to relocate the source.** In addition to citing the source of any text you use in your project, you should properly cite any graphics, audio, or video files included in your work. The elements of citation for electronic sources should include the name of the person responsible (i.e., the author, creator, or maintainer of the site); the title of the work and/or the title of the Web site, if applicable; the date of publication or creation (if known); the protocol and address along with any directions or commands necesssary to access the work; and the date on which you accessed it. Most of the major documentation styles have attempted to present guidelines for citation of electronic sources. A particularly clear and effective style, which conforms to all of the major styles developed for print citation, is presented in Chapter 22.

❑ **If in doubt, ask.** If it is unclear whether or not a given use of electronic material is permitted, ask the owner or author of the site, if possible, explaining the nature of the intended use and noting the portion or portions of the work to be included in your work. If asked by a copyright owner to remove material or links from your project, be prepared to do so promptly.

Note that the WWW is an international publishing space. As such, many of the images, texts, and other files may fall under the copyright laws of other nations, whose attitude toward ownership of intellectual property may be different from our own. Thus, a key word in our own consideration of intellectual property should be *respect*, including respect for the moral and ethical, as well as the economic and legal, rights of authors, creators, and publishers.

15g Establish guidelines for the classroom

With more and more student research projects being published on the World Wide Web or using sources from the Web, it is important that we develop guidelines for using sources. The following suggestions should help you until authors, publishers, legislators, and international policy makers come up with more concrete regulations.

❑ **Always give credit where credit is due.** We deserve credit for our ideas and inventions. Even without laws and teachers' red pens, it would not be ethical to take credit for someone else's ideas. Citing sources serves several purposes beyond avoiding academic penalties and/or lawsuits.

1. It gives credit to the originator of the idea.

2. It shows that you have done your research (you know what you're talking about).

3. It tells readers where to find your sources if they want further information.

❑ **Whenever possible, use primary sources.** *Primary sources* are those sources where the idea or text you are citing (or quoting) originated. *Secondary sources* are those which use the words or ideas of others. For example, an eyewitness to an event testifying in a trial is a primary source. The newspaper account of what the eyewitness said is a secondary source. When writing about literature, the book or story you are writing about is your primary source (for example, Shirley Jackson's "The Lottery"); works *about* the story (Jonathan Burns's "The Hidden Truth: An Analysis of Shirley Jackson's 'The Lottery'") are secondary sources.

In a courtroom, obviously, eyewitness accounts are preferred to hearsay. The same holds true when you are conducting research and compiling research projects: how can you be sure the secondary source has accurately quoted or interpreted the original? The answer is simple: check the original for yourself.

Of course, that is not always possible. Sometimes the original source may not be available or may be too difficult or time-consuming to access. This is especially true with electronic sources; electronic discussion forums, forwarded files, and disappearing Web sites sometimes make it necessary to reference secondary sources. Your citations should always make that clear. (For more information on citing sources, see Chapters 19–20.)

❑ **If it's on the WWW, it's published.** When you make documents and graphics available on the World Wide Web, you are publishing them. In the traditional classroom, students produce papers for an audience of one—the teacher. They are usually free to include graphics, pictures, quotations, and paraphrases from other sources without permission or payment of royalties, provided, of course, the sources are properly cited.

When you publish your work on the Web, on the other hand, it is immediately available to anyone in the world who has access. Intellectual property is considered to have economic value, and publication of someone else's work, even with proper credit, can affect the economic value of that work. Why would people buy a book if they can read it online for free?

When using materials from the Web, you should distinguish between free materials and subscription materials. If you use a graphic from the Internet or another image, such as this photograph of a scene from the play *Androcles and the Lion,* seek permission to use it and provide an appropriate credit line: T. Charles Erickson/Theatre Pix.

Of course, copyrights don't last forever. When they expire, works go into the *public domain.* Many works of literature are now freely available on the WWW, and some newspapers and journals have chosen to make online versions of their publications available for free. Others require a subscription or payment for access. It is important that you know the difference. Works in the public domain may be used without permission or payment of royalties (although it is still necessary—and ethical—to accurately cite the source); copyrighted materials, on the other hand, may not be republished without permission.

GETTING INVOLVED

1. Most schools have formal, written policies on scholastic responsibility and plagiarism. Locate a copy of your institution's official documents or, perhaps, brochures on the subject published by a school office. Do the guidelines make any mention of copyright law? If they do, in regard to what sorts of materials? Do the statements mention electronic texts and materials such as audio and video files?

2. How would you feel about students at other schools linking to a Web site you created—let's say a set of pages decribing your hobby, favorite sports team, or volunteer projects in the community? What reservations might you have about such links? Would you routinely grant permission for links to your site if you received such requests?

3. Imagine that you are running a site for a major political party or interest group. How much control would you want over outside groups linking to your site? What concerns might you have about outside groups tying themselves to your presence on the World Wide Web?

4. The overwhelming majority of newspapers and magazine pieces you read are not written using any of the formal academic systems of documentation described in this book—MLA, APA, CMS, CBE, or COS. In fact, you'd probably be startled to see in-text notes in *Newsweek* or a Works Cited page on the sports page. But look carefully at a serious article in a major publication. How does the piece earn the right to be taken seriously: what signals within and around the article assure readers that it was properly researched and is based on credible materials? Examine several pieces from different types of periodicals: a feature from *The New York Times,* a story from *Popular Science,* a column from *National Review,* a road test from *Car and Driver.* Do you see any differences in the way the periodicals treat information, talk about their sources, or give credit for information that is borrowed?

5. Newspapers and other news media often report information from sources described as "unnamed" or "reliable" or "inside"; the anonymity of such sources is thereby protected. How much faith are you, as a reader, willing to place in an unidentified source? Why do you think news media routinely report off-

the-record information? Discuss the use of such unnamed sources with your colleagues. When—if ever—might such sources appear in a research paper or project?

6. Charges of plagiarism have been attached to the names of numerous public figures over the years—including writers and elected officials. Can you recall any such accusations? Why do you think that such charges are reported even decades after the alleged act of dishonesty?

MANAGING YOUR PROJECT

1. If you expect to rely heavily on materials borrowed from online sources, be sure to acquire permission early in your project. If you wait until the last minute, you may be in trouble if you are denied permission to use material central to your thesis or project. In making such a request in a letter or, more likely, in email, be sure to mention

   - Who you are
   - Your academic institution
   - The character of your work
   - The nature and scope of the material you are borrowing
   - The context in which you intend to use the material

2. What fears and apprehensions about plagiarism and scholastic responsibility do you have when facing a research project or using outside sources in a paper? Discuss these feelings with your colleagues or instructor *before* you turn in a draft of your project. Clear up any doubts you have about how to use sources appropriately.

3. If you are involved in a collaborative project, sit down with your colleagues and discuss how the work will be distributed and then credited. Have this discussion before you get too deeply into the project. Decide not only who will do what but how performance within the group will be monitored during the project and then reported when the project is done.

ABD has entered the language as an acronym describing graduate students who have done all the work required for their Ph.D. degrees—except the final project. In short, they have completed *all but the dissertation*. This final written project proves a hurdle many never leap. The reasons are many and often personal, but the difficulty may rest in translating ideas and research into language. After all, writing can be scary, even for people who write and read a lot. Researchers may fear they don't have enough to say or can't do justice to what they have discovered. Or writing seems less exciting than exploring ideas—in the laboratory, field, or library.

Yet every research project eventually requires a movement from thought to language, from research to dialogue, from creativity to communication. It's natural to feel some resistance to such closure, particularly when one's research is going well and opening new vistas. But sooner or later writers and researchers have to come to terms with practical realities like deadlines and course requirements. That's what this section is all about, gearing up for the push that brings a project to completion, from refining a thesis and organizing your material to choosing quotations and editing a final draft. It's not only necessary work, it is creative too—once you get over that ABD hurdle.

PART

IV

Developing the Project

16

Refining Your Claim

In most cases, you'll want to narrow the scope of your project early in the writing process and give it a design that reinforces clear, though not necessarily simple, points. Some projects will support specific thesis statements or arguments; others may explore alternatives to the status quo or offer proposals to solve problems; still others might invite readers to join in a conversation. Your role is to create whatever framework will work to make your project an effective response to the original assignment. This shaping must be deliberate and strategic. In a research project, you usually can't rely on chance to bring all the parts together.

16a Be sure you have a point to make

It doesn't matter whether your research is supporting a report, an argument, a Web site, or a series of online conversations. You need, eventually, to have a point and purpose. But don't be surprised if you (and your co-authors in collaborative work) have qualms about a project throughout the research process. All the while you're reading, responding, taking notes, and conducting surveys or interviews, you should be testing your preliminary assumptions and objectives. Here are questions to use in testing potential theses or project ideas against the material you are reading or gathering.

- ❏ Does the project focus on a substantial issue, one that deserves readers' attention?
- ❏ Does the project focus on a debatable issue?
- ❏ Will the issue affect or interest the public?
- ❏ Will readers understand how the issue affects them?
- ❏ Does the information you are finding support your hypothesis or research claim?
- ❏ Do you need to qualify your hypothesis and claim?

16b Focus on issues that matter

For many writers, developing a significant point or thesis is the major challenge of a research project. The thesis is the claim you make as the result of your research, the answer to your research question or the confirmation of your original hypothesis (see Chapter 5). It is tempting to rely on thesis statements that only break sprawling research ideas into significant parts because the material then seems easy to organize.

> Child abuse is a serious problem with three major aspects: causes, detection, and prevention.

> Some scientists favor human exploration of the planet Mars while others think robots can do a better job.

> Common types of white-collar crime are embezzlement, mail fraud, and insurance fraud.

Focal points like these can, in fact, work well when you need to divide issues or ideas into their components—as you might when designing a Web site home page or brochure. For example, the page introducing a site on child abuse might quite logically link to additional pages that separately explore "causes," "detection," and "prevention." The simplicity of the design would help to make the Web site coherent. In fact, Web sites designed to provide information are usually designed according to similar "hierarchical" principles of division or classification, beginning with very general categories on the home page and moving down, from page to page, to more and more specific information. The structure of the Web directory *Yahoo!* is an example of hierarchical division (see **http://www.yahoo.com**).

But for research projects that make arguments, theses that just break an idea into parts can seem more like shopping lists than engagements with compelling ideas. The breadth of the statements deadens the argument by preventing readers (and writers too) from considering underlying concepts—how a particular cause of child abuse, for example, might suggest a way to prevent it or why white-collar crime poses a threat to the work ethic. When issues are laid out piece by piece, readers can lose a sense of what connects them.

One way to avoid such loose structures is to focus on problems and conflicts connected to your life or community. Look for claims that demand the attention of readers and that place a burden on you to provide convincing supporting evidence.

TENTATIVE THESIS Students who read extensively may perform no better on academic achievement tests than those who read hardly at all.

You may quickly learn that the point you're developing can't be supported by reliable studies. If that's so, share this discovery with readers.

FINAL THESIS If you think you can do well on achievement tests without cracking a book, you're flat wrong.

Ask basic questions about your topic, particularly *how* and *why*. Get to the heart of a matter in defining a topic. Examine issues that affect people.

LIFELESS	Child abuse is a serious problem with three major aspects: causes, detection, and prevention.
CHALLENGING	Prosecutors in some communities have based charges of child abuse on types of hearsay evidence that now receive tougher scrutiny from judges.
LIFELESS	Common types of white-collar crime are embezzlement, bank fraud, and insurance fraud.
CHALLENGING	White-collar crime is rarely punished severely because many people think that misdeeds aimed at institutions are less serious than crimes against people.

16c Limit your claim

The more you learn about a subject, the more careful you're likely to be in making claims. That's why the thesis that eventually guides your project will almost certainly be more specific, restrictive, and informative than your initial research question or hypothesis. If nothing else, the thesis itself or the paragraph surrounding it should address questions such as *who, what, when, where, under what conditions, with what limits, with what scope?* And topic sentences of paragraphs throughout the project (or other guideposts, such as the headings of Web pages, pamphlets, or information sheets) should relate clearly to this thesis and be equally specific.

Of course, the shape you will give any project will depend on what your thesis promises. One way to understand that commitment is to recall the point of your research inquiry (see Chapter 4). Does it ultimately involve a claim of *fact*, a claim of *definition*, a claim of *value*, a claim of *cause*, or a claim of *policy?* You'll want to refine your thesis to make a distinct and limited claim and then follow through with the appropriate support and evidence.

ORIGINAL CLAIM OF *FACT*
AIDS is the greatest killer of the young.

CLAIM SPECIFIED AND LIMITED BY RESEARCH
In the United States, AIDS has recently replaced automobile accidents as the leading cause of death among teenagers.

COMMITMENTS
- Present figures on mortality rates among young people.
- Find figures on deaths from auto accidents.
- Find figures on deaths from AIDS.
- Draw out the implications of the studies for AIDS prevention.

ORIGINAL CLAIM OF *DEFINITION*
Zoos constitute cruelty to animals.

CLAIM SPECIFIED AND LIMITED BY RESEARCH
Confining large marine mammals in sea parks for public amusement is, arguably, a form of cruelty to animals.

COMMITMENTS
- Define specific criteria for "cruelty."
- Examine what experts say about the condition of animals in marine parks. Or do fieldwork in such a park.
- Find statistics on animal health in and out of marine parks.
- Show that conditions in marine parks meet or do not meet criteria for "cruelty to animals."

ORIGINAL CLAIM OF *VALUE*
The EPA is ruining America.

CLAIM SPECIFIED AND LIMITED BY RESEARCH
Air-quality standards proposed by the U.S. Environmental Protection Agency (EPA) in 1997 may damage the industrial economies of many northern and western states that depend heavily on coal.

COMMITMENTS
- Acquire the actual EPA standards.
- Determine which states may have to comply with the standards. Interview experts in local or state government.
- Explain the possible consequences of compliance.

ORIGINAL CLAIM OF *CAUSE*
Higher speed limits are not the cause of increased traffic deaths.

CLAIM SPECIFIED AND LIMITED BY RESEARCH
The general gradual rise in traffic deaths is not due to recent higher speed limits on interstate and limited-access highways.

COMMITMENTS
- Provide accurate facts on increase in traffic deaths.
- Explain where, when, and by how much speed limits have increased.
- Refute the inference that the rate of traffic deaths has risen uniformly on four-lane limited-access highways.
- Present other potential causes for any observed increase—including increases in travel, number of vehicles and drivers, road rage.

ORIGINAL CLAIM OF *POLICY*
Increases in student fees on campus should be abolished.

CLAIM SPECIFIED AND LIMITED BY RESEARCH
Additional increases in student fees on campus should be capped at a level not to exceed the national rate of inflation unless students approve higher fees in a public referendum.

COMMITMENTS
- Explain how and why fees are increasing on campus.
- Examine the procedure by which fees are currently raised.
- Offer an alternative proposal.
- Defend the advantages and feasibility of the proposal.

GETTING INVOLVED

1. Study the table of contents of one of your textbooks or a major reference tool (one that is not arranged alphabetically). How is the volume arranged? What are the major divisions and subdivisions? Can you appreciate why the book is arranged as it is? Can you imagine alternative arrangements?

2. Working with a team, gather as many examples as you can of claims that are carefully qualified. You can look everywhere, from editorial columns in newspapers to toothpaste packages. What different purposes do these qualifications serve? Summarize your findings in a brief report for all your classmates.

MANAGING YOUR PROJECT

1. Can you connect your project in some way to your world or local community? Why should readers care about what you have discovered? How will they benefit, directly or indirectly? Consider how you can give your project significance.

2. What limits on your thesis can help make your project both more true to the facts you are uncovering and more manageable? Write out your thesis fully, stating both your claim and supporting reasons. Then either add the necessary qualifications or note the qualifications already in the statement.

3. How would you characterize your project and thesis: are you making a claim of *fact*, *definition*, *value*, *cause*, or *policy?* Or does your project fall between categories, combine them, or fit in another realm entirely? (Review Chapter 4, "Establishing a Purpose," for more about these categories.) If you are unable to categorize the nature of your claim, it may be because your claim is either changing or still unfocused. This might be a time to ask an instructor or your colleagues for their suggestions.

4. What commitments does your project make? Writers sometimes underestimate what they have to explain to readers, especially in setting the context for their work and providing background information (or helpful links to related works). Be honest with yourself about enumerating the commitments your work involves. If necessary, plan to do more research to meet those expectations.

Organizing Your Project

From the humblest two-page research report to the most complex Web site, structure matters. Structure helps readers move purposefully from point to point in a project—whether they are heading in straight lines as they usually do in most papers or blazing paths of their own through the nodes of a Web site.

Organizing a project might seem easy. We even have a classic academic design for papers, the five-paragraph essay, that looks like the model of clarity. Make a statement in an introductory paragraph, prove it with at least three paragraphs of supporting evidence, tack on a conclusion, and you've got a paper.

Introduction: Thesis
Argument 1 + examples/illustrations
Argument 2 + examples/illustrations
Argument 3 + examples/illustrations
Conclusion

Unfortunately, a statement isn't proven just because you can line up three ideas in a row to support it. Three or more reasons can be marshaled in favor of most propositions. And using such a pattern of organization can produce sheer nonsense.

THESIS: LARGE DOSES OF RADIATION MUST BE BENEFICIAL TO HUMAN HEALTH.

❑ Atomic power produces useful energy.

❑ Energy powers satellites.

❑ Radiation is used to cure cancer.

As you can see, the supporting "arguments" aren't really related either to the main point or to each other, and they certainly don't prove that radiation in large doses is good for people. Yet some writers believe that they have done their jobs just because they have corralled ideas into a similar five-paragraph structure.

When organizing research materials, you obviously want a plan that reflects the complexity of your ideas while serving your readers' need for clarity. But no single formula will work for all your projects.

17a Create a blueprint for your project

Blueprint may be too precise a term to use early in a project. The design of your paper, brochure, Web site, or other project may initially be too rough to offer the precise lines and dimensions blueprints typically offer. But you do need to sketch out a shape of some kind. For a paper, that shape may be a scratch outline that does no more than list what you know you must cover.

I. Thesis
II. Background information
III. Claim
IV. Evidence
V. Conclusion

The equivalent of a scratch outline for a Web project or brochure might be a *storyboard*—a drawing that positions the major features or elements of a design. Scratch outlines and storyboards help you set large-scale priorities in arranging and positioning information.

Organizing your research effort means deciding what parts or features a project must have and in what order they'll appear. At least five different priorities will typically compete for your attention.

❑ **Logical order.** You will want material to follow a pattern that seems coherent to readers, with claims and reasons backed by evidence. Or you may want to enforce some other logical pattern of induction or deduction. Readers should have the impression that ideas are being presented thoroughly, fairly, and systematically. Even a simple division of a topic into its component parts represents a logical order—the kind you might use in a Web site or field report.

❑ **Chronological order.** In some cases, the structure of a project will follow a sequence: *first, second, third; beginning, middle, end; step 1, step 2, step 3*. Portions of a project may follow chronological order even when the rest of the work doesn't. For example, a section at the beginning of a technical report might review what other researchers have had to say on the subject in past articles, beginning with the oldest sources and working up to the most recent.

❑ **Order defined by genre.** In some cases, the structure of a project will be determined for you by precedent or professional guidelines. This will be the case with laboratory or research reports in many fields. Even items as simple as email messages or business letters have structures dictated by conventions that you violate at your own risk.

❑ **Order of importance or significance.** In some projects, especially papers that present arguments, you may need to present the most compelling evidence near the end of the presentation where readers will remember it. Questions of significance may similarly arise when you have to decide whether information rightly belongs in the body of a paper, in notes, or in an appendix. With a Web site, order of significance may play a major role in determining what goes on the home page and how "deep" the site goes. Readers should be able to find important information with just a few clicks.

❑ **Order of interest.** Depending on your purpose, interest may be a consideration in arranging material. You may decide that it is necessary to present important information early just to keep readers involved. Or, in a Web site or brochure, you may decide to forgo the most logical arrangement in order to present an appealing face.

It's up to you to manage these competing interests as you create a design for your work.

17b Consider general patterns of organization

Projects that prove a thesis can be organized in various ways. Consider, for example, a project that offers a connected sequence of arguments, each claim based on the one that precedes it: "If X is so, then Y is true, and if Y is true, then so is Z." A structure of this kind presents arguments that build on each other. You cannot remove any portion of such a structure without demolishing the whole.

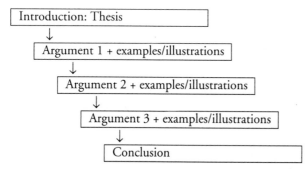

This pattern of organization is potentially more complex than the basic five-paragraph essay because every part of the project depends on its connection to a previous part, not to the thesis statement only. However, the axiom that a chain is only as strong as its weakest link applies here. So a writer has to be sure that readers follow the chain of evidence from link to link. Strong transitions are essential.

Similar organizational patterns may seem simple in outline but will likely grow in complexity as you fill in the blanks. For example, if your project involves **evaluating** something, you know the project has to fulfill commitments.

❑ To provide a rationale for the evaluation
❑ To establish criteria for making evaluative judgments
❑ To measure the subject against the standards
❑ To provide evidence that the standards are or are not met

When you know what the big pieces of a project are, you can begin arranging them. You might test a structure in which you present all the criteria of evaluation first and then apply them to the particular subject of the paper.

Introduction: What's being evaluated

↓

Criteria for evaluation presented

Criterion 1

Criterion 2

Criterion 3

↓

Evaluation/judgment of subject

By criterion 1

Evidence/counterevidence

By criterion 2

Evidence/counterevidence

By criterion 3

Evidence

↓

Conclusions

Or you may decide that readers will be able to follow your evaluation argument more easily if you explain individual criteria of evaluation in the same part of the paper where they are applied. So you craft a different outline.

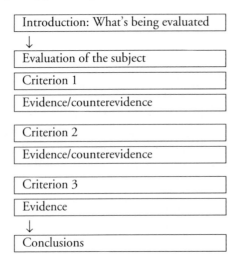

Introduction: What's being evaluated

↓

Evaluation of the subject

Criterion 1

Evidence/counterevidence

Criterion 2

Evidence/counterevidence

Criterion 3

Evidence

↓

Conclusions

Which pattern will work best? That's precisely the kind of question you alone can answer, knowing the purpose of your work, your audience, your evidence, your medium, and your own preferences.

A project that examines a **cause-and-effect** question offers similar structural options. Once again, you'd begin by determining the project's major components. The typical cause-and-effect paper will probably make at least two major commitments.

❏ To examine a phenomenon or event

❏ To explore causes and effects of the event

The first part of such a project might introduce the phenomenon or situation the paper or project will explore, explaining it in some detail (answering the questions *who, what, where, when*). The bulk of the project will then be concerned with interpreting the phenomenon, probably answering the question *why.*

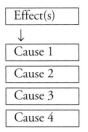

This arrangement is solid and simple, but it still might require arranging the causes from the most obvious, specific, or noncontroversial to the more subtle, abstract, and challenging ones.

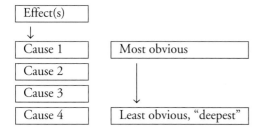

Sometimes the components of a project don't fall to hand as easily as they do for evaluative or cause-and-effect projects. That's often the case when you are **proposing a solution** for a particular problem. The project will likely have several parts, each organized by a different principle: you might have to explain the history of a problem, evaluate the seriousness of the situation, explain the causes of the current situation, enumerate alternatives, and argue for your own solution. Each of these considerations might require a whole section of the project. So, once again, you'd try to set down the essential components of the paper and arrange them in a coherent order—based on the principles described in Section 17a.

| The problem |
| History of the problem |
| Cause of the problem |
| Crisis: need for solution |
| Alternatives to the current situation (rejected) |
| Alternative 1: advantages/disadvantages |
| Alternative 2: advantages/disadvantages |
| Alternative 3: advantages/disadvantages |
| The proposed solution |
| Explanation of solution |
| Feasibility of solution |
| Disadvantages |
| Advantages |
| Implementation of solution |

In research this complex, the key points in the scratch outline may eventually become headings within the project itself.

17c Accommodate dissenting voices

In many projects, you must deal with opposing arguments, presenting them fairly and strategically. If you don't acknowledge them, your project may seem unbalanced, uninformed, or narrow. So the structure of your project must accommodate contrary opinions and deal with them. Counterarguments can be explored anywhere in a project—though generally it is best not to conclude with objections to your thesis since readers often recall best what they have read last. Here are two sample scratch outlines that take counterarguments into account, the first dealing with all objections to a thesis at once and the second dealing with objections one by one.

| Introduction: Thesis |
| Counterarguments |
| Argument 1 + examples/illustrations |
| Argument 2 + examples/illustrations |
| Argument 3 + examples/illustrations |
| Conclusion |

| Introduction: Thesis |
| Argument 1 + examples/illustrations |
| Counterargument 1 |

| Argument 2 + examples/illustrations |
| Counterargument 2 |
| Argument 3 + examples/illustrations |
| Counterargument 3 |
| Conclusion |

Notice that these models suggest that all the components of an essay would receive comparable treatment. This is a distortion: in practice, you would likely give your best points more attention—using all the examples and illustrations you need to make your case. Minor points would obviously receive less coverage than major ones.

17d Follow professional templates

For some projects, you will have to learn and apply conventions of organization already established within a profession or field. For example, if you're asked to prepare a scientific research report, your project may require some or all of the following parts.

Abstract
Introduction
Review of the literature
Methods
Results
Discussion
Summary
References
Appendixes

These parts make up your organization. As you flesh out each section, you create your report. Check carefully with your instructor about the shape of your project. He or she may even provide you with appropriate models or templates. Some software will actually walk you through the task of creating letters, business documents, brochures, and other kinds of presentations.

If your project is a Web site, you will find yourself constricted by the "interfaces" of online communication—the places where you and your readers meet the computer. What you present will be defined by the tools available to you and the expectations readers have for Web sites and Web designs. You'll have many choices to make, but within a fairly limited range.

Even a project as seemingly open-ended as preparing a brochure will quickly be defined by certain expectations. For example, if the brochure is a sheet of paper folded into six panels, readers will expect certain information on the "cover" and other information on the back panel. They will likely peruse the brochure in a certain order, too, and so you have to arrange information to meet such expectations.

In all cases, readers must easily be able to grasp the logic of your design and find information they need.

17e Make connections and use transitions

It is not enough to have a pattern or structure within a project. You must also help readers follow it. In papers and other written work, we describe the components holding a piece together as *transitions*. For the sake of economy, writers often—and understandably—omit such connectors when taking notes simply because they've become so conversant with a subject that they understand a lot of information that was not obvious when they first found the subject.

Unfortunately, writers often fail to restore some of those connections when they write about a subject themselves, mistakenly assuming that readers are just as familiar with these connections as they are. The result can be paragraphs of information unsupported by connective tissue.

> Physicians will usually perform artificial insemination only for married women. When a single woman wants a baby, she will often be rejected. Single parenthood, it is believed, is not good for a child.

Such a cluster of sentences frustrates readers more than it informs them. Readers just about have to rewrite the paragraph to make sense of it. What the writer needs to do is make the connections implied in the sentences much more explicit, spelling out the relationships.

> Physicians will usually perform artificial insemination only for married women **who are having trouble conceiving naturally.** Believing that single parenthood is not good for a child, **doctors** will often reject a single woman who wants to have a baby **by this method.**

The concluding sentence of a paragraph can also function as a kind of connector. Not every paragraph requires a concluding statement that reinforces the thesis of the project. But if, within a paragraph, you have furnished plenty of evidence, don't leave it up to readers—time and again—to reckon how that evidence supports your thesis. Make the connection yourself in a competent concluding sentence.

You can also make connections in an essay by using helpful transitional words and expressions. They seem like small items, but a timely word like *nevertheless* or a phrase such as *on the other hand* can help a reader enormously. So can the strategic placement of headings and subheadings. Even a well-chosen title—one that previews the content of a paper or project—can add to the coherence of a project.

17f Keep track of your subject

You need to reinforce the structure of your project as it progresses so that readers appreciate how each part supports the main point. This principle is easy to understand in on-line documents. It is possible to get lost if, for example, a Web site doesn't provide a clear path back to a home page or if some links lead to dead ends.

But it is almost as easy to go off track in paper documents. For example, in a project presenting research to suggest that student athletes require special academic assistance, it would be important to keep the focus on *athletes*, especially deep in the paper when readers are paragraphs away from the initial statement of the position. Quite often, though, writers begin omitting crucial information, assuming that readers must know what they are talking about.

> CONFUSING   If a person does not receive a good education, he or she will later become a burden to society, and it will leave him or her with nothing at all to contribute to the working world. It is obvious that students, especially in their first year of college, require these benefits to manage their academic and future careers.

What readers need throughout a project are repeated reminders of topic and purpose to give them their bearings. Such signals usually are quite simple.

> SPECIFIC   If a **student athlete** does not receive a good education, he or she will later become a burden to society. **Without a solid education in some field,** the athlete will have nothing to contribute to the working world. It is obvious that **student athletes,** especially in their first year of college, require **academic counseling** to be sure they learn to manage their academic life and future careers.

It is particularly important to reestablish what it is you are trying to prove whenever you offer a new supporting argument. Just because you have stated a thesis clearly once, don't assume readers will recall it. The fact is that they often won't—and they'll resent the expectation.

For example, here's the beginning of a paragraph from deep in an essay arguing that required government and history courses should be removed from the core college curriculum.

> Another aspect of what a waste government and history courses are is time.

The writer probably thinks he is being helpful. After all, he gives readers a transitional signal ("Another aspect") and a reminder of the general topic ("what a waste government and history courses are"), but both assertions are vague, and the new supporting idea is quite mysterious: "time." What does *time* have to do with government and history courses? Whose time? A more helpful topic sentence would move more slowly and spell out ideas with greater care. Here is a possible revision to help readers stay on track.

> Eliminating the government/history requirement from the core curriculum has the added advantage of freeing six credit hours on students' crowded schedules, giving them the time for two more electives.

17g Be sure your project complies with ADA guidelines

If you are creating a Web site, particularly one that may be part of a long-term campus project, get acquainted with the specifications necessary to comply with the Americans with Disabilities Act. The act requires that people with disabilities have reasonable opportunity to use public facilities—which might include the Web site you are creating for a school or corporation. A sightless person, for example, can access a Web site through software that reads the words on a page and which can identify images through "tags" attached to them by the author of the site. But certain types of Web designs make such reading difficult. And those helpful tags do need to be attached to all images.

Most institutions have offices that deal with ADA compliance issues. Contact that office if you would like to be sure your Web site is designed from the outset to serve all people.

GETTING INVOLVED

1. Study the structure of a half-hour television news program. You may need to watch the program several times to grasp its underlying design. Note what comes first in the show, where commercials are typically placed, how credits are presented, how the program typically closes. Once you have uncovered the structure of the program, consider how that design shapes the way news is being presented to viewers. What do viewers see—and not see? How does the program separate what is supposedly important news from what is less significant? What does the regularity of the structure do for (and to) viewers of the news? Programs to consider include the nightly news shows on the networks, the hourly news programs on cable outlets (CNN, Fox, MSNBC), and the weekly Sunday morning political forums on all the major networks.

2. Find a lengthy report or news article, copy it, and then underscore or highlight every paragraph, sentence, phrase, or word that might be considered transitional, defining the term broadly. Hand the piece to a second and even third reader to hunt for transitional devices you may have missed. When you are satisfied that all the transitions have been discovered, estimate what percentage of the entire piece is working to move readers from one thought to another.

MANAGING YOUR PROJECT

1. Create scratch outlines or storyboards for your overall project. Identify the major divisions of your work—the four or five divisions under which all information might be organized. Don't settle too quickly on a single design; try alternatives. Be sure to examine these tentative outlines (or storyboards) from the point of view of readers coming to your project with no idea at the outset of what you may be doing.

2. Once you have settled on the major divisions of your project, you might want to prepare a more formal outline or sketch, subdividing each of the major headings into component parts. You may discover places where a traditional paper might repeat itself or where a Web site might run into navigational problems (such as dead ends, where users might not understand how to return

to a main page). It's easier to see opportunities or eliminate problems at this stage than to revise a project already fully drafted or constructed.

3. If you have had the good sense to keep your notes on cards, you might try now to lay out the entire project. Create note cards for all your major heads and subheads. Then arrange your other cards under those headings in exactly the order you might follow in your actual project. When you have a satisfying design, "read" through it as you might a paper, imagining the transitional paragraphs, sentences, or words you might employ. Modify the design as you see fit. Many writers find that laying out their projects on cards this way helps to keep their thoughts organized.

18

Drafting Your Project

Your desktop is cluttered with *stuff*—books, articles, photocopies, printouts, not-so-floppy disks. Your research question has been refined into a sensible thesis everyone in your group supports. You've drafted a small stack of scratch outlines or a desktop of storyboards. And you've finished brewing a third pot of coffee. Time to *just do it. Do the project—right now!* Pound out a dozen pages. Or crank up *PageMaker* and design that brochure. Or study those HTML tags and start assembling pages. Produce *something*. But that's easier said than done.

There's probably a moment in every major research project when the work *really* begins. You recognize the moment because it often takes so much effort to reach that point and then to push beyond it. You need to have confidence in your ideas, in your hypothesis, in the thoroughness of your research, in your overall design. At this delicate moment, it can be tempting to slide back into more research or reading, or to promise yourself to "think about it tomorrow," or to go to a movie. But that's precisely when you have to gather up your confidence, your determination, and any co-authors and push ahead. You've got to write.

18a Prepare a version of your project early

Think of the first draft or version as the prototype for your project. Many months before new automobiles are introduced to the public, hand-built versions are run thousands of miles on test tracks to simulate road conditions. In a similar way, a draft tests your project under demanding conditions. Will it stand up to demands for facts, evidence, logical argumentation? Will it survive potential counterarguments? Will it keep readers interested and engaged?

Plan on finishing the first version of a project, one on which you can get serious feedback from colleagues, about halfway through the time allotted for the assignment. (See Chapter 2, "Managing Your Project.") If you have a month for a project, resolve to have a draft in hand in two weeks.

Why draft so early? You need to plan ahead because you want plenty of time to revise, fill in gaps, or redesign your presentation. You may have to return to the library or the WWW to gather additional material, or you may need to conduct follow-up experiments or surveys. You may need to reorganize what you have already written, polish the style, or improve the graphics. The more time you give yourself between your prototype and the final version, the better your project is likely to be.

Remember, too, that the final stages of producing a research project involve steps not required in other work: from doing an outline and preparing a Works Cited page to checking Web page links and graphics or tinkering with a color printer. You have to allocate time for all these extra activities, appreciating that something almost always goes wrong.

18b Draft your project for an audience

Tailor your examples, illustrations, and allusions to the group you are addressing. With a professional audience, you can select technical sources and explain them, knowing that many concepts, theoretical assumptions, and terms will be familiar. Among experts, the body of shared common knowledge will be quite large. With a less knowledgeable audience, you'll have to surround technical materials with more detailed explanations or choose less daunting evidence and examples.

You must also write in language suited to your audience. To appreciate how language changes from audience to audience, just pick up a few magazines aimed at different age groups, professions, or economic groups. You'll find differences in the tone, style, organization, and vocabulary (in the professional magazines especially) of these pieces. The differences evident in the periodicals represent the adjustments writers have made to be "heard" by their readers. To address an academic setting, for example, you must master something vaguely described as *college writing*. Managing such an academic style isn't easy when you are a novice in a field—as is typically the case with college writers beginning work in their majors or professional specialties. Yet learning that professional language is one goal of most college research projects. College writing is semiformal in tone, careful about grammar and mechanics, scrupulous about evidence and documentation.

Another aspect of writing for an audience involves convincing readers that your project deserves attention. After spending weeks researching a project, you may simply assume that your subject is important. But readers glancing at a paper, brochure, Web site, or other project still need a reason to take notice. For example, if you've decided (against all advice) to examine the death penalty in the United States, you have to provide a motive for readers to visit that shopworn subject one more time. Maybe you've got a new angle on crime statistics, new survey information, or a newsworthy local case that might compel renewed attention.

In short, you have to give the subject *presence*. Giving a topic presence isn't a matter of grabbing readers with sensational claims or pulsing graphics; it is about supplying a rationale for your work based on your own thoughtful study of an issue or problem. The type of rationale you supply may depend on the audience you must reach: members of a professional audience will attend to your research if it promises to advance what they already know; a general audience may need more coaxing to develop an interest in listening to what you have to say .

18c   Present your material strategically

The organization of your research project (see Chapter 17) will guide many decisions you will make about content and coverage of your subject. But certain general principles and practices are worth remembering as you draft any project.

State ideas clearly. Explain your ideas in language as direct as the facts will allow (see also Section 18d), answering as many basic questions as readers are likely to have. Here, for example, is a topic sentence that would leave most readers puzzling over *who* is doing *what* to *whom*. It's from a paper examining the causes of an increasing pregnancy rate among teenagers.

> The most evident and changeable factor in the pregnancy increase in the past thirty years directly relates to the media.

If you examine the sentence, you won't actually find an explanation for the pregnancy rate, only the suggestion that some evident and changeable factor *relates* to the media. *Relates* is an ambiguous verb. In what sense is this factor connected to the media? Indeed, what is the factor? The topic sentence doesn't tell you. It needs to be revised to make the causal connection much more obvious so that the project (or paragraph) that follows from it can have a direction.

> The clearest blame for the increase in teenage pregnancies in the past thirty years belongs to the national media—newspapers, magazines, films, and television filled daily with articles that make teens believe that early sexual activity is both normal and healthy.

That's quite an indictment. A reader might disagree with the claim, but at least he or she has something to disagree with—an argument stated clearly and directly. Who would react to the original version of the topic sentence in the same way?

Provide evidence for all key claims. You don't prove an assertion merely by restating it or contradicting it—no matter how confident you are of your views. You must take the time to analyze and argue. Be sure readers appreciate how you came to your judgments. If possible, give them an opportunity to arrive at similar conclusions. Consider, for example, this passage from a paper about battered spouses.

> A common belief in society today is that spouses who put up with beatings over a long period of time are probably masochists who come to regard the assaults as signs of love. This belief is obviously not true.

The second sentence, though likely based on the writer's research and probably an accurate statement, carries little weight as part of an argument or proof because it is presented as a mere assertion. In fact, the first sentence is not *obviously* false; if it were, the belief would not be so common. The writer needs to do more work, providing evidence and alternative explanations for the willingness of spouses to put up with long-term abuse.

Qualify generalizations. You'll have a much easier time proving claims that are limited rather than sweeping in scope. If you are writing about conditions in the United

In drafting your project, use precise language that answers basic questions readers might have. For example, readers looking at this photograph might expect a caption to identify who is pictured here (James Meredith), what he did (he changed higher education for minorities in the 1960s), and how this happened (a Supreme Court ruling enabled him to attend and graduate from the University of Mississippi).

States, for instance, be specific; don't assume that readers will understand what you are talking about if you haven't named your scope.

> Throughout history, minorities were barred from institutions of higher learning until the civil rights movement broke those barriers.

College audiences are especially likely to include international students, and so the claim needs to be appropriately qualified.

> In the United States, minorities were barred from most institutions of higher learning until the civil rights movement of the 1960s broke those barriers.

Cite authorities whenever you support assertions with figures or other data. Don't expect readers to take your word for any claim that might be disputed, and don't simply assume that you know what the facts are because you've heard some generalizations. Statements as sweeping as the following would need statistical backing if they appeared in a research project.

> It is a scientific fact that a marijuana cigarette kills more brain cells than a night of free drinks on Bourbon Street.

> There is no evidence that capital punishment serves as a deterrent to crime.

> Athletes perform at the same academic level as students in the general population.

18d Write stylishly

"One size fits all" certainly does not apply to the style of research projects. You'll write one way when you are assembling a research report for a psychology course, another way entirely when posting a Web site designed to help elementary school children understand aspects of African American history. Many of your choices of language will seem fairly obvious. You know better than to joke around in the physics lab report or to present the case for capping tuition in language that insults the very people who have power to change the situation. You've probably been drilled, too, in the virtues of sentence economy—of cutting your prose to a decent bare minimum so readers don't waste their time. Here we'd like to explore more general principles that apply especially to research reports and arguments. As always, the guidelines should be applied judiciously.

Find language that addresses readers intelligently. Be confident about the research you have done, but don't assume that positions other than your own aren't plausible. Remember that some of the readers most interested in your research may be people suspicious of it. So make sure that the language you use welcomes skeptics and doesn't make them personally defensive. Put your own case in positive terms (when that's possible), but don't alienate readers by assuming a lofty moral tone, one that suggests only you have special insight or sensitivity on a given issue.

Avoid vague evaluative terms. Quite often, writers report information in evaluative terms too vague to make much of an impression.

CHART				
Vague terms				
bad	effective	good	little	nice
big	fine	great	neat	poor

The whole point of some research is to make ideas more robust, not to bury claims under vacuous adjectives. So you can't be content with terms quite so vague. Every time you use a vague evaluative term in a draft, circle it, and ask yourself: What do I mean by _____? What exactly makes my subject _____? Then incorporate some of those specifications into your prose.

WHY WRITE . . .	WHEN YOU COULD PROVIDE DETAILS?
good evidence	three refereed articles in *JAMA*
a bad estimate	an estimate 125 percent too high
sort of hot	a surface temperature of 104°F
nice music	lush, romantic orchestration

Avoid expressions that begin with vague qualifiers such as *pretty, sort of, kind of, such a,* and *so.*

Qualify sweeping statements. Can you support all the evaluative statements and judgments you make? Qualifiers help limit your liability.

CHART				
Qualifiers				
almost	many	occasionally	some
in a few cases	most	possibly	sometimes
in many cases	often	probably	with these exceptions

However, a first draft is at least a safe place to overstate your case; in the second draft, take another look and add the necessary qualifiers.

GETTING INVOLVED

1. You know what procrastination is. In a group, talk about the problem as it affects writers and researchers. When do *you* typically procrastinate? What underlies the procrastination: Is it fear of failure? a sense of inadequacy? sheer laziness? How have you suffered in the past from decisions to put off what you might have finished quickly? How have you overcome procrastination?

2. In what ways is most of the research you encounter in journals and magazines argumentative? Are the researchers (or journalists) merely presenting information, or are they expressing opinions through their presentation of research materials? Talk about these questions in small groups, and then present your conclusions to the entire class for further discussion.

MANAGING YOUR PROJECT

1. Clear out both physical and temporal spaces to work on drafting your project: a place to work and a time to work. Don't underestimate the importance of this preparation. Gather all the materials you need in one location so that you don't have to interrupt your writing. Also claim the time you need from friends, other projects, and other concerns. Make yourself comfortable, too.

2. Review the timetable for completing your project, and adjust it to fit any changes in your project to date. (See Chapter 2.) Be sure the schedule remains specific and reasonable. You'll be more successful if you break the project into manageable parts and set goals that you can, in fact, meet.

19

Documenting Your Project

Documentation is the evidence you provide to support the ideas you present in a research project. Effective documentation gives the material you offer readers credibility and authority, and yet it also encourages more dialogue. Anthony Grafton, professor of history at Princeton University, explains this dual mission in "The Death of the Footnote (Report on an Exaggeration)," published in *The Wilson Quarterly* (Winter 1997). Footnotes, he writes, "give us reason to believe that their authors have done their best to find out the truth [. . .] they give us reason to trust what we read." That's the contribution documentation makes to gathering information.

But the dialogic dimension of research—the unending conversation of ideas that makes academic work an adventure—is always present too, as Grafton explains: "[Footnotes] also suggest ways that the author's own formulations can be unraveled. Devised to give texts authority, footnotes in fact undermine. They democratize scholarly writing: they bring many voices, including those of the sources, together on a single page." Footnotes, in-text notes, and electronic hyperlinks encourage the conversation that has become essential to contemporary academic work.

Traditional documentation usually points readers to sources of information: books, articles, statistics, and so on. But it may also cite interviews, software, films, television programs, databases, images, audio files, and online conversations. Various systems for managing sources and documentation have been devised. Presented in this handbook are systems of the Modern Language Association (MLA), the American Psychological Association (APA), the *Chicago Manual of Style* (CMS), the Council of Biology Editors (CBE), and the *Columbia Guide to Online Style* (COS). Specific guidelines for formal documentation appear in Chapters 22 through 26. This section examines more general principles for acknowledging and using sources.

19a Provide a source for every direct quotation

A direct quotation is any material repeated word for word from a source. Direct quotations in college projects often require some form of parenthetical documentation—

that is, a citation of author and page number (MLA) or author, date, and page number (APA).

MLA `It is possible to define literature as simply "that`
`text which the community insists on having repeated`
`from time to time intact"` `(Joos 51-52)`.

APA `Hashimoto (1986)` `questions the value of attention-`
`getting essay openings that "presuppose passive,`
`uninterested (probably uninteresting) readers"`
`(p. 126)`.

Some systems, however, signal notes with raised or highlighted numbers in the body of a text keyed either to individual footnotes (in Chicago Style) or to sources on a References page (in CBE style).

CMS `Achilles can hardly be faulted for taking offense to`
`this incident, as it "threatened to invalidate . . . the`
`whole meaning of his life."`[2]

CBE `Oncologists`[1] `are aware of trends in cancer mortality.`[2]

You are similarly expected to identify the sources for any diagrams, statistics, charts, or pictures in your project. In fact, when you ask for permission to use a copyrighted photograph or illustration, you likely will be asked to provide a credit line as a condition of use. (See Chapter 15 for more on academic responsibility and intellectual property.)

Famous sayings, proverbs, and biblical citations do not need formal documentation. Note that you are likely to quote more often in papers and projects within the humanities and arts than in scientific articles and projects. But all systems of documentation do provide forms for direct quotation.

19b Document all ideas, opinions, facts, and information that you acquire from sources and that cannot be considered common knowledge

Common knowledge includes the facts, dates, events, information, and concepts that an educated person can be assumed to know. You may need to check an encyclopedia to find out that the Battle of Waterloo was fought on June 18, 1815, but that fact belongs to common knowledge and for that reason you don't have to document it.

You may also make some assumptions about *common knowledge within a field*. When you find that a given piece of information or an idea is shared among several of the sources you are using, you need not document it. (For example, if in writing a paper on anorexia nervosa you discovered that most authorities define it the same way, you probably don't have to document that definition.) What experts know collectively constitutes the common knowledge within a field; what they claim individually—their opinions, studies, theories, research projects, and hypotheses—is the material you *must* document in a paper.

19c Document all ideas, opinions, facts, and information in your project that your readers might question or wish to explore further

If your subject is controversial, you may want to document even facts or ideas considered common knowledge. When in doubt, document. Suppose, for example, in writing about witchcraft in colonial America, you make a historical assertion that is well known by historians but likely to surprise nonspecialists. Writing to nonspecialists, you should certainly document the assertion. Writing to historians, you would probably skip the note.

Understand, too, that the documentation you provide should give readers confidence in your source. A traditional citation for a book, for example, usually tells them (at minimum) the name of the author, the title of the book, the place and date of publication, and the identity of the publisher—enough information to support a judgment about the authority of the work.

```
Gass, William. Habitations of the World. Ithaca: Cornell UP,
    1997.
```

But newer electronic sources may provide less information. Some Web sites have no traditional authorship, no pagination, no publisher, no supporting institution. What can a reader deduce from a Works Cited entry such as the following?

```
"Cloning." http://daphne.osu.edu (3 July 1997).
```

The reader won't learn much. The electronic address places the Web site at an educational site (*edu*), but readers will have no clue who "daphne" is, nor will they know whether the material on cloning has much authority. As a writer, you should avoid sources that offer so little documentary information. They will undermine your credibility.

19d Furnish dates, credentials, and other information to assist readers

Provide dates for important events, major figures, and works of literature and art. Also identify any people readers might not recognize.

```
After the great fire of London (1666), the city was . . .

Henry Highland Garnet (1815-82), American abolitionist and
    radical, . . .

Pearl (c. 1400), an elegy about . . .
```

In the last example, the *c.* before the date stands for *circa,* which means "about" or "approximately."

When quoting from literary works, help readers locate any passages you are citing. For novels, identify page numbers; for plays, give act, scene, and line numbers; for long poems, provide line numbers and, when appropriate, division numbers (book, canto, or other divisions).

19e   Use links to document electronic sources

Links in hypertexts (such as World Wide Web pages) can function as a type of documentation: they take readers directly to supporting material or sources. But it's important that readers of hypertexts understand where a highlighted passage is leading them; when they select a link, they should know where they are going.

Hyperlinks should be offered judiciously to provide real information. Don't overwhelm a Web page with links that don't contribute significantly to the project; such a project can seem as fussy as a paper with too many footnotes. Note, too, that you may still be expected to provide a References page or traditional documentation in a scholarly paper that is posted online. The hypertext link may supplement but won't necessarily supplant more traditional documentation—at least not yet.

GETTING INVOLVED

1. Have each member of a small group (four or five people) locate a book or article that uses footnotes or endnotes extensively. Study the way the notes function in these works. What do the notes tell you about the research done to prepare the project? Can you tell how thorough the research has been? Can you tell anything about the field from the sources cited? How up to date were the sources when the piece was published? When does the author use sources? Are the notes in any way "dialogic," as Anthony Grafton claims they might be, "suggest[ing] ways that the author's own formulations can be unraveled"?

2. Which of the following items would be common knowledge? Which would you probably feel the obligation to document? Discuss the examples in class. You may find that you would prefer to document even some items regarded as common knowledge—on the grounds that readers might still prefer to inspect your sources.

   • In a psychology textbook, an informal definition of *split personality*
   • The most recent unemployment figures from the Department of Labor
   • Newton's third law of motion
   • Mae West's comment "When I'm good I'm very good, but when I'm bad, I'm better"
   • The population of Atlanta, Georgia, in 1960
   • Judge Antonin Scalia's dissenting opinion in a Supreme Court case
   • Average price of a quart of milk at three local grocery stores today

- An author's proposal for improving safety of air-traffic control procedures
- Complete text of the Constitution of the United States of America
- Percentage of registered voters who participated in the last presidential election

MANAGING YOUR PROJECT

An important decision for you to make is to determine what system of documentation best suits your project. Here are some matters to consider.

- Did the assignment sheet ask you to use a specific form of documentation? Be sure to check.
- Do you expect to document electronic sources? You may want to use COS style for these electronic items. (See Chapter 22.)
- Are you preparing a project in the arts or humanities? If so, you'll want to choose either MLA (Chapter 23) or CMS style (Chapter 25). Notes in these systems focus on individual authors and on particular passages within these works.
- Are you preparing a project in the social sciences? If so, you'll want to use APA style (Chapter 24). Notes in this system focus on complete research studies (rather than individual passages) and the dates of their publication.
- Are you preparing a project in the natural sciences? If so, you'll want to use CBE style (Chapter 26).
- Do you prefer using in-text notes? If so, your options are MLA (Chapter 23) or APA style (Chapter 24).
- Do you prefer traditional footnotes? If so, use CMS style (Chapter 25).

Benjamin Franklin (1706–1790) founded the first subscription library in America, the Library Company of Philadelphia (pictured here), when he was 25. Subscription libraries collected fees from their members to cover book costs and operating expenses. The libraries were open to the general public for limited hours during the day, but only members were allowed to borrow books. The Library Company of Philadelphia functioned as the unofficial Library of Congress until the Library of Congress was established in 1800.

Today the Library Company of Philadelphia still operates as an independent research library. If your project draws on American colonial history, this library would be an excellent place to find primary source material. Apart from original colonial period texts, the library maintains a collection of American artifacts that date from the colonial period through the nineteenth century. It is open to the public and is online at www.librarycompany.org. The library has indexed 60,000 items of its 500,000-item collection in its database WolfPAC; however, the card catalog remains the best tool for searching this library. Because its stacks are closed, you must actually visit the library to use its resources. Remarkably, the Library Company of Philadelphia still offers subscriptions, and you might consider buying a share, just as the members did in Franklin's day.

◎ DON'T MISS . . .

- **The advice on framing quotations in Section 20b.** If you use direct quotations in a research project, be sure to introduce or frame them in some way. You can't ignore this important detail.

- **The guidelines for punctuating quotation marks in Section 20c.** Placing quotation marks can be tricky; review this section carefully.

- **The guidelines for using ellipsis marks in Section 20e.** The rules have changed for papers written in MLA style.

BOOKMARKS: Web Sites Worth Knowing

"Bartlett's Familiar Quotations,"
http://www.columbia.edu/acis/bartleby/bartlett/

If you can't remember who first noted that "time flies," but you want to correctly cite the statement in your research project, you can find out at "Bartlett's Familiar Quotations." *Project Bartleby* has put the entire text of the 1901 edition of this famous book online. You can even search for a familiar phrase by typing it at the prompt, then using your browser's "find" feature to locate the text you want.

Additional Sites
"Big Dog's Quotation Mechanics Guide," http://gabiscott.com/pages/bigdog_mla_old.html
"Integrating Quotations," http://www.wisc.edu/writing/Handbook/QuoLitIncorporating.html

Handling Quotations

In many research projects—especially those in the arts and humanities—you'll have frequent occasion to quote directly from sources. You will want to do so effectively because quotations can add texture and authority to your project. Think of sources as voices that can confirm your positions, challenge them, or extend them. No stylistic touch makes a research project work quite so well as quotations deftly handled.

20a Select direct quotations strategically

Every quotation in an article should contribute something your own words cannot. Use quotations for various reasons.

- ❏ To focus on a particularly well-stated key idea in a source
- ❏ To show what others think about a subject—either experts, people involved with the issue, or the general public
- ❏ To give credence to important facts or concepts
- ❏ To add color, power, or character to your argument or report
- ❏ To show a range of opinion
- ❏ To clarify a difficult or contested point
- ❏ To demonstrate the complexity of an issue
- ❏ To emphasize a point

Never use quotations to avoid putting ideas in your own words or to pad your work.

20b Introduce all direct and indirect borrowings in some way

Although quotation marks and indentions help to identify direct quotations, these typographical devices don't tell a reader who wrote a passage, why it is important, or how it stands in relationship to the rest of an essay. And, of course, indirect borrowings are not surrounded by quotation marks at all. So short introductions, attributions, or commentaries are needed to orient readers to materials you've gathered from sources. To be sure readers pay attention, give all borrowed words and ideas a context or *frame.*

Such frames can be relatively simple; they can *precede, follow,* or *interrupt* the borrowed words or ideas. The frame need not even be in the same sentence as the quotation; it may be part of the surrounding paragraph. Here are some ways that material can be introduced.

❑ *Frame precedes borrowed material*

A few years ago, my wife and I were startled by a teaser for a story on a network news program, which asked what was meant to be a provocative question: "When is a church more than just a place of worship?"

—Stephen Carter

❑ *Frame follows borrowed material*

"One reason you may have more colds if you hold back tears is that, when you're under stress, your body puts out steroids which affect your immune system and reduce your resistance to disease," **Dr. Broomfield comments.**

—Barbara Lang Stern

❑ *Frame interrupts borrowed material*

"Your best action," **an Atomic Energy Commission booklet read,** "is not to be worried about fallout."

—Terry Tempest Williams

"They are taking away the night," **I thought.** "They are taking away the last moments of mystery. Is nothing sacred?"

—J. Michael Bishop

❑ *Surrounding sentences frame borrowed material*

Even taste is affected by zero gravity. "Body fluids migrate to your upper body, and you end up with engorged tissue around the nasal passages and ear," **explains Gerald Carr, who was commander of the third and longest (84 days) Skylab mission.** "You carry with you a constant state of nasal and head congestion in weightless environment. It feels pretty much like you have a cold all the time."

—Douglas Colligan

If so, says Solow, we should be seeing much warmer temperatures than we have seen so far. "For example, for the planet to warm by 2°C in the next hundred years, the average rate of warming would have to be four times greater than that in the historical record." **Greenhouse warming is expected to be greatest at high latitudes and more rapid in the north than in the south, but this pattern hasn't appeared either, he says.**

—Jane S. Shaw and Richard L. Stroup

❑ *Borrowed material integrated with passage*

The study concludes that a faulty work ethic is not responsible for the decline in our productivity; quite the contrary, the study identifies "a widespread commitment among U.S. workers to improve productivity" and suggests that "there are large reservoirs of potential upon which management can draw to improve performance and increase productivity."

—Daniel Yankelovich

Most borrowings in your research paper should be attributed in similar fashion. Either name (directly or indirectly) the author, the speaker, or the work the passage is from or explain why the words you are quoting are significant. Many phrases of introduction or attribution are available. Here are just a few examples.

President Clinton **claimed** that " . . .

One expert **reported** that " . . .

The members of the board **declared** that " . . .

Representatives of the airline industry **contend** that " . . .

Marva Collins **asserts** that " . . .

Senator Gramm **was quoted** as saying that " . . .

"The figures," **according to** the GAO, "are . . .

CHART
Verbs of Attribution

accept	argue	emphasize	reveal
add	believe	insist	say
admit	confirm	mention	state
affirm	deny	posit	think
allege	disagree	propose	verify

Vary these terms sensibly. You needn't change the verb of attribution with every direct quotation.

20c Handle quotation marks correctly

Quotation marks—which always occur in pairs—draw attention to the words, sentences, or passages they enclose. Use double quotation marks (" ") around most quoted material; use single quotation marks (' ') to mark quotations within quotations. Quotation marks are used around any material you borrow word for word from sources.

Take care with the punctuation before and after quotations. A quotation introduced or followed by *said, remarked, observed,* or similar expressions takes a comma.

> Benjamin Disraeli observed, "It is much easier to be critical than to be correct."

> "Next to the originator of a good sentence is the first quoter of it," said Ralph Waldo Emerson.

Commas are used, too, when a single sentence quotation is broken up by a phrase.

> "If the world were a logical place," Rita Mae Brown notes "men would ride side-saddle."

When a tag line comes between two successive sentences from a single source, a comma and period are required.

> "There is no such thing as a moral book or an immoral book," says Oscar Wilde. "Books are well written or badly written. That is all."

No punctuation is required when a quotation runs smoothly into a sentence you have written.

> Abraham Lincoln observed that "in giving freedom to the slave we assure freedom to the free."

Take care, too, to place quotation marks correctly with other marks of punctuation. Commas and periods go *inside* closing quotation marks except when a parenthetical note is given.

> "This must be what the sixties were like," I thought.

> Down a corridor lined with antiwar posters, I heard someone humming "Blowin' in the Wind."

However, when a sentence ends with in-text documentation, the period follows the parenthetical note.

> Mike Rose argues that we hurt education if we think of it "in limited or limiting ways" (3).

Colons and semicolons go *outside* closing quotation marks.

> Riley claimed to be "a human calculator": he did quadratic equations in his head.

> The young Cassius Clay bragged about being "the greatest"; his opponents in the ring soon learned he wasn't just boasting.

Question marks and exclamation points fall inside the closing quotation marks when they are the correct punctuation for the phrase inside the quotation marks but not for the sentence as a whole.

When Mrs. Rattle saw her hotel room, she muttered, "Good grief!"

She turned to her husband and said, "Do you really expect me to

stay here?"

They fall outside the closing quotation mark when they are the appropriate mark for the entire sentence.

Who was it that said, "Truth is always the strongest argument"?

Quotation marks are also used to mark dialogue. When writing a passage with several speakers, follow convention and start a new paragraph each time the speaker changes.

> Mrs. Bennet deigned not to make any reply; but unable to contain herself, began scolding one of her daughters.
>
> "Don't keep coughing so, Kitty, for heaven's sake! Have a little compassion on my nerves. You tear them to pieces."
>
> "Kitty has no discretion in her coughs," said her father; "she times them ill."
>
> "I do not cough for my own amusement," replied Kitty fretfully.
>
> —Jane Austen, PRIDE AND PREJUDICE

20d Tailor your language so that direct quotations fit into the grammar of your sentences

To make quotations fit smoothly, you may have to tinker with the introduction to the quotation or modify the quotation itself by careful selections, ellipses (see Section 20e), or bracketed additions (see Section 20f).

AWKWARD   The chemical capsaicin that makes chili hot: "it is
so hot it is used to make antidog and antimugger
sprays" (Bork 184).

REVISED   Capsaicin, the chemical that makes chili hot, is so
strong "it is used to make antidog and antimugger
sprays" (Bork 184).

AWKWARD   Computers have not succeeded as translators of
languages because, says Douglas Hofstadter, "nor is
the difficulty caused by a lack of knowledge of
idiomatic phrases. The fact is that translation
involves having a mental model of the world being
discussed, and manipulating symbols in the model."

REVISED   "A lack of knowledge of idiomatic phrases" is not
the reason computers have failed as translators of
languages. "The fact is," says Douglas Hofstadter,
"that translation involves having a mental model of
the world being discussed, and manipulating symbols
in the model" (603).

20e Use ellipses to show where material has been omitted from direct quotations

Three spaced periods or dots mark an ellipsis (. . .), a gap in a sentence or passage. This material may be a word, a phrase, a complete sentence, or more. In MLA style (demonstrated below), ellipses you add to a passage are enclosed in brackets.

COMPLETE PASSAGE   Abraham Lincoln closed his First Inaugural Address
(March 4, 1861) with these words: "We are not
enemies, but friends. We must not be enemies.
Though passion may have strained, it must not
break, our bonds of affection. The mystic chords of
memory, stretching from every battlefield and
patriot grave to every living heart and hearthstone
all over this broad land, will yet swell the chorus
of the Union when again touched, as surely they
will be, by the better angels of our nature."

PASSAGE WITH ELLIPSES   Abraham Lincoln closed his First Inaugural Address
(March 4, 1861) with these words: "We are not
enemies, but friends. [. . .] The mystic chords of
memory [. . .] will yet swell the chorus of the
Union when again touched, as surely they will be,
by the better angels of our nature."

Be sure to use the correct spacing and punctuation before and after ellipsis marks. When an ellipsis mark appears in the middle of a sentence, leave a space before the first and after the last period. Remember that the periods themselves are spaced. If you are following MLA style, note where brackets are placed in the second example.

chords of memory [. . .] will yet swell

If a punctuation mark occurs immediately before the ellipsis, include the mark when it makes your sentence easier to read. The punctuation mark is followed by a space, then the ellipsis mark (or bracket in MLA style).

```
We are not enemies, [ . . . ] must not be enemies
```

When an ellipsis occurs at the end of a complete sentence or when you delete a full sentence or more from a passage, place a period at the end of the sentence, followed by a space and then the ellipsis.

```
We must not be enemies. [ . . . ] The mystic chords
```

```
"These are the times that try men's souls. The summer soldier
and the sunshine patriot will, in this crisis, shrink from the
service of their country [ . . . ] ."
```
--Thomas Paine

When a parenthetical reference follows a sentence that ends with an ellipsis, leave a space between the last word in the sentence and the ellipsis. Then provide the parenthetical reference, followed by the closing punctuation mark.

```
passion may have strained it [ . . . ]" (102).
```

In most cases you should avoid ellipses at the ends of sentences when they indicate only that more material follows. Most readers understand that is likely to be the case whenever you quote. Keep your use of ellipses to a minimum.

Very occasionally, an ellipsis appears at the beginning of quoted sentences to indicate that an opening clause or phrase has been omitted. Three spaced periods precede the sentence, with a space left between the third period and the first letter of the sentence. Any punctuation at the end of the clause or sentence preceding the quotation is retained.

> "The text of the Old Testament is in places the stuff of scholarly nightmares. [. . .] the books of the Old Testament were composed and edited over a period of about a thousand [years]."
> —Barry Hoberman, "Translating the Bible"

You needn't use an ellipsis, however, every time you break into a sentence. The quotation in the following passage, for example, reads more smoothly without the ellipsis.

```
In fact, according to Lee Iacocca, "[ . . . ] Chrysler didn't really
function like a company at all" when he arrived in 1978.
```

```
In fact, according to Lee Iacocca, "Chrysler didn't really
function like a company at all" when he arrived in 1978.
```

Whenever you use ellipses, be sure your shortened quotation still accurately reflects the meaning of the uncut passage. It is scholastically irresponsible and dishonest to alter the meaning of a source by excising critical words or phrases.

20f   Use square brackets to add necessary information to a quotation

Sometimes you may want to explain who or what a pronoun refers to, or you may have to provide a short explanation, furnish a date, and explain or translate a puzzling word. Enclose such material in square brackets [ ].

> Some critics clearly prefer Wagner's Tannhäuser to Lohengrin:
> "the well-written choruses [of Tannhäuser] are combined with solo
> singing and orchestral background into long, unified musical
> scenes" (Grout 629).

> And so Iacocca accepted Chrysler's offer: "We agreed that I would
> come in as president but would become chairman and CEO [Chief
> Executive Officer] on January 1, 1980" (Iacocca 145).

But don't overdo it. Readers will resent the explanation of obvious details. If, for example, most of the prospective readers for the passage about Lee Iacocca were business majors, the explanation of CEO would probably be unnecessary.

20g   Use [sic] to indicate an obvious error copied faithfully from a quotation

Quotations must be copied accurately, word by word from your source—errors and all. To show that you have copied a passage faithfully, place the expression *sic* (the Latin word for *thus* or *so*) in brackets one space after any mistake in the original.

> Mr. Vincent's letter went on: "I would have preferred a younger
> bride, but I decided to marry the old window [sic] anyway."

If *sic* can be placed outside the quotation itself, it appears between parentheses, not brackets.

> Molly's paper was titled "Understanding King Leer" (sic).

20h   Present quotations correctly

Short quotations are arranged differently on a page than longer ones. Place prose quotations shorter than four typed lines (MLA) or forty words (APA) between quotation marks.

> In On Liberty (1859), John Stuart Mill declares, "If all mankind
> minus one were of one opinion, mankind would be no more justified
> in silencing that one person than he, if he had the power, would
> be justified in silencing mankind."

Indent any prose quotations longer than four typed lines (MLA) or forty words (APA). MLA form recommends an indention of ten spaces or one inch from the left-hand margin; APA form requires five spaces. (The right-hand margin is not indented.) Quotation marks are *not* used around the material when it is indented. If the lengthy quotation extends beyond a single paragraph, the first lines of subsequent paragraphs are indented an additional three typed spaces (MLA) or five spaces (APA). In typed papers, the indented material—like the rest of the essay—is always double spaced in MLA. Both APA and Chicago style permit quotations to be single spaced in student projects.

You may also indent passages of fewer than four lines when you want them to have special emphasis. But don't do this with every short quotation or your paper will look choppy.

When you are quoting poetry, indent the lines when the passage runs more than three lines (MLA). Up to three lines of poetry may be handled just like a prose passage, with slashes marking the separate lines. Quotation marks are used when the lines are not indented.

> As death approaches, Cleopatra grows in grandeur and dignity:
> "Husband, I come! / Now to that name my courage prove my title! / I
> am fire and air" (V.ii.287–89).

More than three lines of poetry are indented ten spaces and quotation marks are not used. (If the lines of poetry are unusually long, you may indent fewer than ten spaces.) Double-space the indented passage (MLA), and be sure to copy the passage accurately, right down to the punctuation.

> Among the most famous lines in English literature are those that
> open William Blake's "The Tyger":
>
>> Tyger tyger, burning bright,
>> In the forests of the night;
>> What immortal hand or eye,
>> Could frame thy fearful symmetry? (1–4)

GETTING INVOLVED

1. Comb several full pages of the daily newspaper—including the front, editorial, and lead sports pages—looking for verbs of attribution that introduce direct or even indirect quotations (see Section 20b). Which words or expressions appear most often? What is the most unusual lead-in you find for a quotation?

2. Only recently has the Modern Language Association (MLA) decided that ellipses added to passages should be enclosed in brackets. Given the function of brackets, explained in Section 20f, argue for or against this practice.

MANAGING YOUR PROJECT

1. Review your notes and any photocopied or downloaded material for those passages, tables, charts, or images that you regard as essential to your project. These may be the materials you will either have to quote directly or reproduce entirely in your work. Be sure you have a rationale for each direct borrowing (see Section 20a).

2. After you have drafted a version of your project, check to see that you have framed every direct quotation in some way (see Section 20b) or provided an appropriate label or title for any table, chart, or figure. Remember that no borrowed element should simply be dropped into the paper without an explanation or context.

3. Review every point of entry into a quotation for readability. Be sure that reading is not disrupted by an avoidable shift in verb tense, person, or sentence structure (see Section 20d). Revise your frame or modify the quotation appropriately to make any difficult passage more readable.

Completing Your Project

It is important to remain focused as you bring a long project to completion. Don't be the ballcarrier who begins celebrating before crossing the goal line—only to fumble. Make sure your project meets all its requirements, looks good, and arrives on time. If you created a successful management plan for your project early on (see Chapter 2), you'll reap your reward now with a schedule that can accommodate even inevitable last-minute glitches.

21a Review the structure of your project

Organizing a sizable paper or project is rarely an easy job. That's why you must check that all its final parts fit. Does a home page, for example, provide a logical map or entrance to all the material you've collected in that Web site? Is the information in the body of a report you've written clearly supported by the tables and charts you've placed in its appendixes? Will the separate panels in your brochure or the slides in your presentation work together well in an actual presentation? These are the kinds of questions you face, but sometimes you may be too close to a project to review the material yourself. So it makes sense to encourage others from outside your project group to review your prototype and give you feedback. You might ask yourself and any reviewers the following basic questions.

- ❏ Is the point of the project clear?
- ❏ Are the links between its claims and evidence solid?
- ❏ Will readers understand the relationship between different parts of the project?
- ❏ Are the connections or transitions between parts of the project adequate?
- ❏ Do titles, headings, or other devices contribute to the coherence of the project?
- ❏ Does the project need a more explanatory opening—with more background information?
- ❏ Does the closing require more summary?
- ❏ Do the verbal and visual elements of the project cohere?

For a long academic paper, you may want to use the following method to check the structure.

❑ **Underline the topic idea, or thesis, in your draft.** It should be clearly stated somewhere in the first few paragraphs.

❑ **Underline just the first sentence in each subsequent paragraph.** If the first sentence is very short or closely tied to the second, underline the first two sentences.

❑ **Read the underlined sentences straight through as if they formed an essay in themselves.** Ask whether each sentence advances or explains the main point, or thesis statement. If the sentences—taken together—read coherently, chances are good that the paper is well organized.

❑ **If the underlined sentences don't make sense, reexamine those paragraphs not clearly related to the topic idea.** If the ideas really are not related, delete the whole paragraph. If the ideas are related, consider how to revise the paragraph to make the connection clearer. A new lead sentence for the paragraph will often solve the problem of incoherence. Pay attention to transitions, too—those places in a paper where you can give readers helpful directions: *first of all, on the other hand, to summarize.*

❑ **Test your conclusion against your introduction.** Sometimes the conclusions of essays contradict their openings because of changes that occurred as the project developed. When you've completed a draft, set it aside for a time and then revisit the entire piece. Does it hang together? If not, revise it.

Test the structure of other projects similarly. For example, if you've prepared a brochure, make sure the headings are in the right order, the various sections follow in correct sequence when the brochure is folded, and the panels contain all pertinent information, especially phone numbers and addresses.

In a Web site, try to imagine how a reader encountering it for the first time might search for information: will users find what they are seeking with a minimum number of clicks? Check that all the links work in both directions. Make sure there are no dead ends and that every page on your site provides a way to return to your home page or another helpful location in the site. Make sure you include directions for returning to your site from any external links, if necessary.

2lb Review the design of your project

Again, the format of your projects may vary enormously. Depending on the purpose, audience, and media of a project, you may be expected to accommodate complex textual and visual elements, crop and position photographs on a page, arrange statistics in tables, charts, and graphs, or choose a compatible color scheme. We can offer only very general advice about appropriate document design here. But, fortunately, a bit of common sense goes a long way.

❑ Keep your designs simple and uncluttered.

❑ Design your work so that headings, graphics, and colors highlight, but don't overwhelm, your important ideas.

❑ Don't crowd your designs: allow plenty of white space.

❑ Don't use a distracting array of type fonts and sizes. You rarely need more than two or three.

❑ Don't use colors that distract from your message or make it difficult to read.

❑ Don't push a design beyond your technical skills.

Even traditional academic papers have to meet specific design standards. Be sure any such work is typed cleanly, without distracting strikeovers or whiteouts. Type on only one side of good-quality paper, double-spacing the body of your essay and the notes. If you use a word processor, take advantage of its features. Keep fonts simple, and justify the left-hand margin only. Use a good-quality printer with the correct paper for your printer type.

Specifications for MLA and APA papers are given in Chapters 23 and 24, respectively. These guidelines, which explain where page numbers go, the width of margins, and the placement of headings, can be applied even to projects that don't follow a specific professional style.

21c   Use graphics effectively

Illustrations and other graphics can help readers understand your ideas better than words alone might. Throughout this volume, for example, photographs have been positioned to illustrate the process of research, past and present. In your own work, you might want to use pie charts, graphs, and tables to make statistics easier to interpret or trends easier to spot.

So it makes sense to learn how to manipulate the graphics software available in word-processing or data management programs. In the former, you may be offered a wide range of drawing tools. In the latter, you can typically choose how to present data (in tables, bar graphs, pie charts); the program itself produces the actual image, which you can modify to suit your needs. Presentation programs, too, make it easy to create professional-looking slides and overheads. Some presentation programs even allow you to include sound and may allow you to publish your presentation automatically on the WWW. More complex are the desktop publishing programs, but you can learn to use them to design sophisticated projects, including magazines and books.

If you have access to the World Wide Web, you can download pictures and other visual items for your projects, but you must both document the borrowings and get permission to use them from the authors or owners of the material. Be careful, too, not to clutter your work with what one design expert calls "chartjunk." Just because you have easy access to graphics doesn't mean you must decorate every page. Develop an eye for clean and attractive presentations on paper or screen. For papers, MLA form requires that you label tables (columns of data) and figures (pictures or illustrations), number them, and briefly identify what they illustrate. Spell out the word *table,* and place the head above the table, flush left. Following are a well-prepared table and figure.

Table 1

Economic Dimensions of the Bond Market, 1980-90

Type of Issuer[a]	Year-End Amounts Outstanding (in billions)		
	1980	1985	1990
U.S. Treasury	$159.8	$427.0	$1,023.6
U.S. agencies	17.6	276.1	447.3
States and municipalities	144.4	322.3	734.9
Corporations	181.0	421.7	752.3
Total	$502.8	$1,447.1	$2,958.1

Sources: <u>Federal Reserve Bulletin</u>, <u>U.S. Treasury Bulletin</u>, and <u>Survey of Current Business</u>.

   [a]Excludes institutional issues; data are not available.

Figure, which is usually abbreviated in the caption as *Fig.,* appears below the illustration, flush left.

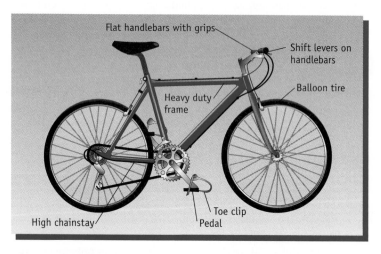

Fig. 1. A well-prepared figure of a mountain bike.

When preparing an APA paper, you may want to check the detailed coverage of figures and tables in the *Publication Manual of the American Psychological Association,* fourth edition. For APA-style student papers, figures (including graphs, illustrations, and photos) and tables may appear in the body of the text itself. Longer tables and all figures are placed on separate pages, immediately following their mention in the the text.

   Chromosomes consist of four different nucleotides or

   bases--adenine, guanine, thymine, and cytosine--which, working

   together, provide the code for different genes (see Figure 1).

Short tables may appear on the same page as text material.

Figures and tables are numbered consecutively. Captions for figures appear below the item. If the illustration is borrowed from a source, you must get permission to reproduce it. Acknowledge the borrowing as shown here.

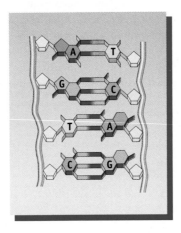

Figure 1. The four bases of the genetic code: adenine (A),
guanine (G), thymine (T), and cytosine (C). Note. From Your
Genes, Your Choice, by C. Baker, 1997. Copyright 1997 by the
American Association for the Advancement of Science. Reprinted
with permission.

Titles for tables appear above the item.

Table 2
Errors by Levels of Difficulty

21d Be consistent with headings

You can use headings to give shape to any project. Titles and headings in brochures, on overheads, and in Web sites require a great deal of attention. A heading has to fit the material it introduces in size and style: a heading too large or gaudy may overwhelm its material while too small a lead-in may diminish important information. When designing multicolumn pages in your projects, you may also have to manipulate space to avoid bumping headings (that is, placing them side by side) or use boxes to break out important information. Again, you should strive for clarity and simplicity.

In academic papers, specific guidelines for headings often apply. A short research paper (five to six pages) ordinarily needs only a first-level head—that is, a title. With longer papers, however, readers will appreciate subheadings that explain the content of major sections. All such heads should be brief, parallel in phrasing, and consistent in format like the items in a formal outline. For most academic papers, you probably won't use more than two levels of headings: a title and one set of subheads.

MLA style (described in more detail in Chapter 23) provides fairly loose standards for headings and subheadings. Titles of MLA papers are ordinarily centered on the first page of an essay while headings and subheadings appear flush with the left-hand margin. If you descend to a third level, you'll have to distinguish between second- and third-level heads by numbering or lettering them or by separating them typographically (usually by variations in capitalization or underlining). MLA style leaves you to decide how you will handle such choices, but in all cases, you must keep the headings clean and unobtrusive. Here are two ways of handling three levels of headings as they might appear in a moderately long MLA-style paper on mountain biking.

Mountain Biking and the Environment	1st level
The Mountain Bike	2nd level
History of Mountain Biking	2nd level
Mountain Bikes and the Environment	2nd level
<u>Trail Damage</u>	3rd level
<u>Conflicts with Hikers</u>	3rd level
Mountain Bikes and Responsible Riding	2nd level

Mountain Biking and the Environment	1st level
1. The Mountain Bike	2nd level
2. History of Mountain Biking	2nd level
3. Mountain Bikes and the Environment	2nd level
3.1. Trail Damage	3rd level
3.2. Conflicts with Hikers	3rd level
4. Mountain Bikes and Responsible Riding	2nd level

APA style (described in more detail in Chapter 24) defines five levels of headings for professional articles—more than you'll likely ever use in a college paper. Here's how to handle three or fewer levels of headings.

❑ First-level heads are centered, using both uppercase and lowercase letters as shown below.

❑ Second-level heads are capitalized like titles but also underlined and placed flush with the left-hand margin.

❑ Third-level heads are underlined, indented, and run as paragraph headings with only their first letters capitalized. Third-level heads conclude with a period.

Here's how those APA guidelines look in operation.

Mountain Biking and the Environment	1st level
<u>The Mountain Bike</u>	2nd level
<u>History of Mountain Biking</u>	2nd level
<u>Mountain Bikes and the Environment</u>	2nd level

<u>Trail damage.</u>	3rd level
<u>Conflicts with hikers.</u>	3rd level
<u>Mountain Bikes and Responsible Riding</u>	2nd level

Any Web pages you create also need accurate, well-focused headings and titles so readers quickly grasp the point of your projects. Succinct and descriptive titles are important, too, if your pages are to be located by Web search engines and directories. Finally, you want titles that will still make sense if they get shortened when added to a Web browser's list of bookmarks or favorites: the first few words of the title should include all important key words. A heading such as "The Beauty and Mystery of Anasazi Cliff Dwellings" might be clipped back to the not very helpful "The Beauty and Mystery." Better to title the Web page "Anasazi Cliff Dwellings: Beauty and Mystery" so that a shortened title would still focus on specific information.

21e Include all the parts your project requires

Before submitting an academic or professional project, reread the specifications either of the instructor or the professional society to which you are submitting a paper. Must you, for instance, include an abstract or an outline? Check to see what leeway (if any) you have in arranging the title page, notes, bibliography, or other features. A research paper, for example, typically follows a specific order.

- ❑ Title page (not recommended in MLA; required in APA)
- ❑ Outline (optional; begins on its own page; requires separate title page)
- ❑ Abstract (optional, but common in APA; usually on its own page)
- ❑ Body of the essay (Arabic pagination begins with the body of the essay in MLA; in APA, Arabic pagination begins with the title page)
- ❑ Content or bibliographic notes
- ❑ Works Cited/References (begins on its own page separate from the body of the essay or any content or bibliographic notes)

The sample research essay on pages 261–271 presents a model paper in MLA style, and the essay on pages 290–304 presents a paper in APA style. For a more complex paper such as a master's thesis or doctoral dissertation, you might follow the order recommended in *The MLA Style Manual* (MLA) or the *Publication Manual of the American Psychological Association* (APA). Many schools also publish their own guidelines for submitting graduate-level theses.

21f Follow the rules for documentation right down to the punctuation and spacing

Accurate documentation is part of professional research. Instructors and editors notice even minor variances in documentation form. Perhaps the two most common errors in handling the MLA format, for example, are forgetting to put a period at the end of entries in the Works Cited list and placing a comma where none is needed in parenthetical documentation.

WRONG	Pluto, Terry. <u>The Curse of Rocky Colavito</u>. New York: Simon, 1994
PREFERRED	Pluto, Terry. <u>The Curse of Rocky Colavito</u>. New York: Simon, 1994.
WRONG	(Pluto, 132-36)
PREFERRED	(Pluto 132-36)

You will survive both errors, but they are easy to avoid.

21g Submit your project professionally

Whether you've written a paper, designed a brochure, or created a Web site, be sure the work meets appropriate standards (see also Section 1b). Examine what you've produced to see that everything looks "detailed"—the writing is sharp and correct, the images are crisp and labeled, the pagination is right, the links are operative, the documentation is solid, and so on.

Don't overdo it. For electronic projects, keep the bells and whistles (and gaudy colors) to a functional minimum. For a paper, bind it modestly with a paper clip. Nothing more elaborate is needed, unless an instructor asks you to place the essay (still clipped) in a folder along with all materials you used in developing it.

If you submit an article for publication, be sure to follow all instructions for submission provided by the editors. Note in particular how many clean copies they require of your work, to whom those copies should be sent, and whether you should furnish a self-addressed, stamped envelope for return of your work.

GETTING INVOLVED

1. Instructors will rarely accept computer failure as an excuse for a late project these days. In a group, share any experiences you may have had with untimely electronic glitches and discuss ways that such problems can be avoided or circumvented.

2. Research papers seem to have lots of extra elements, but that is because they represent preprofessional work. Examine a professional article or scholarly book, listing all the separate parts included either before or after the main body of the piece. You might encounter features such as title pages, publication and copyright information, outlines, tables of contents, prefaces, appendixes, indexes, and author biographies. Discuss the function of each item.

MANAGING YOUR PROJECT

1. To be certain you bring your project to timely completion, decide in advance how you will reward yourself when you are done. Be specific. Give yourself something real to work for—in addition to the satisfaction (not insignificant) of completing a noteworthy research project.

2. If you are writing a paper, perform the test of organization suggested in Section 21b. If you are preparing a different kind of project, carefully examine its structure as well. For example, have friends test-drive a brochure you've designed. Does its arrangement of panels make sense? Are its headings logical? Will readers know where to go for additional information? For a Web site, ask an outsider to navigate the site. Does the structure direct readers logically to important information? Can readers navigate all levels of the site easily? Can they always return quickly to the home page?

3. Before submitting a conventional research paper, ask yourself the following questions.

   - Have you placed your name, the instructor's name, the date, and the course name on the first or title page?
   - Is the title centered? Are only the major words capitalized? (Your title should not be underlined.)
   - Did you number the pages? Are they in the right order?
   - Have you used quotation marks and parentheses correctly and in pairs? (The closing quotation mark and parenthesis are often forgotten.)
   - Have you placed quotation marks around all direct quotations that are shorter than four lines?
   - Have you indented all direct quotations of more than four typed lines (MLA) or of forty words or more (APA)?
   - Have you remembered that indented quotations are not placed between quotation marks?
   - Did you introduce all direct quotations with some identification of their author, source, or significance?
   - Did you use the correct form for parenthetical notes?
   - Have you handled titles correctly, italicizing book titles and putting the titles of articles between quotation marks?
   - Did you include a Works Cited or References list? Is your list of works cited alphabetized? Did you indent the entries correctly?

The very earliest libraries in the Western world, dating from the third millennium BCE, housed mainly clay tablets. These tablets were inscribed with *cuneiform,* an ancient form of writing developed by the Sumerians, which you see pictured here. Cuneiform, derived from the Latin *cuneus,* meaning "wedge," was written with a stylus in wet clay. The tablets were then baked in a kiln if they were highly valued works or dried in the sun if not. Clay tablets lost their usefulness when the Aramaic alphabet was invented in the sixth century BCE—the Aramaic letters were difficult to inscribe on clay. Thus began the development of writing surfaces and tools that would include papyrus, vellum, parchment, paper, and screen; many types of writing instruments, such as the quill pen, the fountain pen, and the ball point pen; and the typewriter, the electric typewriter, and the word processor.

In the following special insert, we address the most recent technology for conveying information—the Web page. It shares with the clay tablet of old the goal of communicating with an audience of readers.

◎ DON'T MISS . . .

- **The quick start template for building a Web page on p. 186.** It demonstrates how easily you can build a Web page from templates.

- **The discussion of patterns used to structure Web sites on p. 188.** We explain linear sequences, gridwork designs, hierarchical structures, and hub or network designs.

- **The table of HTML tags on p. 193.** Refer to this chart to recall the basic HTML tags needed for formatting Web pages.

- **The document design checklist on p. 198.** Consider these guidelines as you design a Web page.

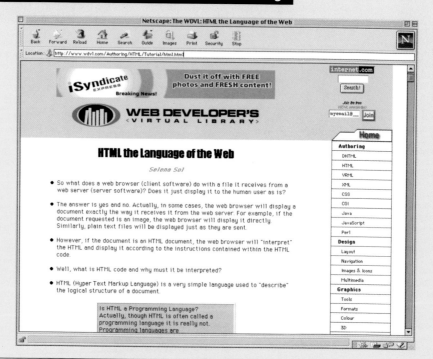

BOOKMARKS: Web Sites Worth Knowing

Tutorials from the Web Developer's Virtual Library,
http://www.wdvl.com/Authoring/Tutorials/

To learn how to make a useful, attractive Web site, take a look at the WDVL Web tutorials. The material guides you from the most basic aspects of HTML through to advanced skills such as CGI programming. The tutorials, written by experts, function like a college course, but all the instructional material is available online, for no charge. Be sure to take a look at Charlie Morris's informative and entertaining guide "Navigation 101."

Additional Sites

"Art and the Zen of Web Sites," http://www.tlc-systems.com/webtips.shtml
"BigNoseBird," http://bignosebird.com/
Creating Killer Web Sites, http://www.killersites.com/
"Yale C/AIM Web Style Guide," http://info.med.yale.edu/caim/manual/contents.html

Authoring Your Own Web Site

Deciding on a format for your project

Almost anyone with access to the Internet can learn to design, create, and publish WWW pages. But not every project belongs on the WWW. You have to decide whether and when the Web is a suitable environment for your project.

❏ **Purpose.** Material on the Web can reach a large audience, so it might be an appropriate place to publish a project when you want to disseminate information widely or make it especially easy for people to respond to your work. But a Web site might not be the best place to post a technical piece of writing or a private meditation.

❏ **Audience.** A college instructor may expect you to turn in a traditional paper, even when the information might be more appropriately presented on the Internet. On the other hand, an employer might expect reports or documents to be accessible online in some form or you may have to combine various formats to reach the widest possible readership.

❏ **Time.** If you have never designed a WWW page before, perhaps you can't afford the time it will take to learn HTML authoring. In that case, stick with more familiar technologies such as presentation software, desktop publishing programs, or word processing. Alternatively, a significant advantage of the Web is speed of publication—if you need to get information to readers quickly, the Web may be your best choice, assuming that your intended audience can access it.

❏ **Medium.** The medium you choose has important design implications. You might decide to stick with print because you are familiar with prescribed formats and with the way your software handles fonts and graphics. Moving to a Web environment will require some new skills. For example, you will need to learn something about creating and formatting graphics, fonts, hypertext links, and other elements of Web design. You may also need some familiarity with advanced programming techniques if you plan to incorporate sophisticated features into your project.

❏ **Access.** To create a Web page, you will need access to a computer and to space on the Internet to publish your work. Depending on your project, you may also need graphics programs, scanning equipment, or other applications. You'll want to be sure, too, that your files load quickly and accurately on a variety of browser types and that your audience knows how to access them. For more information, see "Publishing Your Project" on page 199.

Getting started: a basic template

Many students already have a Web page; if you don't, you can quickly and easily learn to create one. There are many excellent Web page authoring tools available that can simplify what may seem to be a daunting task, and many word processors now allow you to automatically save your work in HTML format for Web publication. Using a graphical Web editor, such as Netscape's *Composer* or Microsoft's *FrontPage*, you can design a Web page with point-and-click ease, or you can use any number of powerful text-based HTML editors that allow you to easily include even advanced features in your designs. However, you don't need any special tools to begin creating a Web page. You can use a simple text editor such as Windows' *Notepad*, available in most Windows platforms, or an online editor such as *Pico* to get started.

Many WWW authoring programs include a selection of templates; as you learn more about HTML authoring, you can design your own. To get started quickly, you can copy the quick start template below into your text or HTML editor. The information shown in blue in the template should be replaced with your own information. Figure 1 shows how this page will appear on the World Wide Web. To see your own page, save the file to disk with the extension *.htm* or *.html,* and then open it in your Web browser. (For more information, see "Publishing Your Project on the Web," p. 199)

Quick Start Template

⟨HTML⟩
⟨HEAD⟩
⟨TITLE⟩Title of Your Site⟨/TITLE⟩
⟨META NAME="Author" CONTENT="Your Name"⟩
⟨META NAME="Title" CONTENT="Title of Your Page"⟩
⟨META NAME="Date of Creation" CONTENT="Day Month Year"⟩
⟨META NAME="URL" CONTENT="http://your.address.edu"⟩
⟨/HEAD⟩
⟨BODY⟩
⟨H1⟩Title on Your Page⟨/H1⟩
⟨A HREF="mailto: your_email_address"⟩Your Name⟨/A⟩
⟨HR⟩

⟨P⟩Insert your text here. You may want to use lists, tables, or other features to help you format your page.⟨/P⟩

⟨P⟩You can also insert graphics, links, and other elements as appropriate.⟨/P⟩

⟨HR⟩
⟨FONT SIZE="−1"⟩© Your Name⟨BR⟩
Date of Creation or Last Modification: Day Month Year⟨BR⟩
URL for this page: http://your.address.edu
⟨/FONT⟩

⟨/BODY⟩
⟨/HTML⟩

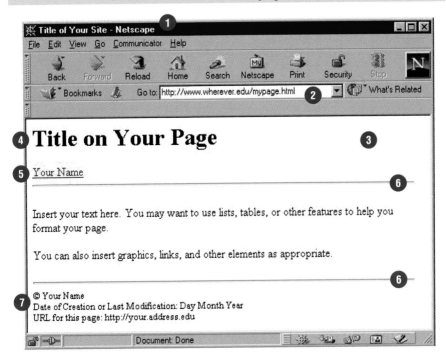

FIGURE I A basic Web page template

1 Information enclosed in the <TITLE> and </TITLE> tags appears in the browser information bar.

2 URL for your home page.

3 The *body* of your file appears in the browser window.

4 The *title of your page*, formatted as a level one header.

5 *Your name* is formatted as an email link.

6 *Horizontal rules* are used to separate sections of the page.

7 Bibliographic information about the page.

For More Information

The Bare Bones Guide to HTML	http://werbach.com/barebones/barebone.html
HTML Quick Reference	http://www.htmlgoodies.com/html_ref.html
Media Builder's HTML Editors	http://www.mediabuilder.com/softwarewebedit.html
Microsoft's *Front Page*	http://www.microsoft.com/frontpage/
Netscape's *Composer*	http://home.netscape.com/communicator/composer/v4.0/index.html
Apple Computer's Internet Publishing	http://www.apple.com/publishing/internet/index.html

Designing your Web site

Web pages offer a great deal of flexibility in design. But just as a traditional essay must follow a logical structure, a Web site needs a coherent system of organization. The design you choose will depend on your purpose and audience as well as on the nature of the information you are presenting. The "Yale C/AIM Web Style Guide" defines four basic structures:

❏ **Linear sequence.** For shorter works, your site may consist of a single page with headings and subheadings to help the reader locate important information and to draw the reader through the page. (See Chapter 21 for more information on headings.) For longer, more complicated projects, you may want to include an index or a table of contents with links to the different parts of your page or to additional pages within your site. You may also want to include "Next" and "Back" links on each page.

❏ **Gridwork design.** A more complicated structure might begin with an index page with links to additional pages that, in turn, link to other pages. Such a pattern forms a kind of gridwork and is useful for presenting information that depends on previous information but does not necessarily follow a linear sequence. Online help manuals for software applications usually follow such a pattern, similar to cross-referencing in an encyclopedia or reference work. In addition to linking pages to related information, you should include links back to the main index page to help keep your reader from getting lost.

❏ **Hierarchical structure.** Sometimes information is dependent on other information. That is, it is necessary to understand one part before moving to another. Construct such a hierarchical structure by connecting your pages to each other following a format similar to a genealogical or organizational chart. Information presented in this format follows a top-down structure, with branches to show relationships between parts at the same level. Each page should include a link back to the main page or to the beginning of each branch.

❏ **Hub or network design.** Sites may also radiate from a central "hub" with spokes (or links) connecting each page to every other page, forming a web or network. This kind of structure works best for information that is interrelated; that is, all parts are related to each other and to the whole but are not dependent on each other. One way to create this kind of site is by including your pages inside a *frame* (a way of dividing the browser window into two or more sections). The frame remains on the screen at all times while other pages appear inside the frame. Keep in mind, however, that not all browsers support frames. Another method that may ensure greater accessibility is to simply link each page in your site back to a main index page.

Figure 2 shows a site designed using frames. The designer offers readers a choice of entering the site using either the frames version or a text-only version without frames. The menu bar on the left side of the page is the frame, with links to other pages appearing in the browser window inside the frame.

FIGURE 2   A page designed using frames

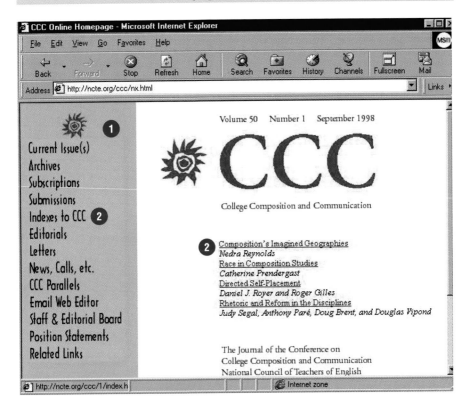

1 A menu bar on the frame offers readers access to links.

2 Linked pages appear inside the frame.

For More Information

"Yale C/AIM Web Style Guide"	**http://info.med.yale.edu/caim/manual/**
Sun Guide to Web style	http://www.sun.com/styleguide/tables/ Welcome.html/
W3C Hyper Text Markup Language	http://www.w3.org/MarkUp
Composing Good HTML	http://www.cs.cmu.edu/~tilt/cgh/
Web Design Group	http://www.htmlhelp.com
Ask Dr. Web	http://www.zeldman.com/askdrweb/

Creating a table of contents

Unless your site consists of only one page, no more than one or two screens in length, you will probably want to include an index (or table of contents) page with links to other parts of your page or to other pages within your site. Figure 3 shows some different ways to format a table of contents or index page. Keep in mind, however, that your reader must be able to access the information you provide, so using graphics or advanced techniques (such as the pull-down menu boxes shown on NCSA's page in Figure 3) might limit who will be able to read your site. The format you choose should make sense for your purpose and audience and should clearly lead the reader to important information. That said, however, a little creativity can go a long way to making your site attractive and appealing to readers without sacrificing clarity and accessibility.

Using the quick start template below, you can create a simple table of contents with links from the table of contents to additional pages in your site. Information shown in blue should be replaced with your own information. For example, replace intro.html with the name of the file to which you want to link, and replace Introduction with the page heading or title to which you are linking.

Quick Start Template

⟨H2⟩Table of Contents⟨/H2⟩

⟨A HREF="intro.html"⟩Introduction⟨/A⟩⟨BR⟩
⟨A HREF="start.html"⟩Getting Started⟨/A⟩⟨BR⟩
⟨A HREF="structure.html"⟩Deciding on a Structure⟨/A⟩⟨BR⟩

To create links to other parts of the same page, create "name references" by inserting the tags ⟨A NAME="name"⟩⟨/A⟩ immediately prior to the text or section to which you want to link. In the table of contents, replace the file name with the name reference preceded by a pound sign (#)—for example, ⟨A HREF="#name"⟩Name⟨/A⟩. You can also create links to external sites, that is, links to other pages or sites on the WWW, by including the complete address for the desired target. For example, to link to the Web site for this book, you could include the tags ⟨A HREF="http://longman.awl.com/bookmarks/"⟩Bookmarks on the Web⟨/A⟩ in your template.

For More Information

NCD HTML Design Guide V. 5.0	http://www.ncdesign.org/html/
AHDS Guides to Good Practice	http://ahds.ac.uk/public/guides.html
CMU's Creating Image Maps	http://www.library.cmu.edu/Unofficial/ WebCourse/imagemaps.html
Alchemy Mindwork's *GIF Construction Set*	http://www.mindworkshop.com/ alchemy/gifcon.html
WWW Image Map Editing Software	http://www.boutell.com/mapedit/

FIGURE 3 **Formatting a table of contents or index page**

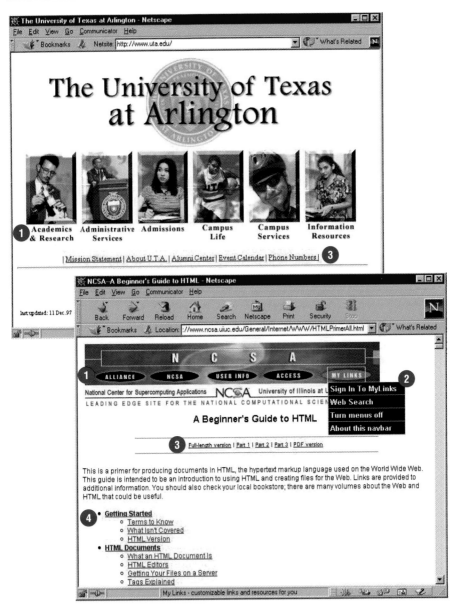

1. A graphic formatted as an "image map" in which areas of the image serve as links to various sites.

2. Pull-down menus (created using advanced techniques) link to specific Web pages within the site.

3. Text-only menu bar offers users a choice of formats, making the site more accessible across various platforms or operating systems.

4. Text links use an outline format to show relationships. Links are to "name references," or designated sections of the same Web page.

Formatting text

One of the things that makes HTML so useful for publication of documents and files is its ability to include *document structure tags*, that is, tags that change the appearance of the document, create headings, emphasize (or de-emphasize) text, or add other useful features. Many Web page authoring programs simplify this process by offering menus or buttons with common formatting options. Some newer word processors will also translate common text formatting into HTML code automatically. You can use the HTML tags shown in Figure 4 to get started.

In the quick start template on page 186, you may have noticed that the name of your page was formatted as large, dark text by enclosing it in the ⟨H1⟩ and ⟨/H1⟩ tags. These tags denote a *header* and are used to set off sections of text in your document (see Chapter 21 for more on using headings in your document). HTML allows for six levels of headers, as shown below.

You can indicate emphasis by changing the appearance of the text on the reader's screen. For example, you can show text in **boldfaced type**, *italicized type*, or even ***bold-faced and italicized type*** simply by enclosing it in the proper tags. Using the ⟨FONT⟩ and ⟨/FONT⟩ tags, you can also change the font size, typeface (for example, Times Roman, Helvetica), or color. In the quick start template on page 186, the copyright statement, date of creation, and URL at the bottom of the page appear slightly smaller than preceding text because these items fall between the ⟨FONT SIZE="−1"⟩ and ⟨/FONT⟩ tags.

Spacing (other than a single space between words), line breaks, tabs, and other such formatting will not show unless you include HTML tags to define these attributes. Figure 4 shows some commonly used HTML tags for formatting text, spacing, and other elements of your Web page.

FIGURE 4 Formatting text in HTML

HTML Tag	Results	Use For:
⟨STRONG⟩ and ⟨/STRONG⟩ or ⟨B⟩ and ⟨/B⟩	**Boldfaced text**	Strong emphasis; headings.
⟨EM⟩ and ⟨/EM⟩ or ⟨I⟩ and ⟨/I⟩	*Italicized text*	Emphasis; foreign words; book and journal titles.
⟨FONT SIZE="−1"⟩ and ⟨/FONT⟩	Reduced point size	Reducing the size of text.
⟨FONT SIZE="+1"⟩ and ⟨/FONT⟩	Enlarged point size	Increasing the size of text.
⟨FONT COLOR ="#FF0000"⟩ and ⟨/FONT⟩	Font color	Drawing the reader's attention to important points, especially to warnings or safety information.
⟨BR⟩	Forces a line break. Text that follows will move to the next line.	Forcing text to appear on a new line.
⟨P⟩ and ⟨/P⟩	Forces a paragraph break. Text that follows will move to the beginning of the second line following.	Separating paragraphs of text or other elements on a page.
	Forces a blank space.	Including blank spaces in a document. Repeat this ASCII code for the number of spaces desired.
⟨CENTER⟩ and ⟨/CENTER⟩	Center elements.	Centering text, graphics, tables, or other elements. Other tags specify alignment within the tag (e.g., ⟨/P ALIGN = "center" ⟩Text ⟨/P⟩ will center a given paragraph of text).
⟨HR⟩	Places a horizontal rule (or line) on your page.	Separating discrete sections of a document. Designate various attributes of the horizontal rule by defining the width (or thickness) and position on the page (e.g., ⟨HR ALIGN = "center" WIDTH = "75%" SIZE = "3"⟩).

For More Information

ASCII ISO Table for HTML   http://www.bbsinc.com/iso8859.html

Character Formatting   http://www.ncsa.uiuc.edu/General/Internet/WWW/HTMLPrimerAll.html#CF

HTML Writer's Guild   http://www.hwg.org/

C/Net's Elements of Web Design   http://builder.cnet.com/Graphics/Design/

Using colors and graphics

Graphics and colors on your pages should make a statement—they are part of the rhetoric or message you convey. Use them to enhance the readability and visual attractiveness of your page, of course, but make sure they also serve a definite purpose. Pages with too many graphics, or with several animated graphics, may not only take too long to load in a browser but may also appear cluttered and thus interfere with your primary purpose: to communicate an idea or information to your reader. You can create your own graphics with a scanner, a simple tool such as *Windows Paintbrush,* or a more advanced graphics program such as Corel *Draw* or Adobe *Photoshop.* You can also find a wide variety of background images available for free on the WWW. (See also Chapter 15 for information on copyright and the WWW.)

A Web page consists of two primary parts: the *head,* which contains information about the page, and the *body,* which defines the structure and appearance of the page itself. Information in the head, such as the site title and "metatag" information, does not appear on your page but is used by many search engines to locate information on the Web. Readers can also access this information by viewing the document's source code. The body of your document appears between the ⟨BODY⟩ and ⟨/BODY⟩ tags and contains the headings, text, links, graphics, and other elements that appear on your page. You can define various attributes of the entire page, such as the background color or image, text and link colors, and fonts, by including these attributes within the ⟨BODY⟩ tags, or you can change the attributes only for specific portions of your document. Graphics-based Web page authoring programs make it easy to add colors and graphics. If you are using a text-based HTML authoring tool (such as *Notepad*), you can simply insert the HTML tags into the body of your document as shown in Figure 5, replacing the information in the tags with your own information.

For More Information

Web Developer's Virtual Library	http://www.WDVL.com/Graphics/
A+ Art	http://www.aplusart.com
Controlling Document Backgrounds	http://www.netscape.com/assist/ net_sites/bg/
Web Color Chart	http://www.maran.com/colorchart/ index.html
Apple Quick Time 4	http://www.apple.com/quicktime
W3C's Graphics on the Web	http://www.w3.org/Graphics
How to Build Lame Web Sites	http://webdevelopersjournal.co.uk/ colums/perpend1.html
Hyper Content, Hyper Junk	http://www.mcs.net/~jorn/html/ hyper.html

FIGURE 5 Adding background colors and graphics

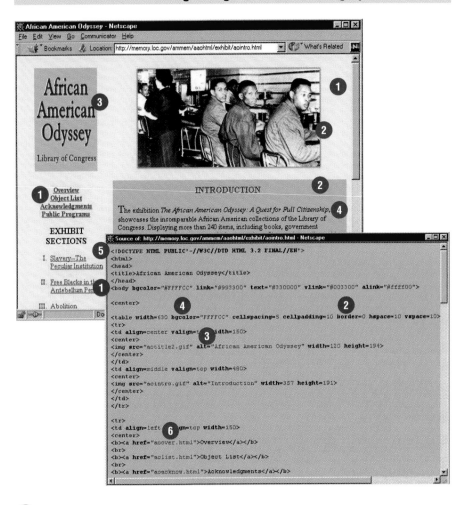

1 Change the background and text colors by defining the attributes in the <BODY> tag.

2 Use tables without borders to lay out text and graphics in the page.

3 ALT tags provide information about graphics for text-only browsers.

4 Define background colors for tables.

5 Comment lines in the source code begin with an exclamation point and provide information only.

6 Links to files and images in the same directory use relative addressing. To link to files and images outside your own directory, include the full URL.

Using lists and tables

Like most word processors, HTML has special codes to format lists and tables. Lists and tables can be *nested* to create a list inside a list or a table within a table. You can create list items with or without bullets or numbers or tables with or without borders, specify the size of cells, and add background graphics or other elements by defining the attributes you want inside the HTML tags. Tables can be used to simulate columns of text, to help align lists, to decrease download time for large graphics, or to emulate the appearance of spreadsheets. Web editors make it easy to include lists and tables. Keep in mind, however, that many text-based browsers and some older graphical browsers cannot handle tables. Using the Quick Start Template below, you can easily create lists or tables like those shown in Figure 6.

Quick Start Template

UNORDERED LISTS
⟨UL⟩
⟨LI⟩An unordered, or bulleted, list is enclosed by the ⟨UL⟩ and ⟨/UL⟩ tags.⟨/LI⟩
⟨LI⟩Each item in the list is enclosed by the ⟨LI⟩ and ⟨/LI⟩ tags.⟨/LI⟩
⟨/UL⟩

ORDERED LISTS
⟨OL⟩
⟨LI⟩Ordered, or numbered, lists are enclosed by the ⟨OL⟩ and ⟨/OL⟩ tags.⟨/LI⟩
⟨LI⟩Each item in the list is enclosed by the ⟨LI⟩ and ⟨/LI⟩ tags.⟨/LI⟩
⟨/OL⟩

DEFINITION LISTS
⟨DL⟩
⟨DT⟩Definition Lists
⟨DD⟩Enclosed by the ⟨DL⟩ and ⟨/DL⟩ tags, definition lists are often used to format glossaries.
⟨DT⟩List terms to be defined following the ⟨DT⟩ tag
⟨DD⟩List the definition for each term following the ⟨DD⟩ tag.
⟨/DL⟩

TABLES
⟨TABLE BORDER="1"⟩
⟨TR⟩
⟨TD⟩Row 1, Column 1⟨/TD⟩
⟨TD⟩Row 1, Column 2⟨/TD⟩
⟨/TR⟩
⟨TR⟩
⟨TD⟩Row 2, Column 1⟨/TD⟩
⟨TD⟩Row 2, Column 2⟨/TD⟩
⟨/TR⟩
⟨/TABLE⟩

FIGURE 6 Formatting lists and tables in HTML

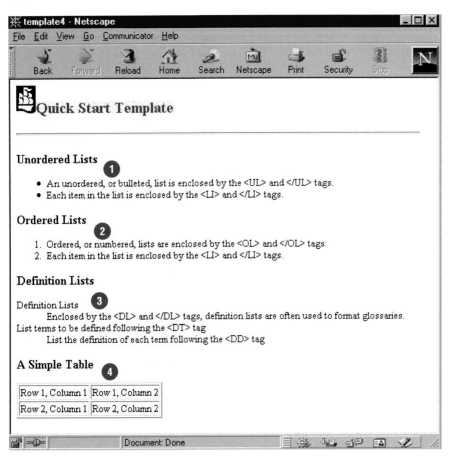

① Use unordered (or bulleted) lists to present items of equal importance.

② Use ordered (or numbered) lists to present items that require a specific order.

③ Use definition lists to format entries in glossaries.

④ Use tables with borders to simulate the appearance of a spreadsheet or form; use tables without borders to locate text and graphics on a Web page.

For More Information

Userland Software's *BBEdit* for MacIntosh	http://www.scripting.com/bbEdit/
Joe Barta's *Table Tutor*	http://www.fix.net/~wmiller/ tabletutor/index.html
The HTML3 Table Model	http://www.w3.org/TR/ WD-tables-951023.html

Keeping the basics of good document design in mind

One of the most important and often overlooked steps in designing any project, including a Web site, is planning. Using paper and pencil, you can sketch your proposed layout, indicating links, navigational features, graphics, headings, or other elements. Keep in mind that your design may (and probably will) change considerably as you actually compose it, so be flexible and consider alternatives.

Many of the features of good Web design are the same as for print documents. Some of these guidelines are presented in the checklist below.

CHECKLIST
Document Design

- **Use contrast for easy readability.** Choose background graphics, colors, and fonts that enhance readability.
- **Break up large blocks of text.** Keep paragraphs short. Use headings and subheadings or other design elements to move the reader's eye to important information. Use white space to provide contrast and legibility.
- **Use graphics or other design elements sparingly.** Too many fancy design elements may distract the reader. Use appropriate graphics to attract attention to important points, to aid the reader in navigation, and to add emphasis or provide additional information.
- **Include a table of contents, links, or other navigational aids.** Use textual transitions as well as clearly explained links and graphics to help your reader navigate your site. Consider using features such as separate browser windows for digressions, explanations, definitions, and/or external links, if you know how.
- **Include bibliographic information.** Provide the information needed to cite your document, including your name and email address, the title of your work, the date of publication or last revision, and your document's URL. MLA's "Draft Guidelines for Providing Web-Site Information" recommends that you also include information on your sponsor, purpose, software requirements, site configuration, and other useful information.
- **Give credit to your sources,** including the source of any graphics or other files you have used. Include full bibliographical information in addition to providing links to online sources.
- **Make your site accessible.** Graphics, frames, and tables may not be readable across platforms, so consider including text-only versions of documents and descriptions of graphics and audio and video files. If applicable, include links to any special software applications needed. Use thumbnail (or reduced) images or text descriptions for large multimedia files, and include interesting but nonessential material as separate linked files. These considerations may also help make your work more accessible to people with impaired vision or hearing.

Publishing your project on the Web

When you are ready to publish your page on the WWW, you will need to transfer, or upload, your files from your disk or hard drive (your *local host*) to your Internet server (your *remote host*). Many HTML editors automate this process, or you may need to use a file transfer protocol (FTP) client program. If you don't have an FTP client or don't know how to use the one you have, check with your Internet service provider (ISP).

Many ISPs allow space for WWW pages on their servers, and some sites on the Internet, such as *GeoCities*, offer free Web space to individuals. Your university may also allow space for students to publish home pages. Check with your provider or university computing service for details, and be sure to follow any posted requirements carefully. Before you publish your pages, however, you will want to see how they will appear online. To view your file, save it, choose the type of file (for example, *.html*), and give it a name. If you are using an application that does not offer *.html* as a choice of file type, choose ASCII or MS-DOS text, and include the file extension after the file name (for example, *index.html*). Follow DOS file-naming conventions to ensure compatibility across programs and platforms: use an eight-character file name, with no spaces, followed by a period and a three-letter extension that designates the type of file (for example, *index.htm*). *Windows95* and Macintosh users can use four letters after the period.

After you have saved your file, open a browser such as Netscape *Navigator* or Microsoft *Internet Explorer,* select "File" in the menu bar at the top of your browser, and then choose "Open" (in most browsers). Locate your file on your disk or hard drive. You do not need to be connected to the Internet to view your page; however, you may not be able to check links or view some graphics on your page unless you are browsing online.

The checklist below offers some guidelines for you to consider in reviewing your Web page.

CHECKLIST

Reviewing Your Web Page

- Make sure all hypertext links are working. Consider including a list describing each external link in case the intended files move or change.
- Make sure your graphics load accurately and quickly. For larger files, consider using thumbnail images or text descriptions with links to the larger file.
- Check the appearance of your work carefully, using a variety of Web browsers if possible. Make sure the file is readable in both text-only and graphical browsers if appropriate.
- Include bibliographical information: your name and a way to contact you (your email address) if appropriate; the title of your work or site; the date of creation or last modification; and the URL for the site.

Continued

CHECKLIST (Cont'd)

- Give credit in the proper format to any sources from which you have borrowed material, including graphics or other files. Make certain you have permission to use those materials.
- Try checking your site using the *Web Site Garage* or *Bobby* sites to make sure your pages are accurate and accessible to the handicapped. (For more information, see "Making Web Pages Universally Accessible.")

For More Information

Bookmarks on the Web	http://www.awlonline.com/researchcentral
Longman "English Pages"	http://longman.awl.com/englishpages/
University of Missouri Online Writery	http://www.missouri.edu/~writery
Purdue University's Online Writing Lab	http://owl.english.purdue.edu/
HTML Writer's Guild	http://www.hwg.org
The Web Developer's Forum	http://WDVL/WDVL/Forum/
Yale Center for Advanced Instructional Media	http://info.med.yale.edu/caim/
Jakob Nielsen's Usable Information Technology	http://www.useit.com
World Wide Web Consortium	http://www.w3.org
Electronic Frontier Foundation	http://www.eff.org
Library of Congress HTML Page	http://lcweb.loc.gov/global/internet/html.html
NCSA's "A Beginner's Guide to HTML"	http://www.ncsa.uiuc.edu/General/Internet/WWW/HTML_Primer.html
"Making Web Pages Universally Accessible"	http://www.december.com/cmc/may/1998/jan/burg.html
Bobby 3.0	http://www.cast.org/bobby/
Web Site Garage	http://www.websitegarage.com
Web Development	http://www.december.com/web/develop.html
GeoCities	http://www.geocities.com
Free Webspace.net	http://freewebspace.net

Documentation

In most respects this section is for reference: by the time you arrive here, you've probably chosen an appropriate system of documentation or an instructor has made that decision for you (see Section 1c). In the arts and humanities, the systems of the Modern Language Association (MLA) or the Chicago Manual of Style (CMS) are often preferred. Projects in the social sciences typically require the style of the American Psychological Association (APA); the natural sciences follow several different style manuals, though that of the Council of Biology Editors (CBE) is particularly influential. These documentation styles in their latest versions appear in the following chapters.

Recently, the editors of these styles have been wrestling with the need to accommodate a growing number of electronic sources—most of them decidedly uncooperative. Over the years, printed sources have usually presented scholars with all the information they needed for documentation: authors, titles, publication information, dates, and pagination. Electronic sources haven't been so helpful. As a result, documentation systems designed for print sources have been stymied by the need to cite nontraditional items such as Web sites without authors, dates, or pages; Web sites with frames, audio clips, and streaming videos; newsgroup musings that disappear in two days; dialogues on MOOs that seem like places but aren't; and worse.

Early attempts to fit electronic sources within conventional documentation forms usually did not adequately describe the sources or help researchers to locate them. Later attempts have been more successful, but electronic items in most documentation systems still seem like afterthoughts. However, an alternative to the traditional documentation systems is offered here: Columbia Online Style (COS). COS has been written specifically to accommodate both electronic sources and conventional systems of documentation. If you are using MLA, APA, CMS, or CBE styles in a paper for conventional sources, you can select an appropriate version (Humanities or Sciences) of COS for all electronic materials.

Like the earliest American computers, the Internet got its start in the military. In 1973, researchers working for the U.S. Defense Advanced Research Projects Agency began exploring ways to network computers that would enable them to communicate across linked networks. The idea was to build a communications grid too vast and decentralized to be destroyed by a nuclear attack. Thus the Internet was born, eventually becoming a channel of communication for researchers and scholars at universities and then, much more recently, for the general public.

The Internet contains vast resources of information, but its materials are not organized for research purposes the way a library collection is. To find material on the Internet for a research project, you will likely use several Web search engines—like the student at work here—and a variety of new search techniques. (Expect some frustrations too.) The Web has also changed the way we view intellectual property and the way we cite information. The following chapter on Columbia Online Style (COS) documentation touches on current copyright debates and provides up-to-date and practical guidelines for citing electronic sources in your projects.

◎ DON'T MISS . . .

- **The rationale for this new system of documentation in Section 22a.** If you expect to use many electronic sources in a project, Columbia Online Style (COS) may be your best choice of documentation system.

- **The index to COS formats for papers in the humanities on page 212.**

- **The index to COS formats for papers in the sciences on page 222.**

InfoJump,
http://www.dominis.com/Zines/

To find Web-based periodicals, search InfoJump's *eZine's* database, a site that tracks the Web for "zines," the Internet equivalent of magazines. Here you'll find regularly updated sites on every conceivable topic, from science and technology to politics. Each zine is rated on a scale of 1 to 5 by visitors who found the site using *eZines*, so you can get a sense of how useful a zine is before you visit.

Additional Sites

The Columbia Guide to Online Style,
   http://www.columbia.edu/cu/cup/cgos/idx_basic.html

FOLDOC (Free On-Line Dictionary of Computing),
   http://wombat.doc.ic.ac.uk/foldoc/index.html

COS Documentation

In preparing a college research project, you may use a wide variety of electronic sources and services—Web sites, listservs, email, full-text databases, electronic reference books, and more. When the time comes to document these items, however, conventional citation systems may prove inadequate. Either they don't mention the types of sources you are using, or the guidelines for documenting them are unwieldy. That's not surprising; most citation systems were originally designed for printed documents, so they wobble as they try to accommodate sources without authors, titles, or even page numbers. Many people have attempted to address these inadequacies by compiling recommendations specifically formulated for electronic sources; however, many of these styles still fail to present a clear, logical, and comprehensive system subtle enough to deal with the complexity of electronic items.

An exception is the system of documentation presented in *The Columbia Guide to Online Style* (1998) by Janice R. Walker and Todd Taylor. Columbia Online Style (COS), designed expressly for electronically accessed material, acknowledges that on-line and computer sources differ from printed ones and yet have a logic of their own that makes reliable citation possible. We recommend that unless specifically instructed otherwise, students should use the appropriate COS style to document electronic sources: COS-humanities style for projects following MLA and CMS guidelines and COS-scientific style for projects following APA and CBE guidelines. For other styles, COS guidelines can easily be adapted to conform to the specific format required.

22a How do you use COS documentation?

Fortunately, you don't have to forget what you have learned about other documentation systems to use COS—it doesn't replace MLA, APA, CMS, or CBE style. Instead, COS is designed to work with all of them so that writers can document electronic sources consistently and appropriately *within* the style they are expected to use in school or at work. To use COS style, simply follow it consistently for all the electronic sources in a project, choosing the COS form best suited to the documentation style you are using for printed sources. To make this adaptation simple, COS offers forms for both major types of documentation, the author–page number form favored in humanities systems (MLA, CMS) and the author-date style preferred in the sciences (APA, CBE). In this chapter, we provide separate COS Form Directories for humanities-style citations (Section 22b) and science-style citations (Section 22d).

Like the MLA and APA systems, Columbia Online Style documentation itself involves just two basic steps: inserting a note at each point where a paper or project needs documentation (Section 22a-1) and then recording all sources used in these notes in a Works Cited or References list (Section 22a-2).

22a-1   **(Step 1) In the body of your paper, place a note in appropriate form for every item you must document.**   For a **humanities** paper in MLA style, the in-text note will usually be an author's last name and a page number in parentheses.

```
(Weinberg 38)
```

But most electronic sources do not have page numbers—which are, after all, a convention of printed texts. Specific references in electronic sources can be easily located using "search" or "find" features built in to most software packages; thus, designating the specific location of a reference within an electronic text is unnecessary. So, for electronic sources without page numbers or other consistent divisions, simply place the author's last name in parentheses after a passage that requires documentation.

```
Jim Lehrer may be America's most trusted newsperson, its new

Walter Cronkite (Shafer).
```

If an electronic source has no conventional author or other person responsible for the information (a common occurrence), identify the source by the title or by a brief description of the file when no title is given (such as for a graphics file). If the title is very long, you may use a shortened version.

```
USA Today was among those to editorialize against the tobacco

industry's continuing influence on Congress ("Tobacco).
```

When you cite a source without page numbers multiple times, repeat the author's name (or short title, if there is no author) for each citation. But try to keep intrusions to a minimum—for example, by using a single note at the end of a paragraph when one source is cited throughout it. You can eliminate a parenthetical note by naming the author or title of a source in the body of the paper.

```
Shafer claims in a Slate column that PBS's Jim Lehrer is the new

Walter Cronkite, America's most trusted newsperson.
```

```
In "Tobacco Wields Its Clout," USA Today editorializes against the

tobacco industry's continuing influence on Congress.
```

When citing a message from email, listservs, or other electronic forums such as MOO or chat room discussions, you may have to cite an author's alias or nickname.

```
In a recent posting to the newsgroup alt.sport.paintball, jireem
argued . . .
```

Note that electronic addresses are not enclosed in parentheses or angle brackets in COS style.

For **scientific** papers, the in-text note will include an author's last name followed by a date of "publication" in parentheses. For most types of publications, give only the year even if the source furnishes day and date.

```
Jim Lehrer may be America's most trusted newsperson, its new
Walter Cronkite (Shafer, 1996).
```

You can also simply name the author in the body of your text, following the name with year of publication in parentheses.

```
Shafer (1996) claims in a Slate column that PBS's Jim Lehrer is
the new Walter Cronkite, America's most trusted newsperson.
```

Some electronic sources such as pages on the World Wide Web may not have dates of publication or any dates at all. In such cases for science-style references, record the date you accessed the source, giving day, month, and year.

```
Slipstream (21 May 1997) argues that the research design is
flawed, but ksmith (22 May 1997) rejects that claim.
```

As a general rule, make all parenthetical notes as brief and inconspicuous as possible. Remember that the point of a note is to identify a source of information, not to distract readers.

For a humanities paper using Chicago Manual of Style (CMS) footnotes or endnotes, the note consists of a raised number in the text keyed to a full note either at the bottom of the page or in a separate "Notes" list at the end.

```
    20. Paul Skowronek, "Left and Right for Rights," Trincoll
Journal, 13 March 1997. http://www.trincoll.edu/~tj/tj03.13.97/
articles/comm2.html (23 July 1997).
```

The COS form for CMS notes can be adapted from the COS Humanities Form Directory in Section 22b. You will need to study both COS forms in that section and the CMS footnote forms in Sections 25a and 25c.

22a-2 (Step 2) On a separate page at the end of your paper, list every source you cited in a parenthetical note. This alphabetical list of sources is usually titled "Works Cited" in humanities projects and "References" in scientific projects. You must have a Works Cited/References list for MLA and APA projects; in Chicago style, such a page is optional because the notes themselves include all essential bibliographical information. (We provide a general Chicago model on p. 210 but do not include specific CMS models in the COS Forms Directories.)

Like citations in other systems, COS items are assembled from a few basic components.

❏ **Author.** In humanities styles, list the full name of the author, last name first, followed by any additional authors listed in the usual order.

```
Walker, Janice R., and Todd Taylor.
```

In scientific styles, list the author's last name and initials, followed by any additional authors.

```
Walker, J. R., & Taylor, T.
```

Many electronic sources do not have authors in the conventional sense. A Web site, for example, may be a collaborative effort or represent an entire institution or a corporation; even for many singly authored electronic sources, the author's name may be missing or may be an alias or nickname. List an "author" when you can clearly identify someone as responsible for a source, text, or message. List an alias if you don't know the actual name of the person. For example, the author of an email message from cerulean@mail.utexas.edu would be cerulean. Do not include the author's email address.

```
cerulean."Re: Bono Rocks." Personal email (25 Jul. 1997).
```

Note that COS style does not hyphenate the word *email.* When no author can be identified, list the source on a Works Cited/References page by its title.

❏ **Title.** Depending on whether you are adapting COS to MLA or APA documentation styles, titles of electronic works might be italicized, placed between quotation marks, or left without any special marking. But titles in COS citations are never underlined because in many computer environments, underlining is used for hypertext links.

❏ **Editor, translator, or compiler.** Include the name of the editor, translator, or compiler, if not listed earlier. In humanities styles, precede the name with the appropriate abbreviations (*Ed., Trans.,* or *Comp.*) immediately followed by the full name. In scientific styles, the abbreviation is enclosed in parentheses and follows the name.

❏ **Print or previous publication information.** Many works online are based on printed sources with conventional publication histories, and this information should be included in a citation just before the electronic publication information. But for other online sources, the electronic address or pathway is the essential publication information. Specifying a "publication medium" (*CD-ROM, Internet, online, WWW*) for an electronic source is usually unnecessary since the information is evident in the electronic address and since the same information may be available in more than one medium. Follow the print information, if applicable, with the online publication information (see below).

❏ **Date of publication and or access.** While print publications are routinely dated and archived, these conventions don't always suit electronic sources, which allow for more frequent revisions or may be moved or even deleted without notice (see Section 11c on the timeliness of research materials). When an online or electronic source is based on a printed source or appears in a dated format (such as the online version of a newspaper or magazine), give the original publication date of the material. For Web sites, check the home page or the source code for information about original dates of posting and updates. For most electronic sources, provide a date of access—the day, month, and year you actually examined the material—enclosed in parentheses and following the electronic address. This date is important for establishing the version of the material you looked at in an environment that might be changing rapidly. When the date of publication of a source is the same as the date of your access to it (as it might be when you're reading an online news source), you need to give only the date of access.

❑ **Electronic address.** In citations of online items, the information most important to a researcher may be the pathway or electronic address, the means by which a given source can be located. For many sources in undergraduate research projects, that electronic address is likely to be a World Wide Web uniform resource locator (URL), that is, the familiar Web address beginning http://www. URLs must be copied accurately so researchers can locate the material you are documenting. To ensure accuracy, you can usually cut and paste an address directly from a Web browser into your project document.

Unfortunately, some URLs are quite long and will produce odd line breaks. Don't, however, introduce a space into a URL just to fill an awkward gap in your citation. That empty space will ruin the citation for researchers who might copy and paste it directly from your document to their Web browsers. Let the word wrap capability of your word processor break the URL (but turn off the auto hyphenation feature).

```
Holmes, Steven. "Black English Debate: No Standard
      Assumptions." The New York Times 30 Dec. 1996.
      http://search.nytimes.com/search/daily/bin/
      fastweb?getdoc+site+site+8836+4+wAAA+%28suspension%29%26OR
      %26%28bridges%29%26OR%26%28%29 (28 July 1997).
```

Sometimes you can avoid long and unwieldy URLs by pointing to the main URL for a given site and then listing the links or search terms followed to access the particular site or document. For example, the *New York Times* article shown above can be located through the paper's searchable index by going directly to the search URL at **http://search.nytimes.com/search/daily/** and typing in the search terms ("Black English Debate").

```
Holmes, Steven. "Black English Debate: No Standard
      Assumptions." The New York Times 30 Dec. 1996.
      http://search.nytimes.com/search/daily/ "Black English
      Debate" (22 Feb. 1998).
```

Note that a single blank space separates the URL from the search terms.

Some newer versions of word processors have incorporated features that automatically reformat URLs and email addresses in a text document. For documents being read on a computer with Internet access, the address in the document becomes a link that automatically opens a browser or email client and connects to the designated URL. For documents in print, the font size and/or color may be changed, and the address is usually underlined automatically to designate a hypertext link.

http://longman.awl.com

When you include this address within a citation, then, the word processor will automatically reformat it for you.

```
Jordan-Henley, Jennifer. "Basic Skills Simulated Search

    Activity." The English Pages. Addison Wesley Longman.

    http://longman.awl.com/englishpages Basic Skills/Activity

    Center (22 Sep. 1998).
```

Unless you are using a color printer, the colored text will appear slightly lighter than the surrounding text. Columbia Online Style recognizes that hypertext is becoming a feature of both print *and* online sources; thus, if your word processor reformats the text for you for an electronic address and automatically treats it as a hypertext link, you should not attempt to change it. However, do not attempt to emulate it on your own either—merely underlining an electronic address will not create a hypertext link in your file.

COS style also suggests that, for works to be published on the WWW, citation entries be listed using the hypertext "unordered list" feature rather than trying to force hanging indents. For traditional print projects, however, COS follows the "hanging indent" feature of other styles, with the first line of each bibliographic entry flush with the left-hand margin and subsequent lines indented one-half inch or five spaces. In the sample COS entries in the Form Directories (Sections 22b and 22d), we follow this convention.

COS style does not surround electronic addresses with angle brackets < >. This additional and potentially confusing punctuation is not necessary to separate an electronic address from other elements in an entry. Moreover, these characters could cause problems if you copy and paste them into a word-processed document or a hypertext composition.

A typical **Columbia Online Style Works Cited entry for an MLA-style paper in the humanities** includes the following basic information.

❑ Author, last name first, followed by a period and one space.

❑ Title of the work, followed by a period and one space. Book titles are italicized; article titles appear between quotation marks.

❏ Publication information (if any), followed by a period and one space. This will ordinarily include a date of publication if different from the date of access. List previous publication information (including print publication information), if known, followed by electronic publication information.

❏ The electronic address and any path or directory information, followed by a space. No period follows the electronic address.

❏ The date you accessed the information, in parentheses, followed by a period.

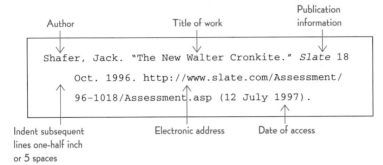

A typical **Columbia Online Style Works Cited entry for a CMS-style paper in the humanities** includes the following basic information.

❏ Author(s), last name first, followed by a period and one space.

❏ Title of the work, followed by a period (or other final punctuation mark) and enclosed between quotation marks.

❏ Publication information, followed by a period. This will ordinarily include a date of publication if different from the date of access. List previous publication information (including print publication information), if known, followed by information on the electronic publication.

❏ The electronic address and any path or directory information, followed by a space. No period follows the electronic address.

❏ The date you accessed the information, in parentheses, followed by a period.

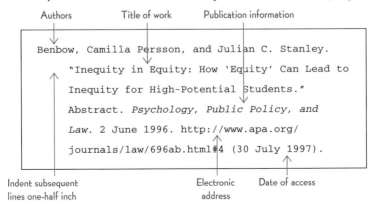

A typical **Columbia Online Style "References" entry for an APA-style paper in the sciences** includes the following basic information.

- ❏ Author(s), last name first, followed by a period and one space.
- ❏ Date of publication in parentheses, followed by a period and one space. Give the year first, followed by the month (do not abbreviate it), followed by the day (if applicable) for periodical publications; give only the year of publication for other works.
- ❏ Title of the work, capitalizing only the first word and any proper nouns, followed by a period and one space.
- ❏ Publication information (if any), followed by a period and one space. List previous publication information (including print publication information), if known, followed by information on the electronic publication.
- ❏ The electronic address and any path or directory information, followed by a space. No period follows the electronic address.
- ❏ The date you accessed the information, in parentheses, followed by a period.

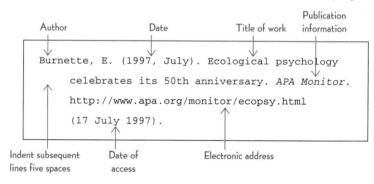

There are so many variations to these general entries, however, that you will want to check the COS Form Directories that follow in Sections 22b (Humanities) and 22d (Sciences) for the correct format of any particular entry.

22b COS Form Directory—HUMANITIES (MLA)

Below you will find the COS humanities-style forms for a variety of electronic sources. Use these forms when you are writing a paper in which you use an author–page number citation system (such as MLA) for nonelectronic sources. Note that the items in this section adhere to MLA style for the names of authors and the titles of works but follow COS guidelines for the electronic portion of the citation.

To find the form you need, simply look in the Format Index for the type of source you need to document and then locate that item by number in the COS Form Directory itself. To handle more complex electronic sources and to learn more about developing standards for online style, consult *The Columbia Guide to Online Style* by Janice

R. Walker and Todd Taylor (New York: Columbia University Press, 1998) or its regularly updated online version at http://www.columbia.edu/cu/cup/cgos/index.html.

COS FORMAT INDEX— HUMANITIES (MLA)

WORLD WIDE WEB CITATIONS

1. Web site—COS/MLA
2. Web site, revised or modified—COS/MLA
3. Web site with a group or institutional author—COS/MLA
4. Web site, no author or institution—COS/MLA
5. Web site maintained by an individual—COS/MLA
6. Web site—government—COS/MLA
7. Web site—corporate—COS/MLA
8. Web site—book, printed, available online—COS/MLA
9. Web site—book, published electronically—COS/MLA
10. Web site—online article—COS/MLA
11. Web site—article from a news service—COS/MLA
12. Web site—article from an archive—COS/MLA
13. Web site—with frames—COS/MLA
14. Web site—graphic, audio, or video file—COS/MLA

EMAIL, LISTSERVS, NEWSGROUPS

15. Personal email—COS/MLA
16. Listserv—COS/MLA
17. Newsgroup—COS/MLA
18. Message from an archive—COS/MLA

GOPHER, FTP, AND TELNET SITES

19. Material from a Gopher or FTP site—COS/MLA
20. Material from a telnet site—COS/MLA
21. Synchronous communications (MOOs, MUDs)—COS/MLA

REFERENCES AND DATABASES

22. Online encyclopedia article—COS/MLA
23. Online dictionary entry—COS/MLA
24. Material from a CD-ROM—COS/MLA
25. Material from an online database—COS/MLA

SOFTWARE

26. Software—COS/MLA

1. **Web Site—COS/Humanities (MLA)** The title of a particular Web page appears in quotation marks, and the title of the entire site is italicized.

```
                        Works Cited
Britton, Fraser. "Fraser's Downhill Domain." Killer Gonzo Bikes.
    1997. http://www.geocities.com/Colosseum/3681/index.html
    (20 June 1997).
```

2. **Web Site, Revised or Modified—COS/Humanities (MLA)** You may specify a date that a page or site was revised or updated if such a date is given. Your date of access follows the electronic address.

Works Cited

Stasi, Mafalda. "Another Deadline, Another Miracle!" *La Pagina*

   Casa Di Mafalda. Rev. Mar. 1997. http://www.cwrl.utexas.edu/

   ~mafi/present/ (5 May 1997).

3. Web Site with a Group or Institutional Author—COS/Humanities (MLA)

Works Cited

Texas Department of Transportation. "Big Bend Ranch State Park:

   General Information." *TourTex 2000*. Rev. 13 June 1996.

   http://www.dot.state.tx.us/travel/tourtex/bigbend/trv0001.htm

   (5 Dec. 1996).

4. Web Site, No Author or Institution—COS/Humanities (MLA)   When no author or institution can be assigned to a site, begin the entry with the title of the page or the site. In the example, the title is italicized because it identifies an entire Web site.

Works Cited

The British Monarchy: The Official Web Site. Rev. 20 June 1997.

   http://www.royal.gov.uk/ (5 July 1997).

5. Web Site Maintained by an Individual—COS/Humanities (MLA)   A maintained site is one that usually contains links, routinely updated, to materials not created by the author(s) of the site. The site can be listed either by the person(s) maintaining it or by its name, depending on which emphasis suits your project.

Works Cited

Clark, Stephen, et al., maint. "Philosophy at Large." University

   of Liverpool Department of Philosophy. http://www.liv.ac.uk/

   ~srlclark/philos.html (15 June 1997).

"Philosophy at Large." Maint. Stephen Clark, et al. University of

   Liverpool Department of Philosophy. http://www.liv.ac.uk/

   ~srlclark/philos.html (15 June 1997).

6. Web Site—Government—COS/Humanities (MLA)   In this example, no date is given for this frequently updated Web site because it would be the same as the date of access.

Works Cited

United States Congress. "Floor Activity in Congress This Week."

   Thomas: Legislative Information on the Internet.

   http://thomas.loc.gov/home/hot-week.html (28 July 1997).

7. **Web Site—Corporate—COS/Humanities (MLA)** The corporation or institution should be listed as the author.

Works Cited

```
Cedar Point, Inc. "The World's Greatest Collection of Roller
    Coasters." 1997. http://www.cedarpoint.com/coast.asp
    (30 June 1997).
```

8. **Web Site—Book, Printed, Available Online—COS/Humanities (MLA)** Give the name of the author, the title of the work, and the publication information for the printed version if known. Then provide the title of the electronic version, if different from the original title, and the electronic publication information.

Works Cited

```
Austen, Jane. Pride and Prejudice. 1813. Pride and Prejudice
    Hypertext. Ed. H. Churchyard. 1994. http://www.pemberley
    .com/janeinfo/prideprej.html (29 July 1997).
```

9. **Web Site—Book, Electronic—COS/Humanities (MLA)** Provide an author, title, and date of publication. In this example, the publication of the book is sponsored by an organization listed after the title.

Works Cited

```
Baker, Catherine. Your Genes, Your Choices. American Association
    for the Advancement of Science. 1997. http://www.nextwave
    .org/ehr/books/index.html (16 July 1997).
```

10. **Web Site—Online Article—COS/Humanities (MLA)** The title of the article in quotation marks is followed by the italicized title of the journal in which it appears. The volume number of the periodical is given, followed by a period and an issue number (if available) and date of publication.

Works Cited

```
University of Texas at Austin Undergraduate Writing Center.
    "Miss Grammars Attacks Sexist Language." The Writer's Block.
    3.2 (1995). http://uwc-server.fac.utexas.edu/wblock/
    dec95.html#TOC (28 July 1997).
```

11. **Web Site—Article from a News Service or Online Newspaper—COS/Humanities (MLA)** If no author's name is given, list the name of the news source (such as Reuters or Associated Press), followed by the title of the article, the name of the

news service or online newspaper, the date of the article if different from the date accessed, the electronic address, and the date accessed.

Works Cited

Associated Press. "Pathfinder's Battery Power Dwindles." *CNN*

   Interactive. http://www.cnn.com/TECH/9707/29/

   pathfinder.ap/index.html (29 July 1997).

12. **Web Site—Article from an Archive—COS/Humanities (MLA)**   Provide author, title, journal, and date as you would for a printed article, followed by the name of the archive site if applicable, the electronic address, and the date of access. In the example below, "The Compost Pile" is the name *Slate* gave to its archive of previously published articles.

Works Cited

Achenbach, Joel. "The Unexamined Game Is Not Worth Watching."

   Slate 9 May 1997. "The Compost Pile." http://www.slate.com/

   goodsport/97-05-09/goodsport.asp (1 June 1997).

13. **Web Site—with Frames—COS/Humanities (MLA)**   A Web site that uses frames may present material from other sites as well as material from within its own site. When you cannot determine the original URL of such material, list the documents by author and title and other publication information, and then give the name of the site where the source appears in a frame. Provide the electronic address of the site with frames, followed by a single blank space, and the path or links necessary to access the specific article or site (separating individual links by a forward slash). Conclude the entry with the date of access.

Works Cited

Burney, Fanny. *Fanny Burney and Dr. Johnson*. London, 1842. *Women*

   of the Romantic Period. http://www.cwrl.utexas.edu/~worp/

   worp.html Frances Burney/Dr. Johnson and Fanny Burney

   (13 July 1997).

14. **Web Site—Graphic, Audio, or Video File—COS/Humanities (MLA)**   You may want to cite a multimedia file one of two ways: either by its own URL (which you can usually find in the Netscape browser by selecting "View Page Info") or by the Web page on which the file appears. For a graphic alone, identify the author, photographer, or artist (if known); then give the title in quotation marks or the file name without quotation marks, followed by the date of publication (if known). Then furnish the electronic address and date of access. For audio and video files, include the name of the artist, composer, or director if known.

Works Cited

Crowley, Stephen. weld-nomination.1.jpg. 1997. http://

www.nytimes.com/library/review/archive/weld-nomination.1.jpg

(22 Feb. 1998).

To cite the file as it appears on a particular page, once again identify the artist and the title of the file. Then name the site on which it appears, followed by any publication information and the electronic address for the page.

Crowley, Stephen. weld-nomination.1.jpg. "Weld Ends Fight over

Nomination by Withdrawing." By Katharine Q. Seelye. *New York*

Times on the Web. 16 September 1997. http://search.nytimes

.com/search/daily/bin/fastweb?getdoc+site+site+29169+0+wAAA+%

22Weld%7Eends%7Efight%22 (22 Feb. 1998).

15. Personal Email—COS/Humanities (MLA)   Identify the author of the email and give the title of the message in quotation marks. Then identify the communication as "Personal email." Usually the date of the message is the same as the date you access (or read) it, so you need only give the access date in parentheses.

Works Cited

Sherman, Lee. "Coffee Shops." Personal email (5 Mar. 1997).

16. Listserv—COS/Humanities (MLA)   Identify the author of the message to a listserv. If no author's name is given, use the author's alias or email name. Then give the subject line of the message (enclosed in quotation marks) as the title, followed by the date of the message (if different from the date of access); the name of the list in italics, if known; the address of the listserv; and the date of access.

Works Cited

Cook, Janice. "Re: What New Day Is Dawning?" 19 June 1997.

Alliance for Computers and Writing Listserv

.acw-l@ttacs6.ttu.edu (21 June 1997).

17. Newsgroup—COS/Humanities (MLA)   Give the author's name (or alias), the subject line of the message as the title (enclosed in quotation marks), the date of the message (if different from the date of access), the address of the newsgroup, and the date of access.

Works Cited

Heady, Christy. "Buy or Lease? Depends on How Long You'll Keep the

Car." 7 July 1997. news:clari.biz.industry.automotive

(14 July 1997).

18. **Message from an Archive—COS/Humanities (MLA)**   Identify the author; the title of the message; the date of posting; the name of the list, if known; and the address of the list. Then give the name of the archive if available; the electronic address, followed by a single blank space; any other access information, separating individual links or commands by a forward slash (/); and the date of access enclosed in parentheses.

Works Cited

Butler, Wayne. "Re: Techno Literacy." 6 June 1996. *Alliance for*

    Computers and Writing Listserv. acw-l@ttacs6.ttu.edu. *ACW-L*

    Archives. http://english.ttu.edu/acw/acw-l/

    archive.htm Volume II (1996)/Issue 6 (29 July 1997).

19. **Material from a Gopher or FTP Site—COS/Humanities (MLA)**   Give the name of the author; the title of the work; publication information if the work appears elsewhere; the date of the document; the protocol (Gopher, FTP); the electronic address, including any directory or path information; and the date of access. If the information is accessed via the World Wide Web, include the electronic address from the browser.

Works Cited

Harnad, Stevan. "Minds, Machines and Searle." *Journal of*

    Experimental and Theoretical Artificial Intelligence 1

    (1989). gopher://gopher.liv.ac.uk:70/00/

    phil/philos-1-files/searle.harnad (30 July 1997).

Or the electronic address can be written to indicate the links that lead to a particular document, separating the links from the URL with a single blank space.

gopher://gopher.liv.ac.uk phil/philos-1-files/searle.harnad (30

    July 1997).

20. **Material from a Telnet Site—COS/Humanities (MLA)**   Give the author of the material you are citing (if available); the title of the material; the date (if available); the protocol (*telnet*); the telnet address, followed by a single blank space and any steps or commands necessary to access the site; and the date of access.

Works Cited

"Manners." *Connections.* telnet://connections.sensemedia.net:3332

    help manners (1 Mar. 1997).

21. **Synchronous Communications (MOOs, MUDs)—COS/Humanities (APA)** Identify the speaker, the type of communication and/or the title of the session,

and the title of the site (if available). Then give the electronic address and date of access. In giving an address, furnish any pathways, directories, or commands necessary.

```
                         Works Cited
Inept Guest. Personal interview. The Sprawl. telnet://sensemedia
     .net:7777/ (21 May 1997).
```

22. Online Encyclopedia Article—COS/Humanities (MLA)   Give the author of the article (if available), the title of the article, and the name of the encyclopedia. If the encyclopedia is based on a printed work, give place of publication, publisher, and date. Give any publication information about the electronic version, including the service offering it (for example, *America Online*) if applicable; the electronic address, including any directories and pathways; and the date accessed.

```
                         Works Cited
Brown, James R. "Thought Experiments." Stanford Encyclopedia of
     Philosophy. Stanford University, 1996. http://plato.stanford
     .edu/entries/thought-experiment/thought-experiment.html
     (30 July 1997).
```

23. Online Dictionary or Thesaurus Entry—COS/Humanities (MLA)   List the entry by the word looked up, followed by the name of the dictionary. If the dictionary is based on a printed work, give place of publication, publisher, and date. Give any publication information about the electronic version, including the service offering it (for example, *America Online*), the electronic address, and the date accessed.

```
                         Works Cited
"Drudge." WWWebster Dictionary. Merriam-Webster, 1996. http://
     www.m-w.com/cgi-bin/netdict (30 July 1997).
```

24. Material from a CD-ROM—COS/Humanities (MLA)   Provide an author (if available), the title of the entry or article, and the name of the CD-ROM program or publication. Furnish any edition or version numbers, a series title if applicable, and available publication information. No date if access is necessary for CD-ROM publications.

```
                         Works Cited
Bruckheim, Allan H. "Basic First Aid." The Family Doctor. Vers. 3.
     Portland: Creative Multimedia, 1993.
```

25. Material from an Online Database—COS/Humanities (MLA)   Identify the author and the title of the entry or article, and give publication information for items that have appeared in print. Identify the database or information service, and furnish retrieval data and a date of access.

Works Cited

```
Vlasic, Bill. "In Alabama: The Soul of a New Mercedes?" Business
     Week 31 Mar. 1997:70. InfoTrac SearchBank. File #A19254659.
     (27 July 1997).
```

26. **Software—COS/Humanities (MLA)**   List software by its individual or corporate author. If no author is given or if the corporate author is the same as the publisher, list the software by its title. Then identify the version of the software unless the version number is part of its name (*Windows 95, Word 6.0*). Give place of publication (if known), publisher, and date of release.

Works Cited

```
The Norton Utilities. Vers. 3.2. Cupertino, CA: Symantec, 1995.
```

22c Sample COS pages—HUMANITIES (MLA)

Page 223 shows excerpts from a research paper written using MLA format for printed sources and COS-humanities style for electronically accessed sources. Unlike the sample paper in MLA style presented in Chapter 23, titles of complete works are italicized rather than underlined, but if you compare the examples, you will notice that the COS entries resemble MLA entries in arrangement, capitalization, and punctuation.

CHECKLIST
Body of the Essay—COS-HUMANITIES Style

Like MLA, COS-humanities style uses parenthetical or in-text citations to designate material from other sources. The parenthetical reference generally includes the author's last name and a page number, if applicable.

- A book is cited following MLA format, including the author's last name and the exact page number of the reference.
- A WWW site is also listed by the author's last name (in this case, the author is a government agency). Since page numbers are not designated in the Web site, this information is omitted from the reference. Even though this source is already named in the text, a parenthetical note is included for direct quotations.
- An article from an electronic encyclopedia on CD-ROM does not include pagination and is listed by the author's last name only.
- Magazine articles, accessed using an online database, are also listed by the author's last name. Page numbers are omitted unless specifically included in the electronic text.
- A posting to an online newsgroup is cited by the author's last name.
- A newspaper article of only one page, following MLA format, may omit the page number from the parenthetical reference.

Although water covers most of the earth's surface, most of this water is not usable for industrial or human consumption (Carson 44). The U.S. Environmental Protection Agency (EPA) estimates as much as 30 to 50 percent of our water in this country is wasted. "Water is so inexpensive," they argue, "that there is little incentive to repair the leaks that needlessly waste our water" (U.S. Environmental Protection Agency). Along with water conservation measures and stricter regulations to preserve water quality, increasing the amount of available freshwater supplies is an urgent concern.

One method often suggested to address this problem is desalination, the process of removing salts from ocean or brackish water to produce fresh, potable water. There are several desalination methods, including reverse osmosis, electrodialysis, flash evaporation, and freezing (Lewin). Reverse osmosis entails pumping salt water at high pressure through special membranes that, while allowing fresh water to pass through, repel the salts (Uehling).

Works Cited

Carson, Rachel. *Silent Spring*. Boston: Houghton, 1962.

Heller, Jean. "Water Woes May Find Salty Solution." *St. Petersburg Times* 2 Apr. 1995, state ed., Tampa Bay and State: 1B.

Kensmark, John. "Re: Desalination." 15 Sep. 1998. news:rec.arts.sf .science (26 Sep. 1998).

Lewin, Seymour Z. "Water." *Microsoft Encarta*. Santa Rosa, CA: Microsoft, 1993.

Uehling, Mark D. "Salt Water on Tap." *Popular Science* Apr. 1991: 82–85. *SIRS Researcher on the Web*. http://researcher .sirs.com/cgi-bin/res-article-display?003387 (26 Sep. 1998).

U.S. Environmental Protection Agency. "Water Conservation." http://www.epa.gov/rgytgrnj/kids/lawater1.htm (28 Sep. 1998).

CHECKLIST
Works Cited Page—COS-HUMANITIES Style

The Works Cited list (see p. 223) contains full bibliographic information on all sources used in composing the paper. Electronic sources are cited using COS-humanities format; other sources are cited using MLA style. Titles are italicized rather than underlined for both types of sources.

- Begin the list of works cited on a separate page immediately following the body of the essay; number the pages sequentially throughout the paper (including the Works Cited page).
- Center the title "Works Cited" at the top of the page.
- Include full bibliographic information for all sources actually mentioned in the paper.
- Arrange the items in the list alphabetically by the last name of the author, or, if no author is given, by the first major word of the title.
- Use the "hanging indent" feature of your word processor to format entries, with the first line of each entry flush with the left-hand margin and subsequent lines indented five spaces or one-half inch.
- Double-space the entire list. Do not add extra spacing between entries.
- Use MLA style to cite nonelectronic sources; for electronic sources, follow COS-humanities style.

22d COS Form Directory—SCIENCES (APA)

Following you will find the COS science-style forms for a variety of electronic sources. Use these forms when you are writing a paper in which you use an author-date citation system (such as APA) for nonelectronic sources. Note that the items in this section adhere to APA style for the names of authors and the titles of works but follow COS guidelines for the electronic portion of the citation.

To find the form you need, simply look in the Format Index for the type of source you need to document and then locate that item by number in the COS Form Directory that follows. To handle more complex electronic sources and to learn more about developing standards for online style, consult *The Columbia Guide to Online Style* by Janice R. Walker and Todd Taylor (New York: Columbia University Press, 1998) or its regularly updated online version at http://www.columbia.edu/cu/cup/cgos/index .html.

COS Format Index—**SCIENCES (APA)**

WORLD WIDE WEB CITATIONS
27. Web site—COS/APA
28. Web site, revised or modified—COS/APA
29. Web site with a group or institutional author—COS/APA
30. Web site, no author or institution—COS/APA
31. Web site maintained by an individual—COS/APA
32. Web site—government—COS/APA
33. Web site—corporate—COS/APA
34. Web site—book, printed, available online—COS/APA
35. Web site—book, published electronically—COS/APA
36. Web site—online article—COS/APA
37. Web site—article from a news service—COS/APA
38. Web site—article from an archive—COS/APA
39. Web site—with frames—COS/APA
40. Web site—graphic, audio, or video file—COS/APA

EMAIL, LISTSERVS, NEWSGROUPS
41. Personal email—COS/APA
42. Listserv—COS/APA
43. Newsgroup—COS/APA
44. Message from an archive—COS/APA

GOPHER, FTP, AND TELNET SITES
45. Material from a Gopher or FTP site—COS/APA
46. Material from a telnet site—COS/APA
47. Synchronous communications (MOOs, MUDs)—COS/APA

REFERENCES AND DATABASES
48. Online encyclopedia article—COS/APA
49. Online dictionary entry—COS/APA
50. Material from a CD-ROM—COS/APA
51. Material from an online database—COS/APA

SOFTWARE
52. Software—COS/APA

27. **Web Site—COS/Sciences (APA)** Capitalize the first word and any proper names in the title. The title of the site is italicized.

References

Britton, F. (1997). Fraser's downhill domain. *Killer gonzo bikes.*
http://www.cwrl.utexas.edu/~mafi/present/ (20 June 1997).

28. **Web Site, Revised or Modified—COS/Sciences (APA)** You may specify a date that a page or site was revised or updated if such a date is given. Your date of access follows the electronic address.

References

Stasi, M. (1997, March). Another deadline, another miracle! *La
pagina casa di Mafalda* (Rev. ed.). http://www.cwrl
.utexas.edu/~mafi/present/ (5 May 1997).

29. Web Site with a Group or Institutional Author—COS/Sciences (APA)

References

Texas Department of Transportation. (1996, June 13). "Big

    Bend Ranch State Park: General information." *TourTex*

    2000 (Rev. ed.). http://www.dot.state.tx.us/travel/

    tourtex/bigbend/trv0001.htm (5 Dec. 1996).

30. Web Site, No Author or Institution—COS/Sciences (APA) When no author or institution can be assigned to a site, begin the entry with the title of the page or the site. In the example, the title is italicized because it identifies an entire Web site.

References

The British monarchy: The official Web site. (1997, June 20).

    (Rev. ed.). http://www.royal.gov.uk/ (5 July 1997).

31. Web Site Maintained by an Individual—COS/Sciences (APA) A maintained site is one that contains links, routinely updated, to materials not created by the author(s) of the site. The site can be listed either by the person(s) maintaining it or by its name, depending on which emphasis suits your project. Because this site is undated, no date follows the name of the author. In a parenthetical citation, however, give the date of access: (*Clark, 15 June 1997*).

References

Clark, S., et al. (Maint.). Philosophy at large. University of

    Liverpool Department of Philosophy.

    http://www.liv.ac.uk/~srlclark/

    philos.html (15 June 1997).

32. Web Site—Government—COS/Sciences (APA) In this example, no date is given for this frequently updated Web site because it would be the same as the date of access.

References

U.S. Congress. Floor activity in Congress this week. *Thomas:*

    Legislative information on the Internet. http://

    thomas.loc.gov/home/hot-week.html (28 July 1997).

33. Web Site—Corporate—COS/Sciences (APA) The corporation or institution should be listed as the author.

References

Cedar Point, Inc. (1997). The world's greatest collection of

    roller coasters. http://www.cedarpoint.com/coast.asp

    (30 June 1997).

34. Web Site—Book, Printed, Available Online—COS/Sciences (APA)   Give the name of the author, the title of the work, and the publication information for the printed version if known. Then provide the title of the electronic version, if different from the original title, and the electronic publication information.

References

Austen, J. (1813). *Pride and prejudice. Pride and prejudice*

    hypertext. H. Churchyard (Ed.). 1994. http://www.pemberley

    .com/janeinfo/prideprej.html (29 July 1997).

35. Web Site—Book, Electronic—COS/Sciences (APA)   Provide an author, title, and date of publication. In this example, the publication of the book is sponsored by an organization listed after the title.

References

Baker, C. (1997). *Your genes, your choices*. American Association

    for the Advancement of Science. http://www.nextwave

    .org/ehr/books/index.html (16 July 1997).

36. Web Site—Online Article—COS/Sciences (APA)   In this entry, the author of the piece is an institution. Notice also that in APA style, the volume number of the periodical is italicized. Provide an issue number (if available) in parentheses after the volume number. The issue number is not italicized.

References

University of Texas at Austin Undergraduate Writing Center.

    (1995). Miss Grammars attacks sexist language. *The Writer's*

    Block, 3 (2). http://uwc-server.fac.utexas.edu/wblock/

    dec95.html#TOC (28 July 1997).

37. Web Site—Article from a News Service or Online Newspaper—COS/Sciences (APA)   If no author's name is given, list the name of the news source (such as Reuters or Associated Press), followed by the date of the article if different from the date accessed, the title of the article, the name of the news service or online newspaper, the electronic address, and the date accessed.

References

Associated Press. (1997, July 29). Pathfinder's battery power

   dwindles. *CNN Interactive*. http://www.cnn.com/TECH/9707/

   29/pathfinder.ap/index.html (30 July 1997).

38. **Web Site—Article from an Archive—COS/Sciences (APA)**   Provide author, title, journal, and date as you would for a printed article, followed by the name of the archive site if applicable, the electronic address, and the date of access. In the example below, "The Compost Pile" is the name *Slate* gave to its archive of previously published articles.

References

Achenbach, J. (1997, May 9). The unexamined game is not worth

   watching. *Slate*. The Compost Pile. http://www.slate.com/

   goodsport/97-05-09/goodsport.asp (1 June 1997).

39. **Web Site—with Frames—COS/Sciences (APA)**   A Web site that uses frames may present material from other sites as well as material from within its own site. When you cannot determine the original URL of such material, list the documents by author and title and other publication information, and then give the name of the site where the source appears in a frame. Provide the electronic address of the site with frames, followed by a single blank space, and the path or links necessary to access the specific article or site. Conclude the entry with the date of access.

References

Burney, F. (1842). *Fanny Burney and Dr. Johnson*. London. *Women of*

   the Romantic Period. http://www.cwrl.utexas.edu/~worp/

   worp.html Frances Burney/Dr. Johnson and Fanny Burney

   (13 July 1997).

40. **Web Site—Graphic, Audio, or Video File—COS/Sciences (APA)**   You may want to cite a multimedia file one of two ways: either by its own URL (which you can usually find in the Netscape browser by selecting "View Page Info") or by the Web page on which the file appears. The first citation is for the file itself. The second citation is to the page on which it appears. APA style permits a description of the source in brackets, useful in this case.

References

Savoia, S. (1997). William F. Weld [Photograph]. http://

   www.washtimes.com/news/images/news2.gif (29 July 1997).

Savoia, S. (1997). William F. Weld [Photograph]. *The Washington*

   Times. http://www.washtimes.com/index.html (29 July 1997).

Audio or video files can be treated the same way as graphics, either as separate documents or as files set in the context of particular Web pages.

41. **Personal Email—COS/Sciences (APA)**   In APA style, you do not include personal email messages in the References list.

42. **Listserv—COS/Sciences (APA)**   Identify the author of the message to a listserv. If no author's name is given, use the author's alias or email name. Then give the date followed by the subject line of the message as the title; the name of the list, if known, in italics; the address of the listserv; and the date of access.

References

```
Cook, J. (1997, June 19). Re: What new day is dawning? Alliance
     for Computers and Writing Listserv. acw-l@ttacs6.ttu.edu
     (21 June 1997).
```

43. **Newsgroup—COS/Sciences (APA)**   Give the author's name (or alias), the date of the posting, the subject line of the message as the title, the address of the newsgroup, and the date of access.

References

```
Heady, C. (1997, July 7). Buy or lease? Depends on how long you'll
     keep the car. news:clari.biz.industry.automotive (14 July
     1997).
```

44. **Message from an Archive—COS/Sciences (APA)**   Give the name of the author, the date of the message, the title of the message, the name of the listserv (if applicable), and the address of the newsgroup or listserv (if known). Next, list the title of the archive site (if available), the electronic address followed by a single blank space and any directory path or access information, and the date of access.

References

```
Butler, W. (1996, June 6). Re: Techno literacy. Alliance for
     Computers and Writing Listserv. acw-l@ttacs6.ttu.edu. ACW-L
     Archives. http://english.ttu.edu/acw/acw-l/archive.htm Volume
     II (1996)/Issue 6 (29 July 1997).
```

45. **Material from a Gopher or FTP Site—COS/Sciences (APA)**   Give the name of the author; the date; the title of the work; publication information if the work appears elsewhere; the protocol (*gopher, FTP*); the electronic address, including any directory or path information, and the date of access. If the information is accessed via the World Wide Web, you may include the electronic address from the browser.

References

Harnad, S. (1989). Minds, machines and Searle. *Journal of*
   Experimental and Theoretical Artificial Intelligence 1.
   gopher://gopher.liv.ac.uk:70/00/phil/philos-1-files/
   searle.harnad (30 July 1997).

Or the electronic address can be written to indicate the links that lead to a particular document, separating the electronic address from the directory or path information by a single blank space.

gopher://gopher.liv.ac.uk phil/philos-1-files/searle.harnad
   (30 July 1997).

46. **Material from a Telnet Site—COS/Sciences (APA)** Give the author of the material you are citing (if available); the date (if available); the title of the material; the protocol (*telnet*); the telnet address, including any steps or commands necessary to access the site; and the date of access.

References

Manners. *Connections.* telnet://connections.sensemedia.net:3333
   help manners (1 Mar. 1997).

47. **Synchronous Communications (MOOs, MUDs)—COS/Sciences (APA)** Identify the speaker, the type of communication and/or the title of the session, and the title of the site (if available). Then give the electronic address and date of access. In giving an address, furnish any pathways, directories, or commands necessary. Note that personal communications are not usually included in the References list in APA style. However, they must be noted within the body of the paper (see Section 24b).

References

Inept Guest. Personal interview. *The Sprawl.* telnet://sensemedia
   .net:7777/ (21 May 1997).

48. **Online Encyclopedia Article—COS/Sciences (APA)** Give the author of the article (if available), the date of the edition, the title of the article, and the name of the encyclopedia. If the encyclopedia is based on a printed work, identify the place of publication and the publisher. Give any publication information about the electronic version such as the service offering it (for example, *America Online*); the electronic address, including any directories and pathways; and the date accessed.

References

Brown, J. R. (1996). Thought experiments. *Stanford encyclopedia of*
   philosophy. Stanford University. http://plato.stanford.edu/

entries/thought-experiment/thought-experiment.html
(30 July 1997).

49. Online Dictionary or Thesaurus Entry—COS/Sciences (APA) List the entry by the word looked up, followed by the date of publication and the name of the dictionary. If the dictionary is based on a printed work, give the place of publication and the publisher. Give any publication information about the electronic version, including the service offering it (for example, *America Online*), the electronic address, and the date accessed.

References

Drudge. (1996). *WWWebster dictionary*. Merriam-Webster. http://
    www.m-w.com/cgi-bin/netdicte (30 July 1997).

50. Material from a CD-ROM—COS/Sciences (APA) Provide an author (if available), the date of publication, the title of the entry or article, and the name of the CD-ROM program or publication. Furnish any edition or version numbers, a series title, and available publication information.

References

Bruckheim, A. H. (1993). Basic first aid. *The family doctor*
    (Version 3). Portland, OR: Creative Multimedia.

51. Material from an Online Database—COS/Sciences (APA) Identify the author, the date of publication, and the title of the entry or article, and give publication information for items that have appeared in print. Identify the database or information service, and furnish retrieval data and a date of access.

References

Vlasic, B. (1997, March 31). In Alabama: The soul of a new
    Mercedes? *Business Week, 70. InfoTrac SearchBank*. File
    #A19254659. (27 July 1997).

52. Software—COS/Sciences (APA) List software by its individual or corporate author. If no author is given or if the corporate author is the same as the publisher, list the software by its title. APA style does not italicize the title of software in a References list. Note also the placement of the version number in parentheses and the description of the source in brackets, both following the title.

References

The Norton utilities (Version 3.2) [Computer software]. (1995).
    Cupertino, CA: Symantec.

22e   Sample COS pages—SCIENCES (APA)

On page 233 we present excerpts taken from a research paper written using APA format for printed sources and COS-sciences style for electronically accessed sources. Unlike the case in the sample paper in APA style presented in Chapter 24, titles of complete works are italicized rather than underlined, but if you compare the examples, you will notice that the COS entries resemble APA entries in arrangement, capitalization, and punctuation. However, COS electronic entries are more compact than comparable APA entries.

CHECKLIST
Body of the Essay—COS-SCIENCES Style

Like APA, COS-sciences style uses parenthetical or in-text citations to designate material from other sources. The parenthetical reference generally includes the author's last name and the year of publication. APA requires that page numbers be included for citing a specific part of a text and for direct quotations. In COS-sciences style, however, page numbers may be omitted for electronically accessed sources that do not specifically designate pagination.

- An article in a print journal is cited in the paper by the author's last name and the year of publication, separated by a comma. Since this reference is to the work as a whole, no page number is given.

- A WWW page with no author specified is cited by a shortened version of the title, followed by a comma and the year of publication.

- A Web site authored by an organization (in this case, a government agency) is listed by the name of the organization, followed by the year of publication.

- For both print and electronic sources, when the author's name is included in the essay, the parenthetical reference directly follows it and includes only the year of publication.

- A book published online is cited as for a print book, by author's last name followed by the year of publication.

Sanders 2

The human genome project began a decade ago in 1988 when the
Congress of the United States allocated approximately $3 billion to
support a 15-year multi-university endeavor to complete the mapping of
the human genome (Caskey, 1994). The human genome is the set of
23 chromosomes and 60,000 to 80,000 genes that provide the blueprint
for our bodies ("Human genome," 1997). . . .

Throughout the project, scientists also hope to identify some of
the key ethical issues in gene research, to address the societal
implications of the research, to bring genetic issues to public
attention, and to formulate policy options designed to benefit both
individuals and society (U.S. Department of Energy, 1995). Swinbanks
(1992) observes, however, that since many scientists believe that they

Sanders 10

References

Baker, C. (1997). *Your genes, your choices.* American Association for
the Advancement of Science. http://www.nextwave.org/ehr/books/
index.html (16 July 1997).

Caskey, T. C. (1994). Human genes: The map takes shape. *Patient Care,
28,* 28-32.

Human genome project frequently asked questions. [FAQ]. http://www
.ornl.gov/hgmis/faq/faqsl.html#q1 (5 July 1997).

Matsubara, K. (1993). Background of human genome analysis. *The human
genome: Toward understanding ourselves.* http://www.genome.ad.jp/
brochure/english/Background.html#part4 (5 May 1997).

Swinbanks, D. (1992). When silence isn't golden. *Nature, 368,* 368-370.

U.S. Department of Energy. (1995). Understanding our genetic
inheritance: The U.S. Human Genome Project. *Human Genome Project
research.* http://www.ornl.gov/TechResources/Human_Genome/
project/5yrplan/science2.html (1 July 1997).

CHECKLIST
References Page—COS-SCIENCES Style

List sources used in the paper alphabetically by the last name of the author or, if no author is given, by the first major word of the title (see p. 233). Use italics rather than underlining for titles throughout.

- Begin the list of references on a separate page immediately following the body of the essay; number the pages sequentially throughout (including the References page).
- Center the title "References" at the top of the page.
- Include full bibliographic information for all sources actually mentioned in the paper.
- Use the "hanging indent" feature of your word processor to format entries, with the first line of each entry flush with the left-hand margin and subsequent lines indented five spaces or one-half inch.
- Double-space the entire list. Do not add extra spacing between entries.
- Use APA style to cite nonelectronic sources; for electronic sources, follow COS-sciences style.

The mainframe computer pictured here, the ENIAC (Electronic Numerator, Integrator, Analyzer and Computer), was a general-purpose calculator developed in 1945 in a U.S. Army Ballistics Research Lab by John W. Mauchly and J. Presper Eckert (both standing in the foreground of this photo). This early computer weighed 30 tons and covered 1,000 square feet of floor space—a far cry from today's space-conscious desktop designs. The ENIAC's plugboard made it easy to run a continuous program, a revolutionary feature at the time. However, when a new program was needed, the plugs had to be reconfigured because the ENIAC lacked storable memory.

Transistors, invented in 1947, increased computer storage power exponentially, and when researchers began using silicon semiconductors in the late 1950s, computers became smaller and more efficient. The 30-ton dinosaurs of the early computer age were now extinct.

When microprocessors became economical to produce in the mid–1980s, computer technology reached the masses. Computer chips could be found in digital watches, microwaves, telephones, TVs, and thermostats, to name just a few items. Computer chips are now small enough to contain more than 20 million transistors in 2 square centimeters. With ongoing technological advances like these, you may wonder what's next. Perhaps you'll soon see computers that fit in the palm of your hand and are completely mobile—never needing an outlet, a battery recharge, or a phone connection. Such miniature computers with super storage power might change, yet again, the way we write and research.

◎ DON'T MISS . . .

- **The explanation of MLA documentation in Section 23a.** If you are preparing a paper in language, literature, or the humanities, you may want to use MLA documentation.

- **The index to MLA formats on page 242.** Note that the formats provided include samples of both Works Cited entries and in-text parenthetical notes.

- **The sample MLA paper beginning on page 261.** The sample paper shows how to use short quotations, long quotations, figures and tables, and many different kinds of sources, including electronic items.

BOOKMARKS: Web Sites Worth Knowing About

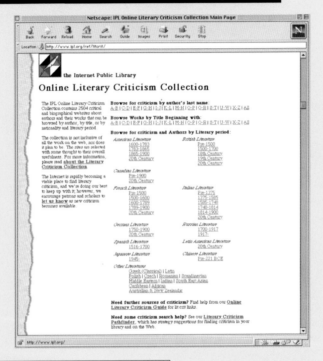

"IPL Online Literary Criticism Collection,"
http://www.ipl.org/ref/litcrit/

If you've been frustrated searching for serious literary criticism on the Web, try the "IPL Online Literary Criticism Collection." The *Internet Public Library's* librarians screen each Web page for scholarly relevance before adding it to their listings. At this site, you'll find links organized by author, time period, and literary genre. Many links point to complete works of criticism rather than just abstracts or ads for books.

Additional Sites
"Using Modern Language Association (MLA) Format,"
    http://owl.english.purdue.edu/files/33.html
Project Gutenberg, http://promo.net/pg/ (thousands of public-domain texts available online, at no charge)
The Zuzu's Petals Literary Resource, http://www.zuzu.com/

MLA Documentation

In many professional fields in the humanities (including both English and rhetoric and composition), writers are expected to follow the conventions of documentation and format recommended by the Modern Language Association (MLA). The basic procedures for MLA documentation are spelled out in this chapter. If you encounter documentation problems not discussed here, you may want to refer to the *MLA Handbook for Writers of Research Papers,* fifth edition, by Joseph Gibaldi. Style updates are also available at the MLA Web site at <http://www.mla.org/main_mla-nf.htm>.

23a How do you use MLA documentation?

MLA documentation involves just two basic steps: inserting an in-text note at each point that a paper or project needs documentation (Section 23a-1) and then recording all sources used in these notes in a Works Cited list (Section 23a-2).

Citing Electronic Sources in the Humanities

MLA guidelines do not currently include forms for many electronic sources and environments, and there is considerable debate over the forms they do present. When citing electronic sources, you can use MLA format or you may instead want to use the documentation style recommended by the *Columbia Guide to Online Style;* it was developed explicitly for electronic environments. Columbia Online Style (COS) for humanities papers is described on pages 204 through 231. MLA items that have a Columbia equivalent are marked in the MLA Form Directory (Section 23b) with a distinctive icon: COS p. 000 . Consult your instructor about using Columbia style for electronic and computerized sources.

Note an important difference between MLA and Columbia Online Style (COS) styles: for college papers, MLA continues to recommend (at an instructor's discretion) that the titles of books and other major works be underscored rather than italicized. COS requires italics for all such titles to avoid confusion between underscored text and hypertext links. MLA's use of angle brackets < > to surround electronic addresses can also cause problems in some applications. You may need to change the default settings in your word processor to deal with them or use special characters in HTML files (for more information, see Chapter 22). COS style, of course, avoids these problems. But consistency in citation formats is important if the elements are to be easily understood by readers. COS-humanities style is designed to *replace* MLA style for citation of electronic sources and to work *with* MLA's forms for citing conventional print sources.

23a-1 **(Step 1) In the body of your paper, place a note in parentheses to identify the source of each passage or idea you must document.** Such a note ordinarily consists of an author's last name and a page number—or a paragraph number for the few electronic sources that have them. For example, here is a sentence that includes a direct quotation from *Ralph Bunche: An American Life* by Brian Urquhart.

```
Ralph Bunche never wavered in his belief that the races in America
had to learn to live together: "In all of his experience of racial
discrimination Bunche never allowed himself to become bitter or to
feel racial hatred" (Urquhart 435).
```

The author's name and the page number of the source are separated by a single typed space.

In MLA documentation, page numbers are not preceded by *p.* or *pp.* or by a comma.

```
(Urquhart 435)

(Bly 253-54)
```

You can shorten a note by naming the author of the source in the body of the essay; then the note consists only of a page number. This is a common and readable form, one you should use regularly.

```
Brian Urquhart, a biographer of Ralph Bunche, asserts that
"in all of his experience of racial discrimination Bunche never
allowed himself to become bitter or to feel racial hatred"
(435).
```

As a general rule, make all parenthetical notes as brief and inconspicuous as possible. Remember that the point of a note is to identify a source of information, not to distract or impress readers.

The parenthetical note is usually placed after a passage needing documentation, typically at the end of a sentence and inside the final punctuation mark. However, with a quotation long enough (more than four typed lines) to require indention, the parenthetical note falls outside the final punctuation mark. Compare the following examples.

SHORT QUOTATION (NOT INDENTED)

```
Ralph Bunche never wavered in his belief that the races in America
had to learn to live together: "In all of his experience of racial
discrimination Bunche never allowed himself to become bitter or to
feel racial hatred" (Urquhart 435). He continued to work . . .
```

The note is placed inside the final punctuation mark.

LONG QUOTATION (INDENTED TEN SPACES)

```
Winner of the Nobel Peace Prize in 1950, Ralph Bunche, who died in
1971, left an enduring legacy:

          His memory lives on, especially in the long struggle for

          human dignity and against racial discrimination and

          bigotry, and in the growing effectiveness of the United

          Nations in resolving conflicts and keeping the peace.

     (Urquhart 458)
```

The note is placed outside the final punctuation mark.

Following are guidelines to use when preparing in-text notes.

1. **When two or more sources are cited within a single sentence,** the parenthetical notes appear right after the statements they support.

```
While the budget cuts might go deeper than originally reported
(Kinsley 42), there is no reason to believe that "throwing more
taxpayers' dollars into a bottomless pit" (Doggett 62) will do
much to reform "one of the least productive job training
programs ever devised by the federal government" (Will 28).
```

Notice that a parenthetical note is always placed outside any quotation marks but before the period that ends the sentence.

2. **When you cite more than one work by a single author in a paper,** a parenthetical note listing only the author's last name could refer to more than one book or article on the Works Cited page. To avoid confusion, place a comma after the author's name and identify the particular work being cited, using a shortened title. For example, a Works Cited page (see Section 23a-2) might list the following four works by Richard D. Altick.

```
                    Works Cited
Altick, Richard D. The Art of Literary Research. New York:
     Norton, 1963.
---. The Shows of London. Cambridge: Belknap-Harvard, 1978.
```

---. <u>Victorian People and Ideas</u>. New York: Norton, 1973.

---. <u>Victorian Studies in Scarlet</u>. New York: Norton, 1977.

The first time—and every subsequent time—you refer to a work by Richard Altick, you need to identify it by a shortened title in the parenthetical note.

(Altick, <u>Shows</u> 345)

(Altick, <u>Victorian People</u> 190-202)

(Altick, <u>Victorian Studies</u> 59)

3. **When you need to document a work without an author**—an unsigned article in a magazine or newspaper, for example—simply list the title, shortened if necessary, and the page number.

("In the Thicket" 18)

("Students Rally" A6)

Works Cited

"In the Thicket of Things." <u>Texas Monthly</u> Apr. 1994: 18.

"Students Rally for Academic Freedom." <u>The Chronicle of Higher

    Education</u> 28 Sept. 1994: A6.

4. **When you need to cite more than a single work in one note,** separate the citations with a semicolon.

(Polukord 13-16; Ryan and Weber 126)

5. **When a parenthetical note would be awkward,** refer to the source in the body of the essay itself.

In "Hamlet's Encounter with the Pirates," Wentersdorf

argues . . .

Under "Northwest Passage" in <u>Collier's Encyclopedia</u> . . .

The Arkansas State Highway Map indicates . . .

Software such as Microsoft's <u>FoxPro</u> . . .

Occasions when parenthetical notes might be awkward include the following.

❏ When you wish to refer to an entire article, not just to a passage or several pages

❏ When the author is a group or institution—for example, the editors of *Time* or the Smithsonian Institution

❏ When the citation is to a personal interview or an unpublished speech or letter

❏ When the item doesn't have page numbers—for example, a map, a cartoon, a work of art, a videotape, or a play in performance

❏ When the item is a reference work arranged alphabetically

❏ When the item is a government document with a name too long for a convenient in-text note

❏ When the item is computer software or an electronic source without conventional page numbers (see also Section 22a-1 for more on using parenthetical notes with electronic sources)

Individual entries in the MLA Form Directory (Section 23b) indicate when to avoid an in-text parenthetical note.

23a-2 **(Step 2) On a separate page at the end of your paper, list every source cited in a parenthetical note.** This alphabetical list of sources is titled "Works Cited." The Works Cited entry for Brian Urquhart's biography of Bunche discussed in Section 23a-1 would look like this.

> Urquhart, Brian. <u>Ralph Bunche: An American Life</u>. New York: Norton,
>
> 1993.

The first few entries on a full Works Cited page might look like this.

Subsequent lines indented
one-half inch or five spaces   "Works Cited" centered   All items double spaced

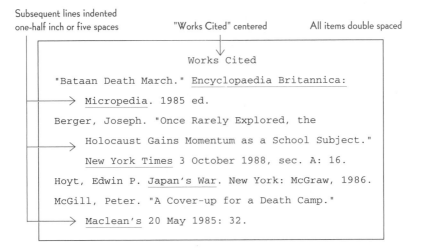

> Works Cited
>
> "Bataan Death March." <u>Encyclopaedia Britannica:</u>
>   <u>Micropedia</u>. 1985 ed.
>
> Berger, Joseph. "Once Rarely Explored, the
>   Holocaust Gains Momentum as a School Subject."
>   <u>New York Times</u> 3 October 1988, sec. A: 16.
>
> Hoyt, Edwin P. <u>Japan's War</u>. New York: McGraw, 1986.
>
> McGill, Peter. "A Cover-up for a Death Camp."
>   <u>Maclean's</u> 20 May 1985: 32.

A typical **MLA Works Cited entry for a book** includes the following basic information.

❏ Author, last name first, followed by a period and one space

❏ Title of the work, underlined, followed by a period and one space

❏ Place of publication, followed by a colon

❏ Publisher, followed by a comma and one space

❏ Date of publication, followed by a period

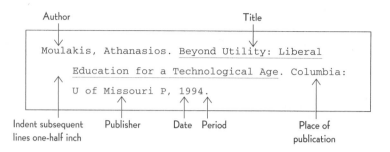

Author   Title

Moulakis, Athanasios. Beyond Utility: Liberal
        Education for a Technological Age. Columbia:
        U of Missouri P, 1994.

Indent subsequent   Publisher   Date   Period   Place of
lines one-half inch   publication

A typical **MLA Works Cited entry for an article in a scholarly journal** (where the pagination is continuous throughout a year) includes the following basic information.

❏ Author, last name first, followed by a period and one space.

❏ Title of the article, followed by a period (or other final punctuation mark) and enclosed between quotation marks.

❏ Name of the periodical, italicized or underlined, followed by one space.

❏ Volume number, followed by one space.

❏ Date of publication in parentheses, followed by a colon.

❏ Page or location, followed by a period. Page numbers should be inclusive, from the first page of the article to the last, including notes and bibliography.

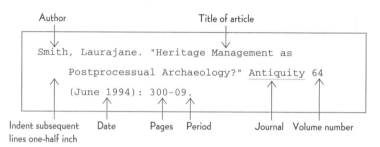

Author   Title of article

Smith, Laurajane. "Heritage Management as
        Postprocessual Archaeology?" Antiquity 64
        (June 1994): 300-09.

Indent subsequent   Date   Pages   Period   Journal Volume number
lines one-half inch

A typical **MLA Works Cited entry for an article in a popular magazine or newspaper** includes the following basic information.

❏ Author, last name first, followed by a period and one space.

❏ Title of the article, followed by a period and enclosed between quotation marks.

❏ Name of the periodical or newspaper, underlined, followed by one space.

❏ Date of publication, followed by a colon and one space. Abbreviate all months except May, June, and July.

❏ Page and/or location (section number for newspapers), followed by a period. Pages should be inclusive.

Author   Title of article

```
Fragnoli, Delaine. "Mountain Biking in Muir
      Country." Bicycling Apr. 1998: 36-39.
```

Indent subsequent   Periodical   Date   Pages   Period
lines one-half inch

A typical **MLA Works Cited entry for an electronic source** may include the following information, though few will require all the elements. (See also COS-humanities style in Chapter 22.)

- ❑ Author, last name first, followed by a period and one space.
- ❑ Title of the work, followed by a period and one space. Book titles are underlined; article titles appear between quotation marks.
- ❑ Print publication information (if any), followed by a period and one space.
- ❑ Title of the electronic site, underlined, followed by a period and one space.
- ❑ Editor (if any) of the electronic site, database, or text, with role indicated (for example, *Ed.*), followed by a period and a space.
- ❑ Version or volume number (if any) of the source, usually followed by a period.
- ❑ Date of electronic publication or most recent update, followed by a period.
- ❑ Identity of institution or group (if any) sponsoring the electronic site, followed by a period and a space.
- ❑ The date you accessed the information, followed by a space.
- ❑ The electronic address between angle brackets < >, followed by a period.

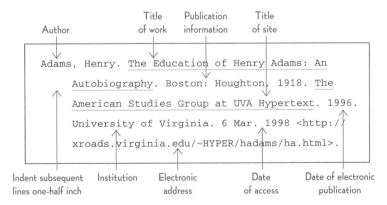

There are so many variations to these general entries, however, that you will want to check the MLA Form Directory that follows in Section 23b for the correct format of any unusual entry.

The Works Cited page itself follows the body of the essay (and endnotes, if there are any). It lists bibliographical information on all the materials you used in composing an essay. You do not, however, include sources you examined but did not cite in the body of the paper itself. For a sample Works Cited list, see page 270.

When an author has more than one work on the Works Cited list, those works are listed alphabetically under the author's name, using this form.

```
Altick, Richard D. The Shows of London. Cambridge: Belknap-
     Harvard, 1978.

---. Victorian People and Ideas. New York: Norton, 1973.

---. Victorian Studies in Scarlet. New York: Norton, 1977.
```

Works published since 1900 include a publisher's name. Publishers' names should be shortened whenever possible. Drop words such as *Company, Inc., Ltd., Bros.,* and *Books.* Abbreviate *University* to *U* and *University Press* to *UP.* When possible, shorten a publisher's name to one word. Here are some suggested abbreviations.

Barnes and Noble Books	Barnes
Doubleday and Co., Inc.	Doubleday
Harvard University Press	Harvard UP
University of Chicago Press	U of Chicago P
The Viking Press	Viking

23b MLA Form Directory

Below you will find the MLA Works Cited and parenthetical note forms for more than sixty kinds of sources. Simply find the type of source you need to cite in the Format Index and then locate that item by number in the list that follows. "COS" next to an entry indicates that a Columbia Online Style (COS) form is available for that source (see Chapter 22 for more on COS).

MLA FORMAT INDEX

BOOKS AND DISSERTATIONS
53. Book, one author
54. Book, two or three authors or editors
55. Book, four or more authors or editors
56. Book, revised by a second author
57. Book, edited—focus on the editor
58. Book, edited—focus on the editor, more than one editor
59. Book, edited—focus on the original author
60. Book, written by a group

61. Book with no author
62. Book, focus on a foreword, introduction, preface, or afterword
63. Work of more than one volume
64. Book, translation—focus on the original author
65. Book, translation—focus on the translator
66. Book in a foreign language
67. Book, republished
68. Book, part of a series
69. Book, a reader or anthology
70. Book, a second, third, or later edition

71. Book, a chapter in
72. Book published before 1900
73. Book, issued by a division of a publisher—a special imprint
74. Dissertation or thesis—published
75. Dissertation or thesis—unpublished
76. Book review

ARTICLES AND MAGAZINE PIECES

77. Article in a scholarly journal
78. Article in a popular magazine
79. Article in a weekly or biweekly magazine
80. Article in a monthly magazine— author named
81. Article or selection from a reader or anthology

NEWSPAPERS

82. Article in a newspaper
83. Editorial in a newspaper
84. Letter to the editor
85. Cartoon

REFERENCE WORKS

COS 86. Reference work or encyclopedia (familiar or online)
87. Reference work (specialized or less familiar)
88. Bulletin or pamphlet
89. Government document

ELECTRONIC SOURCES

COS 90. Computer software
COS 91. WWW page, generic

COS 92. WWW page, online book
COS 93. WWW page, online scholarly journal
COS 94. WWW page, online popular magazine
COS 95. WWW page, online newspaper editorial
COS 96. WWW page, personal home page
COS 97. Listserv/Newsgroup/Usenet newsgroup
COS 98. Synchronous communication (MOOs, MUDs) newsgroup
COS 99. Email
COS 100. CD-ROM/diskette database or publication

MISCELLANEOUS ENTRIES

101. Microfilm or microfiche
102. Biblical citation
103. Videotape
104. Movie
105. Television program
106. Radio program
107. Personal interview
108. Musical composition
109. Recording
110. Speech—no printed text
111. Speech—printed text
112. Lecture
113. Letter—published
114. Letter—unpublished
115. Artwork
116. Drama or play

53. Book, One Author—MLA

Works Cited

Weinberg, Steven. Dreams of a Final Theory. New York: Pantheon, 1992.

Parenthetical note: (Weinberg 38)

54. **Book, Two or Three Authors or Editors—MLA**   The names of second and third authors are given in normal order, first names first.

Works Cited

Collier, Peter, and David Horowitz. <u>Destructive Generation: Second</u>

    <u>Thoughts About the '60s</u>. New York: Summit, 1989.

Parenthetical note: (Collier and Horowitz 24)

55. **Book, Four or More Authors or Editors—MLA**   You have two options. You may name all the authors in both the Works Cited entry and any parenthetical notes.

Works Cited

Guth, Hans P., Gabriele L. Rico, John Ruszkiewicz, and Bill

    Bridges. <u>The Rhetoric of Laughter: The Best and Worst of</u>

    <u>Humor Night</u>. Fort Worth: Harcourt, 1996.

Parenthetical note: (Guth, Rico, Ruszkiewicz, and Bridges 95)

Alternatively, you may name just the first author on the title page and use the Latin abbreviation *et al.,* which means "and others."

Works Cited

Guth, Hans P., et al. <u>The Rhetoric of Laughter: The Best and Worst</u>

    <u>of Humor Night</u>. Fort Worth: Harcourt, 1996.

Parenthetical note: (Guth et al. 95)

56. **Book, Revised by a Second Author—MLA**   Sometimes you may need to cite a book by its original author, even when it has been revised. In such a case, place the editor's name after the title of the book.

Works Cited

Guerber, Hélène Adeline. <u>The Myths of Greece and Rome</u>. Ed. Dorothy

    Margaret Stuart. 3rd ed. London: Harrap, 1965.

Parenthetical note: (Guerber 20)

57. **Book, Edited—Focus on the Editor—MLA**   If you cite an edited work by the editor's name, identify the original author after the title of the work.

Works Cited

Noyes, George R., ed. <u>The Poetical Works of John Dryden</u>. By John

    Dryden. Boston: Houghton, 1950.

Parenthetical note: (Noyes v-vi)

58. Book, Edited—Focus on the Editor, More Than One Editor—MLA Treat multiple editors just as you do multiple authors, but place the abbreviation for editors (*eds.*) after their names.

```
                          Works Cited
Detweiler, Robert, John N. Sutherland, and Michael S. Werthman,
      eds. Environmental Decay in Its Historical Context. Glenview:
      Scott, 1973.
```
Parenthetical note: (Detweiler et al. 3)

59. Book, Edited—Focus on the Original Author—MLA Notice that because the sample Works Cited entry shown here is an edition of Shakespeare, the parenthetical note furnishes the act, scene, and line numbers for a particular play—not the author and page numbers one might expect with another kind of book.

```
                          Works Cited
Shakespeare, William. The Complete Works of Shakespeare. Ed. David
      Bevington. 4th ed. New York: Longman, 1997.
```
Parenthetical note: (Ham. 4.5.179-85)

60. Book, Written by a Group—MLA In the Works Cited entry, treat the group as the author. But to avoid a confusing parenthetical note, identify the group author in the body of your paper and place only relevant page numbers in parentheses. For example, you might use a sentence such as this: "The Reader's Digest *Fix-It-Yourself Manual* explains the importance of a UL label (123)."

```
                          Works Cited
Reader's Digest. Fix-It-Yourself Manual. Pleasantville: Reader's
      Digest, 1977.
```

61. Book with No Author—MLA List the book by its title, alphabetized by the first major word (excluding *The, A,* or *An*).

```
                          Works Cited
Illustrated Atlas of the World. Chicago: Rand, 1985.
```
Parenthetical note: (Illustrated Atlas 88)

62. Book, Focus on a Foreword, Introduction, Preface, or Afterword—MLA The note below, for instance, refers to information in Tanner's introduction, not to the text of Jane Austen's novel.

```
                          Works Cited
```
Tanner, Tony. Introduction. <u>Mansfield Park</u>. By Jane Austen.

    Harmondsworth, Eng.: Penguin, 1966. 7-36.

Parenthetical note: (Tanner 9-10)

63. **Work of More Than One Volume—MLA**   When you use only one volume of a multivolume set, identify both the volume you have used and the total number of volumes in the set.

```
                          Works Cited
```
Spindler, Karlheinz. <u>Abstract Algebra with Applications</u>. Vol. 1.

    New York: Dekker, 1994. 2 vols.

Parenthetical note: (Spindler 17-18)

If you use more than one volume of a set, list only the total number of volumes in that set. Then, in your parenthetical notes, identify the specific volumes as you cite them.

```
                          Works Cited
```
Spindler, Karlheinz. <u>Abstract Algebra with Applications</u>. 2 vols.

    New York: Dekker, 1994.

Parenthetical notes: (Spindler 1: 17-18); (Spindler 2: 369)

64. **Book, Translation—Focus on the Original Author—MLA**

```
                          Works Cited
```
Freire, Paulo. <u>Learning to Question: A Pedagogy of Liberation</u>.

    Trans. Tony Coates. New York: Continuum, 1989.

Parenthetical note: (Freire 137-38)

65. **Book, Translation—Focus on the Translator—MLA**

```
                          Works Cited
```
Swanton, Michael, trans. <u>Beowulf</u>. New York: Barnes, 1978.

Parenthetical note: (Swanton 17-18)

66. **Book in a Foreign Language—MLA**   Copy the title of the foreign work exactly as it appears on the title page, paying special attention both to accent marks and capitalization.

```
                          Works Cited

Bablet, Denis, and Jean Jacquot. Les Voies de la création
        théâtrale. Paris: Editions du Centre National de la Recherche
        Scientifique, 1977.
```
Parenthetical note: (Bablet and Jacquot 59)

67. **Book, Republished—MLA**   Give original publication dates for works of fiction that have been through many editions and reprints.

```
                          Works Cited

Herbert, Frank. Dune. 1965. New York: Berkeley, 1977.
```
Parenthetical note: (Herbert 146)

68. **Book, Part of a Series—MLA**   Give the series name just before the publishing information. Do not underline or italicize a series name.

```
                          Works Cited

Kirk, Grayson, and Nils H. Wessell, eds. The Soviet Threat: Myths
        and Realities. Proceedings of the Academy of Political
        Science 33. New York: Academy of Political Science, 1978.
```
Parenthetical note: (Kirk and Wessell 62)

69. **Book, a Reader or Anthology—MLA**   When you quote from the front matter of the collection, the page numbers for a parenthetical note may sometimes be Roman numerals. (To cite a selection within an anthology, see model 81.)

```
                          Works Cited

Lunsford, Andrea, and John Ruszkiewicz, eds. The Presence of
        Others: Voices That Call for Response. 2nd ed. New York: St.
        Martin's, 1997.
```
Parenthetical note: (Lunsford and Ruszkiewicz xvii-xix)

70. **Book, a Second, Third, or Later Edition—MLA**

```
                          Works Cited

Rombauer, Marjorie Dick. Legal Problem Solving: Analysis,
        Research, and Writing. 5th ed. St. Paul: West, 1991.
```
Parenthetical note: (Rombauer 480-81)

71. Chapter in a Book—MLA

Works Cited

Owens, Delia, and Mark Owens. "Home to the Dunes." The Eye of

the Elephant: An Epic Adventure in the African Wilderness.

Boston: Houghton, 1992: 11-27.

Parenthetical note: (Owens and Owens 24-27)

72. Book Published Before 1900—MLA Omit the name of the publisher in citations to works published prior to 1900.

Works Cited

Bowdler, Thomas, ed. The Family Shakespeare. 10 vols. London,

1818.

Parenthetical note: (Bowdler 2: 47)

73. Book Issued by a Division of a Publisher—a Special Imprint—MLA Attach
the special imprint (Vintage in this case) to the publisher's name with a hyphen.

Works Cited

Hofstadter, Douglas. Gödel, Escher, Bach: An Eternal Golden Braid.

New York: Vintage-Random, 1980.

Parenthetical note: (Hofstadter 192-93)

74. Dissertation or Thesis—Published (Including Publication by UMI)—MLA
If the dissertation you are citing is published by University Microfilms Interna-
tional (UMI), be sure to provide the order number as the last item in the Works
Cited entry.

Works Cited

Rifkin, Myra Lee. Burial, Funeral and Mourning Customs in

England, 1558-1662. Diss. Bryn Mawr, 1977. Ann Arbor: UMI,

1977. DDJ78-01385.

Parenthetical note: (Rifkin 234)

75. Dissertation or Thesis—Unpublished—MLA Note that the titles of unpublished dissertations appear between quotation marks. *Diss.* indicates that the source
is a dissertation.

```
                              Works Cited
Altman, Jack, Jr. "The Politics of Health Planning and

     Regulation." Diss. Massachusetts Institute of Technology,

     1983.
```
Parenthetical note: (Altman 150)

76. Book Review—Titled or Untitled—MLA   Not all book reviews have titles, so the Works Cited form for a book review can vary slightly. Notice that a book title (*Uncle Tom's Cabin*) within a book title is not underscored or italicized (Uncle Tom's Cabin *and American Culture*).

```
                              Works Cited
Baym, Nina. Rev. of Uncle Tom's Cabin and American Culture, by

     Thomas F. Gossett. Journal of American History 72 (1985):

     691-92.
Keen, Maurice. "The Knight of Knights." Rev. of William Marshall:

     The Flower of Chivalry, by Georges Duby. New York Review of

     Books 16 Jan. 1986: 39-40.
```
Parenthetical notes: (Baym 691-92); (Keen 39)

77. Article in a Scholarly Journal—MLA   Scholarly journals are usually identified by volume number or season (rather than day, week, or month of publication). Such journals are usually paginated year by year, with a year's work treated as a volume.

```
                              Works Cited
Pratt, Mary Louise. "Humanities for the Future: Reflections on the

     Western Cultural Debate at Stanford." South Atlantic

     Quarterly 89 (1990): 7-25.
```
Parenthetical note: (Pratt 24)

If a scholarly journal is paginated issue by issue, place a period and an issue number after the volume number.

78. Article in a Popular Magazine—MLA   Magazines are paginated issue by issue and identified by the monthly or weekly date of publication (instead of by volume number). If an article does not appear on consecutive pages in the magazine, give the first page on which it appears, followed by a plus sign—for example, *64+*.

Works Cited

Sabbag, Robert. "Fear & Reloading in Gun Valley." Men's Journal
    Oct. 1994: 64+.

Parenthetical note: (Sabbag 64)

79. **Article in a Weekly or Biweekly Magazine—MLA**   Give the date of publication as listed on the issue.

Works Cited

Smolowe, Jill. "When Violence Hits Home." Time 18 July 1994:
    18-25.

Parenthetical note: (Smolowe 20)

80. **Article in a Monthly Magazine—MLA**

Works Cited

Hudson, Elizabeth. "Hanging Out with the Bats." Texas Highways
    Aug. 1994: 14-19.

Parenthetical note: (Hudson 15)

81. **Article or Selection from a Reader or Anthology—MLA**   List the item on the Works Cited page by the author of the piece you are actually citing, not the editor(s) of the collection. Then provide the title of the particular selection, the title of the overall collection, the editor(s) of the collection, and publication information. Conclude with the page numbers of the selection.

Works Cited

Rohrer, Matthew. "Found in the Museum of Old Science." The
    Presence of Others: Voices That Call for Response. Ed. Andrea
    Lunsford and John Ruszkiewicz. 2nd ed. New York: St.
    Martin's, 1997. 290-91.

Parenthetical note: (Rohrer 290)

When you cite two or more selections from a reader or an anthology, list that collection fully on the Works Cited page.

Lunsford, Andrea, and John Ruszkiewicz, eds. The Presence of
    Others: Voices That Call for Response. 2nd ed. New York: St.
    Martin's, 1997.

Then, elsewhere in the Works Cited list, identify the authors and titles of all articles you cite from that reader or anthology, followed by the name of the editors and page numbers of those selections.

Himmelfarb, Gertrude. "The Victorians Get a Bad Rap." Lunsford and

    Ruszkiewicz 528-32.

Rohrer, Matthew. "Found in the Museum of Old Science." Lunsford

    and Ruszkiewicz 290-91.

When necessary, provide the original publication information first and then give the facts about the collection.

Hartman, Geoffrey. "Milton's Counterplot." ELH 25 (1958): 1-12.

    Rpt. in Milton: A Collection of Critical Essays. Ed. Louis L.

    Martz. Twentieth Century Views. Englewood Cliffs: Spectrum-

    Prentice, 1966: 100-08.

Parenthetical note: (Hartman 101)

82. Article in a Newspaper—MLA   For page numbers, use the form in the newspaper you are citing; many papers are paginated according to sections.

Works Cited

Rorty, Richard. "The Unpatriotic Academy." New York Times 13 Feb.

    1994: E15.

Parenthetical note: (Rorty E15)

A plus sign following the page number (for example, 7+) indicates that an article continues beyond the designated page, but not necessarily on consecutive pages.

Works Cited

Peterson, Karen S. "Turns Out We Are 'Sexually Conventional.'" USA

    Today 7 Oct. 1994: 1A+.

Parenthetical note: (Peterson 2A)

83. Editorial in a Newspaper—Author Not Named—MLA

Works Cited

"Negro College Fund: Mission Is Still Important on 50th

    Anniversary." Editorial. Dallas Morning News 8 Oct. 1994,

    sec. A: 28.

Parenthetical note: ("Negro College" 28)

84. Letter to the Editor—MLA

```
                         Works Cited
Cantu, Tony. Letter. San Antonio Light 14 Jan. 1986, southwest
     ed., sec. C: 4.
```

Parenthetical note: (Cantu 4)

85. Cartoon—MLA   To avoid a confusing parenthetical note, describe any cartoon in the text of your essay. For example, you might use a reference such as this: "In 'Squib' by Miles Mathis . . ."

```
                         Works Cited
Mathis, Miles. "Squib." Cartoon. Daily Texan 15 Jan. 1986: 19.
```

86. Reference Work or Encyclopedia (Familiar or Online)—MLA   With familiar reference works, especially those revised regularly, identify the edition you are using by its date. You may omit the names of editors and most publishing information. No page number is given in the parenthetical note when a work is arranged alphabetically.

```
                         Works Cited
Benedict, Roger William. "Northwest Passage." Encyclopaedia
     Britannica: Macropaedia. 1974 ed.
```

Parenthetical note: (Benedict)

COS
p. 219

A citation for an online encyclopedia article would include a date of access and electronic address. However, the online version might not list an author.

```
                         Works Cited
"Northwest Passage." Britannica Online. Vers. 98.1. 1 Nov. 1997.
     Encyclopaedia Britannica. 30 Nov. 1997
     <http://www.eb.com:180/cgibin/g?DocF=micro/430/12.html>.
```

87. Reference Work (Specialized or Less Familiar)—MLA   With less familiar reference tools, a full entry is required. (See model 86 for a comparison with familiar reference works.)

```
                         Works Cited
Kovesi, Julius. "Hungarian Philosophy." The Encyclopedia of
     Philosophy. Ed. Paul Edwards. 8 vols. New York: Macmillan,
     1967.
```

Parenthetical note: (Kovesi)

88. Bulletin or Pamphlet—MLA   Treat pamphlets as if they were books.

Works Cited

Morgan, Martha, ed. Campus Guide to Computer Services. Austin:

U of Texas, 1997.

Parenthetical note: (Morgan 8-9)

89. Government Document—MLA   Give the name of the government (national, state, or local) and the agency issuing the report, the title of the document, and publishing information. If it is a congressional document other than the *Congressional Record,* identify the Congress and, when important, the session (for example, *99th Cong., 1st sess.*) after the title of the document. Avoid a lengthy parenthetical note by naming the document in the body of your essay and placing only the relevant page numbers between parentheses, as in this sentence: "This information is from the *1985–86 Official Congressional Directory* (182–84)."

Works Cited

United States. Cong. Joint Committee on Printing. 1985-86 Official

Congressional Directory. 99th Cong., 1st sess. Washington:

GPO, 1985.

To cite the *Congressional Record,* give only the date and page number.

Cong. Rec. 8 Feb. 1974: 3942-43.

90. Computer Software—MLA   Give the author if known, the version number if any (for example: *Microsoft Word.* Vers. 7.0), the manufacturer, the date, and (optionally) the system needed to run it. Name the software in your text rather than use an in-text note. For example, you could begin a sentence like this: "With software such as Microsoft's *FoxPro.* . . ."

Works Cited

FoxPro. Vers. 2.5. Redmond: Microsoft, 1993.

91. WWW Page—Generic—MLA   The variety of Web pages is staggering, so you will have to adapt your documentation to particular sources. In general, provide author; title of the work; print publication information (if any); title of the electronic site, underlined; editor, with role appropriately indicated (for example, *Ed.*); version or volume number (if any) of the source; date of electronic publication or most recent update; identity of the institution or group (if any) sponsoring the electronic site; date you accessed the information; and electronic address between angle brackets < >. Since most Web sites do not have page numbers, avoid in-text parenthetical citations by identifying the site in your paper itself. A citation for a particular page within a site might look like the following.

Works Cited

"Hubble Catches Up to a Blue Straggler Star." Space Telescope
Science Institute. 29 Oct. 1997. NASA. 28 Nov. 1997
<http://oposite.stsci.edu/pubinfo/PR/97/35/>.

A citation of the entire site might be somewhat different.

Works Cited

Space Telescope Science Institute Home Page. 20 Nov. 1997. NASA.
28 Nov. 1997 <http://www.stsci.edu/>.

92. WWW—Online Book—MLA   Since most online books do not have page numbers, avoid in-text parenthetical citations by identifying the site in your paper itself. Give both an original date of publication of the electronic source and the date you accessed the information.

Works Cited

Dickens, Charles. A Christmas Carol. London, 1843. The Electronic
Text Center. Ed. David Seaman. Dec. 1997. U of Virginia
Library. 4 Feb. 1998 <http://etext.lib.virginia.edu/
cgibin/browse-mixed?id=DicChri&tag=public&images=images/
modeng&data=/lv1/Archive/eng-parsed>.

93. WWW—Online Scholarly Journal—MLA   Since most online articles do not have page numbers, avoid in-text parenthetical citations by identifying the site in your paper itself.

Works Cited

Katz, Seth, Janice Walker, and Janet Cross. "Tenure and Technology:
New Values, New Guidelines." Kairos 2.1 (1997). 20 July 1997
<http://english.ttu.edu/kairos/2.1/index_f.html>.

94. WWW—Online Popular Magazine—MLA   Since most online articles do not have page numbers, avoid in-text parenthetical citations by identifying the site in your paper itself.

Works Cited

Shafer, Jack. "The New Walter Cronkite." Slate 18 Oct. 1996.
12 July 1997 <http://www.slate.com/Assessment/96-10-18/
Assessment.asp>.

95. WWW—Online Newspaper Editorial—MLA Since most online newspaper stories or editorials do not have page numbers, avoid in-text parenthetical citations by identifying the site in your paper itself. Here the date of the editorial and the date of access to it are the same.

Works Cited

```
"The Proved and the Unproved." Editorial. New York Times on the
     Web 13 July 1997. 13 July 1997 <http://www.nytimes.com/
     yr/mo/day/editorial/13sun1.html>.
```

96. WWW—Personal Home Page

Works Cited

```
Yumibe, Joshua. Home page. 3 Mar. 1997 <http://www.dla.utexas.edu/
     depts/drc/yumibe/homeward.html>.
```

97. Listserv/Newsgroup/Usenet Newsgroup—MLA When citing material from a listserv, identify the author of the document or posting; put the subject line of the posting between quotation marks, followed by the date on which the item was originally posted and the words *Online posting;* give the name of the listserv, followed by the date you accessed the item, and the electronic address in angle brackets. Because there will be no page number to cite, avoid an in-text parenthetical citation by naming the author in the text of your paper, with a sentence such as "Cook argues in favor of. . . ."

Works Cited

```
Cook, Janice. "Re: What New Day Is Dawning?" 19 June 1997. Online
     posting. Alliance for Computers and Writing Listserv. 4 Feb
     1998 <acw-l@ttacs6.ttu.edu>.
Heady, Christy. "Buy or Lease? Depends on How Long You'll Keep the
     Car." 7 July 1997. Online posting. ClariNet. 14 July 1997
     <news:clari.biz.industry.automotive>.
```

98. Synchronous Communication (MOOs, MUDs)—MLA Provide the speaker and/or site, the title of the session or event, the date of the session, the forum for the communication (if specified), the date of access, and the electronic address.

Works Cited

```
Inept_Guest. Discussion of disciplinary politics in rhet/comp.
     12 Mar. 1998. LinguaMOO. 12 Mar. 1998
     <telnet://lingua.utdallas.edu:8888>.
```

99. Email—MLA   Identifying the communication in the essay itself is preferable to a parenthetical citation. Note the hyphen in *e-mail.*

Works Cited

Pacheco, Miguel. "Re: R-ball?" E-mail to the author. 14 Apr.

    1997.

100. CD-ROM/Diskette Database or Publication—MLA   To cite a CD-ROM or similar electronic database, provide basic information about the source itself—author, title, and publication information. Identify the publication medium (*CD-ROM; Diskette; Magnetic tape*) and the name of the vendor if available. (The vendor is the company publishing or distributing the database.) Conclude with the date of electronic publication.

Works Cited

Bevington, David. "Castles in the Air: The Morality Plays." The

    Theater of Medieval Europe: New Research in Early Drama. Ed.

    Simon Eckchard. Cambridge: Cambridge UP, 1993. MLA

    Bibliography. CD-ROM. SilverPlatter. Feb. 1995.

Parenthetical note: (Bevington 98)

For a CD-ROM database that is often updated (ProQuest, for example), you must provide publication dates for the item you are examining and for the data disk itself.

Works Cited

Alva, Sylvia Alatore. "Differential Patterns of Achievement Among

    Asian-American Adolescents." Journal of Youth and Adolescence

    22 (1993): 407-23. Proquest General Periodicals. CD-ROM. UMI-

    Proquest. June 1994.

Parenthetical note: (Alva 407-10)

Cite a book, encyclopedia, play, or other item published on CD-ROM or diskette just as if it were a printed source, adding the medium of publication (*Diskette* or *CD-ROM,* for example). When page numbers aren't available, use the author's name in the text of the paper to avoid a parenthetical citation. For example, you might use a sentence that begins "Bolter argues . . . ."

Works Cited

Bolter, Jay David. Writing Space: A Hypertext. Diskette.

    Hillsdale: Erlbaum, 1990.

101. Microfilm or Microfiche—MLA Treat material on microfilm exactly as if you had seen its original hard-copy version.

Works Cited

"How Long Will the Chemise Last?" Consumer Reports. Aug. 1958:

434-37.

Parenthetical note: ("How Long?" 434)

102. Biblical Citation—MLA Note that titles of sacred works, including all versions of the Bible, are not underlined.

Works Cited

The Jerusalem Bible. Ed. Alexander Jones. Garden City: Doubleday,

1966.

Parenthetical note: (John 18:37-38)

103. Videotape—MLA Cite a video entry by title in most cases. You may include information about the producer, designer, performers, and so on. Identify the distributor, and provide a date. Avoid in-text parenthetical citations to items on videocassette by naming the work in the body of your essay—for example, "In Oliveri's video *Dream Cars of the 50s & 60s . . . .*"

Works Cited

Dream Cars of the 50s & 60s. Compiled by Sandy Oliveri.

Videocassette. Goodtimes Home Video, 1986.

104. Movie—MLA In most cases, list a movie by its title unless your emphasis is on the director, producer, or screenwriter. Provide information about actors, producers, cinematographers, set designers, and so on, to suit your readers. Identify the distributor, and give a date of production. Avoid in-text parenthetical citations to films by naming the works in the body of your paper. You might use a reference such as "In Lucas's film *American Graffiti . . . .*"

Works Cited

American Graffiti. Dir. George Lucas. Perf. Richard Dreyfuss and

Ronny Howard. Universal, 1973.

105. Television Program—MLA List the TV program by episode or name of program. Avoid in-text parenthetical citations to television shows by naming the programs in the body of your paper.

```
                        Works Cited
"No Surrender, No Retreat." Dir. Mike Vejar. Writ. Michael
     Straczynski. Perf. Bruce Boxleitner, Claudia Christian, and
     Mira Furlan. Babylon #5 KEYE-42, Austin. 28 July 1997.
```

106. Radio Program—MLA Avoid in-text parenthetical citations to radio shows by naming the programs in the body of your paper.

```
                        Works Cited
Death Valley Days. Created by Ruth Cornwall Woodman. NBC Radio.
     WNBC, New York. 30 Sept. 1930.
```

107. Personal Interview—MLA Refer to the interview in the body of your essay rather than in a parenthetical note, as suggested here: "In an interview, Peter Gomes explained . . . ."

```
                        Works Cited
Gomes, Rev. Peter. Personal interview. 23 Apr. 1997.
```

108. Musical Composition—MLA List the work on the Works Cited page by the name of the composer. If you have sheet music or a score, you can furnish complete publication information.

```
                        Works Cited
Joplin, Scott. "The Strenuous Life: A Ragtime Two Step."
     St. Louis: Stark Sheet Music, 1902.
```

If you don't have a score or sheet music to refer to, provide a simpler entry. In either case, naming the music in the essay itself is preferable to a parenthetical citation.

```
Porter, Cole. "Too Darn Hot." 1949.
```

109. Recording—MLA Naming the recording in the essay itself is preferable to a parenthetical citation.

```
                        Works Cited
Pavarotti, Luciano. Pavarotti's Greatest Hits. London, 1980.
```

110. Speech—No Printed Text—MLA Give the location and date of the address. Naming the work in the essay itself is preferable to a parenthetical citation.

Works Cited

Reagan, Ronald. "The Geneva Summit Meeting: A Measure of
       Progress." U.S. Congress. Washington. 21 Nov. 1985.

111. Speech—Printed Text—MLA

Works Cited

O'Rourke, P. J. "Brickbats and Broomsticks." Capital Hilton.
       Washington. 2 Dec. 1992. Rpt. American Spectator Feb. 1993:
       20-21.

Parenthetical note: (O'Rourke 20)

112. Lecture—MLA Naming the lecture in the essay itself is preferable to a parenthetical citation.

Works Cited

Cook, William W. "Writing in the Spaces Left." Chair's Address.
       Conf. on Coll. Composition and Communication. Cincinnati.
       19 Mar. 1992.

113. Letter—Published—MLA

Works Cited

Eliot, George. "To Thomas Clifford Allbutt." 1 Nov. 1873. In
       Selections from George Eliot's Letters. Ed. Gordon S. Haight.
       New Haven: Yale UP, 1985: 427.

Parenthetical note: (Eliot 427)

114. Letter—Unpublished—MLA Identifying the letter communication in the essay itself is preferable to a parenthetical citation.

Works Cited

Newton, Albert. Letter to Agnes Weinstein. 23 May 1917. Albert
       Newton Papers. Woodhill Lib., Cleveland.

115. Artwork—MLA Naming the artwork in the essay itself is preferable to a parenthetical citation.

Works Cited

Fuseli, Henry. Ariel. Folger Shakespeare Lib., Washington, DC.

116. **Drama or Play—MLA** Citing a printed text of a play, whether individual or collected, differs from citing an actual performance. For printed texts, provide the usual Works Cited information, taking special care when citing a collection in which various editors handle different plays. In parenthetical notes, give the act, scene, and line numbers when the work is so divided; give page numbers if it is not.

Works Cited

Stoppard, Tom. Rosencrantz and Guildenstern Are Dead. New York:

    Grove, 1967.

Shakespeare, William. The Tragedy of Hamlet, Prince of Denmark.

    Ed. Frank Kermode. The Riverside Shakespeare. 2nd ed. Ed. G.

    Blakemore Evans and J. J. M. Tobin. Boston: Houghton, 1997.

    1183-1245.

Parenthetical notes: (Stoppard 11-15); (Ham. 5.2.219-24)

For actual performances of plays, give the title of the work, the author, and then any specific information that seems relevant—director, performers, producers, set designer, theater company, and so on. Conclude the entry with a theater, location, and date. Refer to the production directly in the body of your essay to avoid a parenthetical citation.

Timon of Athens. By William Shakespeare. Dir. Michael Benthall.

    Perf. Ralph Richardson, Paul Curran, and Margaret Whiting.

    Old Vic, London. 5 Sept. 1956.

23c Sample MLA paper

The sample paper that follows is accompanied by checklists designed to help you set up a paper correctly in MLA style. When your work meets the specifications on the checklists, it should be in proper form.

AUTHOR'S NOTE

I wrote "Mountain Bikes on Public Lands: Happy Trails?" (under an alias) to test how well various online sources would support an undergraduate research topic. Electronic indexes proved particulary helpful in locating up-to-date magazine articles while the Internet and Web furnished numerous interesting references—and could have supplied many more. Unfortunately, the topic did not lend itself to articles in scholarly journals, so only one such source is included.

I was able to download several of the magazine articles used in the paper directly from the library's online catalog, which provides complete texts of recent articles from major publications. But there was a catch. Although it was possible to download and print the text of these articles in my office, they arrived without page numbers. To cite these materials accurately, I still had to hotfoot it to the library to find the original articles. Like any new technology, online research still has its frustrations.

JR

Curt Bessemer

Professor Ruszkiewicz

English 306

31 July 1997

            Mountain Bikes on Public Lands: Happy Trails?

     Imagine that you have driven hundreds of miles to enjoy the

serenity of one of America's national parks. Without a care in the

world, you are hiking through a tranquil canyon. Suddenly from around

a bend in the trail comes a whooping gang of men and women mounted on

thick-framed, knobby-tired bicycles. Kicking up dust, climbing logs,

leaping boulders, scattering wildlife, they push you into the

underbrush as they whirl past, screaming obscenities. Welcome to the

sport of mountain biking--at least the way angry hikers and

environmentalists sometimes portray it (Coello 148).

     Imagine, now, that you are a rider on a lightweight, sturdy

machine designed to take you safely and comfortably across isolated

roads and trails miles from automobile traffic and madding crowds. Fat

tires soften the trail over which you travel at a sober speed,

enjoying the wilderness your tax dollars support. You come up on a

group of hikers and courteously indicate that you will pass them on

the left. But the hikers reply with curses and maybe even a slap on

the back or a board with nails (Drake). This, too, is mountain biking

from the point of view of its enthusiasts, who feel victimized by

environmentalists eager to preserve public lands for themselves.

     Somewhere between these two portraits lies the truth about the

conflict currently raging between mountain bikers and trail hikers

(with equestrians caught somewhere in between) when it comes to access

to public land. Conservation groups, ecologists, and equestrians would

just as soon lump bikers with the drivers of motorized vehicles

already banned from many off-road areas, especially park trails. These

groups want to keep parks and wilderness areas in as natural a state

as possible and don't regard mechanical vehicles of any kind as

compatible with their goal. On the other hand, mountain bikers

consider these lands--especially the narrow hiking trails--their

First Page of the Essay—MLA

MLA does not require a separate cover sheet or title page. If your instructor expects one, center the title of your paper and your name in the upper third of the paper. Center the course title, your instructor's name, and the date of submission on the lower third of the sheet, double-spacing between the elements.

The first page of a paper without a separate title page will look like the facing page. Be sure to check all the items in this list.

- Place your name, your instructor's name, the course title, and the date in the upper left-hand corner, beginning one inch from the top of the page. These items are doubled spaced.

- Identify your instructor by an appropriate title. When uncertain about academic rank, use *Mr.* or *Ms.*

  Dr. James Duban   Professor Rosa Eberly
  Ms. Joanna Wolfe   Mr. Eric Lupfer

- Center the title a double space under the date. Capitalize the first and last words of the title. Capitalize all other words *except* articles (*a, an, the*), prepositions, the *to* in infinitives, and coordinating conjunctions—unless they are the first or last words.

  RIGHT   Mountain Bikes on Public Lands: Happy Trails?

  Do not underline the title of your paper, use all capital letters, place it between quotation marks, or end it with a period. Titles may, however, end with question marks or include words or phrases that are italicized, underlined, or between quotation marks.

  RIGHT   Violence in Shakespeare's Macbeth

  RIGHT   Dylan's "Like a Rolling Stone" Revisited

- Begin the body of the essay two lines (a double space) below the title. Double-space the entire essay, including quotations.

- Use one-inch margins at the sides and bottom of this page.

- Number pages in the upper right-hand corner, one-half inch from the top, one inch from the right margin. Precede the page number with your last name. Use the "automatic header" feature in your word processor, if available.

natural environment. While admitting that some bikers have been irresponsible, they also believe that problems with mountain biking have been greatly exaggerated. The Mountain Bike Book author Rob van der Plas, for example, claims to have witnessed public officials and hikers "manipulating or circumventing facts to find justification for attempts to deny cyclists access" to trails (107). When all is said and done, if mountain bikers wish to use trails in public lands and wilderness, they must organize politically to defend their rights and, according to the International Mountain Biking Association (IMBA), demonstrate "environmentally sound and socially responsible riding practices."

What some have characterized as a war between bikers and environmental groups is due in part to the explosive popularity of mountain bikes (see fig. 1). More comfortable and sturdy than the drop-handled 10-speed racing bikes dominant just a generation ago, mountain bikes now represent half the sales in what has become a $3.5 billion industry in the United States, with 25 million Americans riding their bikes at least once a week (Castro 43).

Distinguishing mountain bikes from touring or racing bikes are flat handlebars for upright posture, high chainstays for greater road clearance, wide balloon tires for durability, and stout frames for

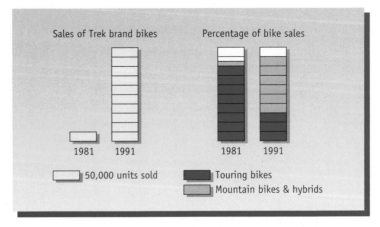

Fig. 1. U.S. sales of mountain bikes.

CHECKLIST
Body of the Essay—MLA

The body of an MLA research paper continues uninterrupted until the separate Notes page (if any) and the Works Cited page. Be sure to use good-quality paper for print projects.

- Use margins of at least one inch all around. To keep the right-hand margin reasonably straight use the automatic word-wrap feature of your word processor. Do not hyphenate words at the end of lines or right-justify your margins.

- Place page numbers in the upper right-hand corner, one inch from the right edge of the page and one-half inch from the top. Precede the page number with your last name.

- Indent the first line of each paragraph one-half inch, or five spaces if you use a typewriter.

- Indent long quotations one inch, or ten spaces if you use a typewriter. In MLA documentation, long quotations are any that exceed four typed lines in the body of your essay. Double-space these indented quotations.

overall performance (see fig. 2). These features contribute to the
ruggedness of the vehicles as well as to rider comfort. The sturdy
structures and bulging tires that give trail bikes their off-road
capacity also make them strong and comfortable on-road vehicles. This
versatility probably accounts for the mountain bike's current
domination of the market. For if early mountain bikers developed the
sport for the thrill of racing downhill, most bikers today take their
rides for the same reason that hikers hoist a backpack--to enjoy the
great outdoors. Rob van der Plas explains it well:

> What's nice about riding off road is not a function of the
> roughness, the dirt, or any of the other characteristics of
> the terrain. Instead what you'll relish most is the
> remoteness, the solitude, the experience of nature and the
> lack of traffic. (104)

In effect, the mountain bike has become the all-terrain, off-road
trail bike of choice, the most civilized, economical, and inexpensive
machine for getting away from it all.

But how to get away from it all has now become the problem,
especially in National Wilderness and Wilderness Study Areas, where
the government controls access to thousands of potential recreational
acres and where the 1964 Wilderness Act forbids "motor vehicles and
other forms of mechanical transport" (van der Plas 108). In most other

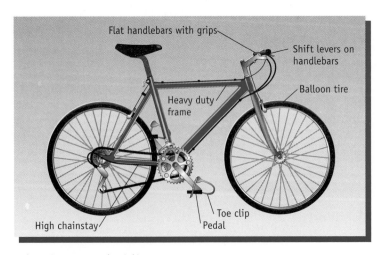

Fig. 2. Mountain bike.

natural areas, service and fire roads provide the perfect routes for biking, though an important distinction is made between double-track and single-track trails. Double-track trails--which are usually just unpaved roads--are ordinarily open to bikers because they are wide enough to be shared comfortably with other users. Single-track trails--narrower and more challenging paths through wilderness areas-- are both preferred by experienced trail bikers and more likely to be closed to them. It is on these trails that bikers compete with pedestrian or equestrian traffic and where most conflicts occur.

Mountain bikes have been accused of damaging trails and causing soil erosion, their knobby tires eating away at the terrain, especially after rains (Schwartz 75). Officials in natural areas have shown increasing concern over such damage, going so far as to consider banning even horses on park trails, let alone bikes (O'Keefe). Yet horses at least remain on trails and move slowly while aggressive bikers often do not (Coello 148). Traditional environmental coalitions have been eager to lobby against permitting bikers on trails, and such groups have had considerable success in California, where the mountain biking craze originated.

It isn't just environmental dangers that have made some people angry at the bikers; it is their unconventional and sometimes outrageous behavior. As David Schwartz puts it, "To traditional trail users, the new breed of bicycle was alien and dangerous, esthetically offensive and physically menacing" (75). Rob Buchanan describes the situation in Marin County, California, this way:

> At first Marin's old guard, the equestrians and Sierra clubbers who'd always had the place to themselves, grudgingly put up with the new fad. Then the whole thing got out of hand. Weekends the hills were overrun with "wheeled locusts," as the San Francisco Chronicle put it, "driven by speed-crazed yuppies in Day-Glo Lycra." (80)

The new bikers come from a generation that environmentalists from the 1960s and earlier don't understand or like. But that impression isn't always true, as mountain biking activist and writer Geoff Drake explains, complaining about attacks on him for defending biking:

You can't imagine how strange this is. A lifelong hiker and
environmentalist, I find myself a renegade--an expatriate in
the woods I love. What about my years of membership in
Greenpeace and the Nature Conservancy? [. . .] Now,
incredibly, I'm receiving the ire of environmentalists
everywhere.

Bicyclists have begun to respond to the threat that the more
politically experienced environmentalists pose to their sport and
recreation. They point to the politically correct character of the
mountain bike as "an ideal vehicle for global ecological change"
(Buchanan 82). They challenge unproven conclusions about trail erosion
in the absence of hard evidence that bikes have actually caused it. In
fact, they argue that the erosion of trails may be caused largely by
runoff from rain and snow (van der Plas 108). They even poke fun at
the extremism of some environmentalists; Mike Garlinski, for example,
wonders about the damage a NASA Martian rover must be causing on Mars:

These NASA Mountain Bike types are not content to destroy
the pristine environment of the earth, or even the moon.
They have to continuously attack Mars. [. . .] Now, the
ultimate insult has occured [sic]. We have a device that is
the equivalent of THREE Mountain Bikes (That's right, six
wheels) tearing up the terrain for miles in every direction!

Bikers have also begun to clean up their image and to organize in
order to claim their rights to responsible use of the country's
natural resources. An associate editor of Mountain Biking Magazine
warns that "land access and liability problems [. . .] could ensue if
the majority of the population thinks mountain biking as a whole is a
gonzo activity for those with more muscle fibers than brain cells"
(Fragnoli). To change that perception, groups such as the National
Off-Road Bicycle Association (NORBA) have written codes to encourage
members to behave responsibly, while the Women's Mountain Bike and Tea
Society (WOMBATS) have, as Sara Corbett reports, moved aggressively to
prove bikers can share trails with hikers. Biking groups and magazines
have also been leaders in urging everyone to wear helmets while riding
to prevent some of the almost 200,000 bike-related head injuries that
occur each year (Goldsmith).

Trail riders, appreciating that all politics is local, have begun to take their civic responsibilities seriously. For example, in Austin, Texas, an off-road bicycle group called the Ridge Riders made allies in the local environmental community by helping to build trails in a state park and to clean and maintain trails in other local recreational areas (Skinner). Perhaps the most aggressive efforts are being made in the San Francisco Bay Area by groups such as ROMP (Responsible Organized Mountain Pedalers), which explains its mission in civic terms:

> ROMP is a group of over 250 local, energetic mountain biking volunteers who have discovered the need for an active representation for the mountain biking public. Mountain biking is becoming even more popular, increasing the need for volunteers to work at maintaining or improving access to trails. ROMP needs YOUR support to help these changes come about.

As a result of such political action, biking groups that have demonstrated their willingness to protect the natural environment are beginning to have success in negotiating with environmental groups. In spring 1994, the International Mountain Bicycling Association (IMBA) and the powerful Sierra Club jointly endorsed the principle that "mountain biking is a legitimate form of recreation and transportation on trails, including singletrack, when and where it is practiced in an environmentally sound and socially responsible manner" (Stein 86). Several months later, the IMBA persuaded the U.S. Forest Service to acknowledge that bicycles, unlike motorized vehicles, have a legitimate place on trails, their agreement potentially opening up more tracks for mountain riders in the 191 million acres of land controlled by the Forest Service ("IMBA Breaks"). The agreements signed at Park City, Utah, and West Dover, Vermont, represent the kinds of compromises that we are likely to see more of in the future between people who wish to use our natural resources and those sworn to protect them. When such groups begin to realize their common interests and when groups such as mountain bikers earn their political clout through community action, we're likely to discover that there's room on the trail for everyone.

Works Cited

Buchanan, Rob. "Birth of the Gearhead Nation." <u>Rolling Stone</u>
     9 July–23 Aug. 1992: 80+.

Castro, Janice. "Rock and Roll." <u>Time</u> 19 Aug. 1991: 42+.

Coello, Dennis. <u>Touring on Two Wheels: The Bicycle Traveler's
     Handbook</u>. New York: Lyons, 1988.

Corbett, Sara. "Ride with Pride: Practice Rolling Acts of Kindness."
     <u>Outside Magazine</u> Mar. 1995. 1 May 1997
     <http://outside.starwave.com/magazine/0395/3f_bkind.html>.

Drake, Geoff. "Trouble on the Mountain." <u>Bicycling</u> Aug. 1992: 106.

Fragnoli, Delaine. "Are We Extreme?" <u>Mountain Biking Magazine</u> Sept.
     1994: 13.

Garlinski, Mike. "Re: Pathfinder Causing Martian Erosion." 5 July
     1997. Online posting. 15 July 1997 <alt.mountain-bike>.

Goldsmith, Marsha F. "Campaigns Focus on Helmets as Safety Experts
     Warn Bicycle Riders to Use—and Preserve—Heads." <u>JAMA</u> 15 July
     1992: 308.

"IMBA Breaks Through—Twice!" <u>Mountain Bike</u> Oct. 1994: 16.

International Mountain Biking Association. <u>IMBA</u>. 1996. 23 Apr. 1997
     <http://www.outdoorlink.com/imba/index.html>.

O'Keefe, Eric. "Destabilized." <u>Texas Monthly</u> Sept. 1994: 82.

<u>Responsible Organized Mountain Pedalers Home Page</u>. 14 July 1997.
     18 July 1997 <http://www-leland.stanford.edu/~scoop/romp/>.

Schwartz, David M. "Toward Happy Trails: Bikers, Hikers and
     Olympians." <u>Smithsonian</u> June 1994: 74-87.

Skinner, Dawn. <u>Austin Cycling Notes</u> Aug. 1994: 8.

Stein, Theo. "The New MBA: Is It Finally in the Driver's Seat?" <u>MTB</u>
     Oct. 1994: 85-89.

van der Plas, Rob. <u>The Mountain Bike Book: Choosing, Riding and
     Maintaining the Off-Road Bicycle</u>. 3rd ed. San Francisco: Bicycle,
     1993.

The Works Cited Page—MLA

The Works Cited list contains full bibliographical information on all the books, articles, and other resources used in composing the paper. For more information about the purpose and form of this list, see Section 23a–2.

- Center the title "Works Cited" at the top of the page.

- Include in the Works Cited list all the sources actually mentioned in the paper. Do not include materials you examined but did not cite in the body of the paper itself.

- Arrange the items in the Works Cited list alphabetically by the last name of the author. If no author is given for a work, list it according to the first word of its title, excluding articles (*The, A, An*).

- Be sure the first line of each entry touches the left-hand margin. Subsequent lines are indented five spaces.

- Double-space the entire list. Do not quadruple-space between entries unless that is the form your instructor prefers.

- Punctuate items in the list carefully. Don't forget the period at the end of each entry.

- Follow this form if you have two or more entries by the same author.

    van der Plas, Rob. The Mountain Bike Book: Choosing, Riding and
        Maintaining the Off-Road Bicycle. 3rd ed. San Francisco:
        Bicycle, 1993.
    ---. Mountain Bike Magic. Mill Valley: Bicycle, 1991.

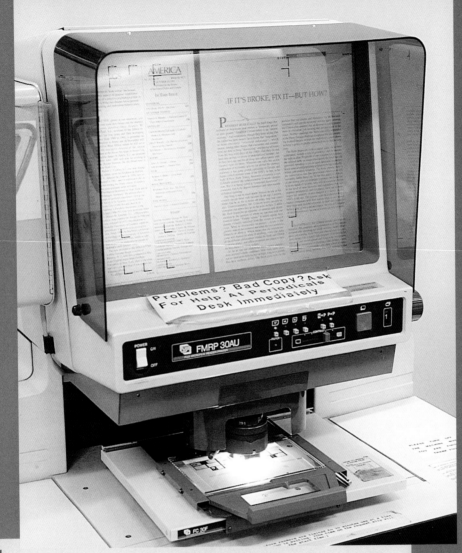

In the late 1920s, banks and other businesses began to store information on rolls of film. This microfilming technique enables documents to be reduced photographically and to be stored compactly. Microfiche, more common than microfilm today, is a 4-by-6-inch card with 98 images arranged in rows. With advances in photographic technique and reader magnification, some kinds of microfiche can now contain 3,000 to 4,000 document images per 4-by-6-inch film. Reading these reduced documents, however, requires machines to project the image in enlarged form. Pictured above is a microfiche reader; you've no doubt encountered one at some point during your career as a student. Libraries use microfilm and microfiche to save space. Such items are also easy to copy, and they help with document preservation. For example, it is much easier to preserve old newspapers on film than on crumbling newsprint.

Library storage and technology has changed considerably in the last decade as computers have made electronic images easy to make and share. Today microfilm has to share the limelight with optical disk technology. And the availability of articles on the Internet has reduced the need for microfilm; now that digitized text is available with the click of a button, today's researchers rarely need to thumb through drawers of microfiche.

- **The explanation of APA documentation in Section 24a.** If you are preparing a paper in the social sciences, you may want to use APA documentation.

- **The index to APA formats on page 281.** Note that the formats provided include samples of both References entries and in-text parenthetical notes.

- **The sample APA paper beginning on page 290.** The sample paper includes an abstract and an illustration and shows how to integrate many different kinds of sources, including electronic items.

BOOKMARKS: Web Sites Worth Knowing

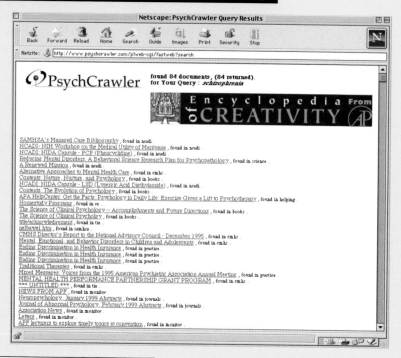

PsychCrawler,
http://www.psychcrawler.com

To find the best sites for serious psychology research, start with *PsychCrawler*. The site works just like any other Web search engine but limits its scope to academic sites. A search for "schizophrenia," for example, will return only abstracts and articles dealing with scientific research on the subject. Unlike the major commercial search engines, *PsychCrawler* lists only sites that have been submitted by their authors. For an exhaustive search after you've narrowed your topic, use a universal search engine such as *AltaVista* or *HotBot*.

Additional Sites

Anthromorphemics anthropology glossary, http://www.anth.ucsb.edu/glossary/index2.html
CyberPsychLink, http://cctr.umkc.edu/user/dmartin/psych2.html
"Using American Psychological Association (APA) Format,"
    http://owl.english.purdue.edu/files/34.html

APA Documentation

In many social science and related courses (anthropology, education, home economics, linguistics, political science, psychology, sociology), writers are expected to follow the conventions of documentation recommended by the American Psychological Association (APA). The basic procedures for APA documentation are spelled out in this chapter. A full explanation of APA procedures is provided by the *Publication Manual of the American Psychological Association,* 4th edition (1994), available in most college libraries.

Citing Electronic Sources in the Social Sciences

APA documentation offers forms for documenting some electronic sources, which we present on pages 281 through 289. For electronic items not covered by specific APA forms, you may want to use the documentation style recommended by the *Columbia Guide to Online Style.* The citation examples in COS-sciences style were developed explicitly for electronic forms and cover more different types of sources than any other style. But consistency in citation formats is essential if the elements of the citation are to be readily understood. COS-sciences style is designed to *replace* APA style for citation of electronic sources and *work with* APA forms for citing conventional print sources. However, when necessary to use APA format for citing electronically accessed and published sources, this chapter presents examples following the guidelines in the *Publication Manual.* Columbia Online Style (COS) for science papers is described on pages 222 through 232. APA items that have a Columbia equivalent are marked in the APA Form Directory (Section 24b) with a distinctive icon: COS p. 000 . Consult your instructor about using COS for electronic and computerized sources.

24a How do you use APA documentation?

APA documentation involves just two basic steps: inserting an in-text note at each point where a paper or project needs documentation (Section 24a-1) and then recording all sources used in these notes in a References list (Section 24a-2).

24a-1 **(Step I) In the body of your paper, place a note to identify the source of each passage or idea you must document.** In its most common form, this APA note consists of the last name of the source's author, followed immediately by the year the material was published, in parentheses. For example, here is a sentence derived from information in an article by E. Tebeaux titled "Ramus, Visual Rhetoric, and the Emergence of Page Design in Medical Writing of the English Renaissance," published in 1991.

```
According to Tebeaux (1991), technical writing developed in
important ways in the English Renaissance.
```

Another basic form of the APA parenthetical note places the author's last name and a date between parentheses. This form is used when the author's name is not mentioned in the sentence itself. Notice that a comma follows the author's name within the parentheses.

```
Technical writing developed in important ways during the English
Renaissance (Tebeaux, 1991).
```

A page number may be given for indirect citations and *must* be given for direct quotations. A comma follows the date if page numbers are given. Page numbers are preceded by *p.* or *pp.*

```
During the English Renaissance, writers began to employ "various
page design strategies to enhance visual access" (Tebeaux, 1991,
p. 413).
```

When appropriate, the documentation may be distributed throughout a passage.

```
Tebeaux (1991) observes that for writers in the late sixteenth
century, the philosophical ideas of Peter Ramus "provided a
significant impetus to major changes in page design" (p. 413).
```

APA parenthetical notes should be as brief and inconspicuous as possible. Following are some guidelines to use when preparing in-text notes.

1. **When two or more sources are used in a single sentence,** the notes are inserted as needed after the statements they support.

```
While Porter (1981) suggests that the ecology of the aquifer
might be hardier than suspected, "given the size of the
drainage area and the nature of the subsurface rock"
(p. 62), there is no reason to believe that the county needs
another shopping mall in an area described as "one of the
last outposts of undisturbed nature in the state"
(Martinez, 1982, p. 28).
```

Notice that a parenthetical note is placed outside quotation marks but before the period ending the sentence.

2. **When a single source provides a series of references, you need not repeat the name of the author until other sources interrupt the series.** After the first reference, page numbers are sufficient until another citation intervenes. Even then, you need repeat only the author's last name, not a date, when the reference occurs within a single paragraph.

> . . . The council vetoed zoning approval for a mall in an area described by Martinez (1982) as the last outpost of undisturbed nature in the state. The area provides a "unique environment for several endangered species of birds and plant life" (p. 31). The birds, especially the endangered vireo, require breeding spaces free from encroaching development (Harrison & Cafiero, 1979). Rare plant life is similarly endangered (Martinez).

3. **When you cite more than one work written by an author in a single year,** assign a small letter after the date to distinguish between the author's two works.

> (Rosner, 1991a)
>
> (Rosner, 1991b)
>
> The charge is raised by Rosner (1991a), quickly answered by Anderson (1991), and then raised again by Rosner (1991b).

4. **When you need to cite more than a single work in a note,** separate the citations with a semicolon and list them in alphabetical order.

> (Searle, 1993; Yamibe, 1995)

5. **When you are referring to a Web site** (though not a particular Web document), you can give the electronic address directly in the paper. The site does not need to be added to the References list according to APA. (See also Chapter 22 on COS-sciences style for more on citing electronically accessed sources.)

> More information about psychology as a profession is available on the American Psychological Association's World Wide Web site at http://www.apa.org/.

24a-2 **(Step 2) On a separate page at the end of your paper, list every source cited in an in-text note.** This alphabetical list of sources is titled "References." A References page entry for an article on medical writing in the Renaissance by

E. Tebeaux would look like the following if it were in a *professional paper* submitted for publication to an APA journal.

```
Tebeaux, E. (1991). Ramus, visual rhetoric, and the emergence
of page design in medical writing of the English Renaissance.
Written Communication, 8, 411-445.
```

This form, indented like a paragraph, makes typesetting a professional article easier.

However, most college papers won't be typeset; in fact, APA style describes them as "final copy." (See *Publication Manual of the American Psychological Association,* 4th ed., pp. 334–36, for an explanation of this principle.) Consequently, **References list items in student essays ought to look the way such entries appear in APA journal articles themselves—with hanging indents of five spaces rather than paragraph indents.** APA also permits the titles of books and comparable works to be italicized rather than underlined. (See page 208 for a discussion of italics versus underlining.)

Here, then, is how Tebeaux's article would appear in the References list of a *college paper* in APA "final copy" style.

```
Tebeaux, E. (1991). Ramus, visual rhetoric, and the emergence of
     page design in medical writing of the English Renaissance.
     Written Communication, 8, 411-445.
```

We use hanging indents for APA References entries throughout the handbook.

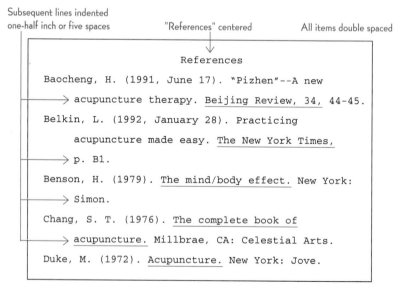

Subsequent lines indented one-half inch or five spaces   "References" centered   All items double spaced

```
                           References
     Baocheng, H. (1991, June 17). "Pizhen"--A new
          acupuncture therapy. Beijing Review, 34, 44-45.
     Belkin, L. (1992, January 28). Practicing
          acupuncture made easy. The New York Times,
          p. B1.
     Benson, H. (1979). The mind/body effect. New York:
          Simon.
     Chang, S. T. (1976). The complete book of
          acupuncture. Millbrae, CA: Celestial Arts.
     Duke, M. (1972). Acupuncture. New York: Jove.
```

A typical **APA References entry for a book** includes the following basic information.

❏ Author(s), last name first, followed by a period and one space. Initials are used instead of first and middle names unless two authors mentioned in the paper have identical last names and initials.

❏ Date in parentheses, followed by a period and one space.

❏ Title of the work, underlined, followed by a period, also underlined (unless some other information separates the name of the title from the period), and one space. Only the first word of the title, the first word of a subtitle, and proper nouns and adjectives are capitalized.

❏ Place of publication, followed by a colon and one space.

❏ Publisher, followed by a period.

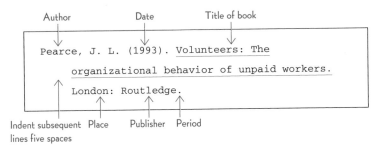

A typical **APA References entry for an article in a scholarly journal or magazine** includes the following basic information.

❏ Author(s), last name first, followed by a period and one space.

❏ Date in parentheses, followed by a period and one space.

❏ Title of the article, followed by a period and one space. Only the first word of the title, the first word of a subtitle, and proper nouns and adjectives are capitalized. The title does not appear between quotation marks.

❏ Name of the periodical, underlined, followed by a comma and one space. All major words are capitalized.

❏ Volume number, underlined, followed by a comma and space, also underlined without interruption.

❏ Page numbers, followed by a period.

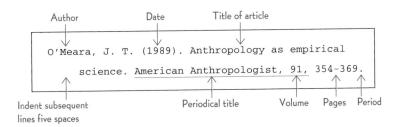

A typical **APA References entry for an article in a popular magazine or newspaper** includes the following basic information.

❏ Author(s), last name first, followed by a period.

❏ Date in parentheses, followed by a period and one space. Give the year first, followed by the month (do not abbreviate it) and the day, if necessary.

❏ Title of the work, followed by a period and one space. Only the first word and proper nouns and adjectives are capitalized. The title does not appear between quotation marks.

❏ Name of the periodical, underlined, followed by a comma, also underlined. All major words are capitalized.

❏ Page or location indicated by the abbreviation *p.* or *pp.*, followed by a period.

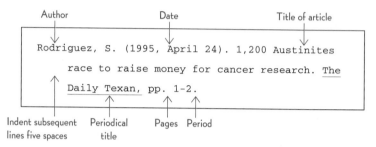

A typical **APA References entry for an online or WWW document** includes the following basic information.

❏ Author(s), last name first, followed by a period and one space.

❏ Date of publication in parentheses, followed by a period and one space. Give the year first, followed by the month (do not abbreviate it), followed by the day, if necessary.

❏ Title of the work, followed by a period and one space.

❏ Information about the form of the information—*On line, CD-ROM, Computer software*—in brackets, followed by a period and one space. Note that *on line* is spelled as two words in APA style.

❏ Path statement or electronic address, including the date of access. No period follows the path statement.

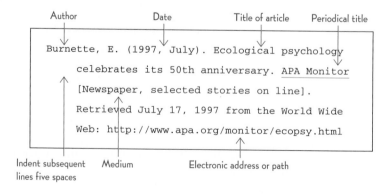

There are many variations to these generic entries, however, so you should check the *Publication Manual of the American Psychological Association* (1994) when you do a major APA-style project. For advice on writing a student paper, consult pages 331 through 340 of the APA manual. For the latest updates on electronic documentation, check the APA Web site at http://www.apa.org/students. APA provides only a limited number of types of electronic sources and examples. For other types of electronic sources, you will need to review the elements above to determine how to cite the specific type of source. You may also want to review COS-sciences style in Chapter 22.

The References list itself appears on its own page following the body of the essay (and a footnote page if there is one). It lists bibliographical information on all the materials you used in composing an essay. See page 303 for a checklist on setting up a References list.

24b APA Form Directory

In this section, you will find the APA References page and parenthetical note forms for a variety of sources. Locate the type of source you need to cite in the Format Index and then locate the item by number in the list that follows. The "COS" icon next to an entry indicates that a Columbia Online Style (COS) form is available for that source (see Chapter 22 for more on COS).

APA FORMAT INDEX

117. Book, one author
118. Book, two authors
119. Book, three or more authors
120. Book, revised
121. Book, edited
122. Book with no author
123. Book, a collection or anthology
124. Work within a collection, anthology, or reader
125. Chapter in a book
126. Book review
127. Article in a scholarly journal paginated by year or volume, not issue by issue
128. Article in a monthly periodical paginated issue by issue
129. Article in a weekly or biweekly periodical

130. Article in a newsletter
131. Article in a periodical—author not named
132. Newspaper article—author named
133. Newspaper article—author not named
COS 134. Computer software
COS 135. Online source
COS 136. WWW page—generic
COS 137. WWW page—online scholarly article
COS 138. WWW page—online newspaper article
COS 139. WWW page—online abstract
COS 140. Email
141. Movie/videotape
142. Musical recording

117. Book, One Author—APA

References

Pearson, G. (1949). <u>Emotional disorders of children.</u> Annapolis,

    MD: Naval Institute Press.

Parenthetical notes:

Pearson (1949) found . . .

(Pearson, 1949)

(Pearson, 1949, p. 49)

118. Book, Two Authors—APA
Notice the ampersand (&) between authors' names in the References list item and parenthetical notes. Note also that *and* is used when the authors are identified in the text itself.

References

Lasswell, H. D., & Kaplan, A. (1950). <u>Power and society: A</u>

    <u>framework for political inquiry.</u> New York: Yale University

    Press.

Parenthetical notes:

Lasswell and Kaplan (1950) found . . .

(Lasswell & Kaplan, 1950)

(Lasswell & Kaplan, 1950, pp. 210-213)

119. Book, Three or More Authors—APA

References

Rosenberg, B., Gerver, I., & Howton, F. W. (1971). <u>Mass society in</u>

    <u>crisis: Social problems and social pathology</u> (2nd ed.). New

    York: Macmillan.

Parenthetical notes:

First note. Rosenberg, Gerver, and Howton (1971) found . . .

Subsequent notes. Rosenberg et al. (1971) found . . .

First note. (Rosenberg, Gerver, & Howton, 1971)

Subsequent notes. (Rosenberg et al., 1971)

If a work has six or more authors, use the first author's name followed by *et al.* for all parenthetical references, including the first. In the References list, however, identify all the authors.

120. Book, Revised—APA

References

Edelmann, A. T. (1969). <u>Latin American government and politics</u>
(Rev. ed.). Homewood, IL: Dorsey.

Parenthetical notes:

Edelmann (1969) found . . .

(Edelmann, 1969)

(Edelmann, 1969, p. 62)

121. Book, Edited—APA   Notice that APA uses an ampersand (&) to join the names of two editors or authors.

References

Journet, D., & Kling, J. (Eds.). (1984). <u>Readings for technical</u>
<u>writers.</u> Glenview, IL: Scott, Foresman.

Parenthetical notes:

Journet and Kling (1984) observe . . .

(Journet & Kling, 1984)

122. Book, No Author—APA

References

<u>Illustrated atlas of the world.</u> (1985). Chicago: Rand McNally.

Parenthetical notes:

In <u>Illustrated Atlas</u> (1985) . . .

(<u>Illustrated Atlas,</u> 1985, pp. 88-89)

When the author of a work is actually listed as "Anonymous," cite the work that way in the References list and parenthetical note.

(Anonymous, 1995)

123. Book, a Collection or Anthology—APA

References

Feinstein, C. H. (Ed.). (1967). <u>Socialism, capitalism, and</u>
<u>economic growth.</u> Cambridge, England: Cambridge University
Press.

Parenthetical notes:

Feinstein (1967) found . . .

(Feinstein, 1967)

124. Work within a Collection, Anthology, or Reader—APA List the item on the References page by the author of the piece you are actually citing, not the editor(s) of the collection. Then provide the title of the particular selection, its date, the editor(s) of the collection, the title of the collection, pages on which the selection appears, and publication information.

References

Patel, S. (1967). World economy in transition (1850-2060). In C.

    H. Feinstein (Ed.), <u>Socialism, capitalism, and economic</u>

    <u>growth</u> (pp. 255-270). Cambridge, England: Cambridge

    University Press.

Parenthetical notes:

Patel (1967) found . . .

(Patel, 1967)

125. Chapter in a Book—APA

References

Clark, K. (1969). Heroic materialism. In <u>Civilisation</u> (pp. 321-

    347). New York: HarperCollins.

Parenthetical notes:

Clark (1969) observes . . .

(Clark, 1969)

126. Book Review—APA Notice that brackets surround the description of the article, which in this case has no title. A title would precede the bracketed description, which would still be included in the entry.

References

Farquhar, J. (1987). [Review of the book <u>Medical power and social</u>

    <u>knowledge</u>]. <u>American Journal of Psychology, 94,</u> 256.

Parenthetical notes:

Farquhar (1987) observes . . .

(Farquhar, 1987)

127. Article in a Scholarly Journal—APA Scholarly journals are usually identified by volume number or season (rather than day, week, or month of publication) and are paginated year by year, with a full year's work gathered and treated as a volume. Cite articles from such scholarly journals by providing author, date, title of article, journal, volume, and page numbers.

References

Tebeaux, E. (1991). Ramus, visual rhetoric, and the emergence of

page design in medical writing of the English Renaissance.

Written Communication, 8, 411-445.

Parenthetical notes:

Tebeaux (1991) observes . . .

(Tebeaux, 1991, p. 411)

128. Article in a Monthly Periodical—APA To cite a magazine published monthly, give the author's name, date (including month), title of the article, name of the magazine and volume number if available (underlined), and page numbers.

References

Bass, R. (1995, May/June). The perfect day. Sierra, 80, 68-78.

Parenthetical notes:

Bass (1995) notes . . .

(Bass, 1995)

129. Article in a Weekly or Biweekly Periodical—APA To cite a weekly or biweekly periodical or magazine, give the author's name, date (including month and day), title of the article, name of the magazine, and volume number if available (underlined), and page numbers.

References

Moody, J. (1993, December 20). A vision of judgment. Time, 142,

58-61.

Parenthetical notes:

Moody (1993) observes . . .

(Moody, 1993)

(Moody, 1993, p. 60)

130. Article in a Newsletter—APA To cite a newsletter, give the author's name, date, title of the article, name of the magazine and volume number if available (underlined), and page numbers. If no volume number is given, give as full a date as possible.

References

Piedmont-Marton, E. (1997, July 20). Schoolmarms or language

paramedics? The Writer's Block, 4, 6.

Parenthetical notes:

Piedmont-Marton (1997) argues . . .

(Piedmont-Marton, 1997)

131. Article in a Periodical, No Author Named—APA Note that quotation marks are used around shortened titles in the parenthetical notes.

References

```
Aladdin releases desktop tools. (1993, October). Macworld, 10, 35.
```
Parenthetical notes:
```
In "Aladdin releases" (1993) . . .

("Aladdin releases," 1993)
```

132. Newspaper Article, Author Named—APA If the article does not appear on consecutive pages in the newspaper, give all the page numbers, separated by a comma. Note that abbreviations for *page* (*p.*) and *pages* (*pp.*) are used with newspaper entries.

References

```
Bragg, R. (1994, October 15). Weather gurus going high-tech. San
     Antonio Express-News, pp. 1A, 7A.
```
Parenthetical notes:
```
Bragg (1994) reports . . .

(Bragg, 1994, p. 7A)
```

133. Newspaper Article, No Author Named—APA

References

```
Scientists find new dinosaur species in Africa. (1994, October
     14). The Daily Texan, p. 3.
```
Parenthetical notes:
```
In the article "Scientists find" (1994) . . .

("Scientists find," 1994)
```

134. Computer Software—APA Do not underline the titles of software. List authors only when they own the product.

References

```
Adobe Pagemill 1.0 [Computer software]. (1995). Mountain View, CA:
     Adobe Systems.
```
Parenthetical note:
```
In Adobe Pagemill (1995) . . .
```

135. Online Source, Archived Listserv, or Usenet Newsgroup—APA For all online sources, provide the same information you would give for printed sources (author, date, title of article, publication information). Then identify the "medium" of the source in brackets, that is, the kind of material it is. Finally, furnish the date of access and a path statement to guide readers to the material, usually an electronic address or the protocol, directory, and file name of the source.

References

Dubrowski, J. (1994, October 18). Mixed signals from Washington leave automakers puzzled [ClariNet news item]. Retrieved October 20, 1995 from C-reuters@clarinet.com. Directory: biz/industry/automotive

Parenthetical notes:

Dubrowski (1994) reports . . .

(Dubrowski, 1994)

136. WWW Page—Generic—APA

References

Johnson, C. W., Jr. (1997, February 13). How our laws are made [Article posted on Web site Thomas]. Retrieved May 27, 1997 from the World Wide Web: http://thomas.loc.gov/ home/lawsmade.toc.html

Parenthetical notes:

Johnson (1997) explains . . .

(Johnson, 1997)

137. WWW Page—Online Scholarly Article—APA
Because it is immediately obvious that the source is an article from a scholarly journal, no bracketed explanation of the medium is necessary.

References

Fine, M. A., & Kurdek, L. A. (1993). Reflections on determining authorship credit and authorship order on faculty-student collaborations. American Psychologist, 48, 1141-1147. Retrieved July 17, 1997 from the World Wide Web: http://www.apa.org/journals/amp/kurdek.html

Parenthetical notes:

Fine and Kurdek (1993) report . . .

(Fine & Kurdek, 1993)

COS
p. 225

138. WWW Page—Online Newspaper Article—APA

References

Cohen, E. (1997, January 17). Shrinks aplenty online but are they
credible? The New York Times [Newspaper, article in
archives]. Retrieved May 5, 1997 from the World Wide Web:
http://search.nytimes.com/search/daily/bin/fastweb?getdoc
+site+site+4842+4+wAAA+%28psychology%29%26OR%26%28%29%26OR
%26%28%29

Parenthetical notes:

Cohen (1997) asks . . .

(Cohen, 1997)

COS
p. 225

139. WWW Page—Online Abstract—APA

References

Shilkret, R., & Nigrosh, E. (1997). Assessing students' plans for
college [Abstract]. Journal of Counseling Psychology, 44,
222-231. Retrieved July 1, 1997 from the World Wide Web:
http://www.apa.org/journals/cou/497ab.html#10

Parenthetical notes:

Shilkret and Nigrosh (1997) report . . .

(Shilkret & Nigrosh, 1997)

COS
p. 227

140. Email—APA
Electronic communications not stored or archived have limited use for researchers. APA style treats such information (as well as email) like personal communication. Because personal communications are not available to other researchers, no mention is made of them in the References list. Personal communications should, however, be acknowledged in the body of the essay in parenthetical notes.

Parenthetical note:

According to Rice (personal communication, October 14,
1994) . . .

141. Movie/Videotape—APA
This is also the basic form for films, audiotapes, slides, charts, and other nonprint sources. The specific medium is described between brackets, as shown here for a film. In most cases, APA references are listed by identifying the screenwriter, though that varies, as the example shows.

References

Zeffirelli, F. (Director). (1968). <u>Romeo and Juliet</u> [Film].

  Hollywood, CA: Paramount.

Parenthetical notes:

Zeffirelli (1968) features . . .

(Zeffirelli, 1968)

142. Musical Recording—APA Ordinarily, music is listed by the composer.

References

Dylan, B. (1989). What was it you wanted? [Recorded by Willie

  Nelson]. On <u>Across the borderline</u> [CD]. New York: Columbia.

Parenthetical note:

In the song "What Was It You Wanted?" (Dylan, 1989,

  track 10) . . .

24c   Sample APA paper

In the social sciences, articles published in professional journals often follow a form designed to connect new findings to previous research. Your instructor will usually indicate whether you should follow this structure for your paper or report.

The sample APA paper that follows is not a formal social science research report. It does, however, include an abstract, and its headings conform to APA form. The paper by Gerald J. Reuter, an undergraduate at the University of Texas at Austin, has been revised, updated, and slightly expanded to enhance its usefulness as a model, especially in the area of online sources. The paper was written for a course taught by James Kinneavy.

Note that the sample paper is accompanied by checklists designed to help you set up a paper correctly in APA style. When your work meets the specifications on the checklists, it should be in proper form.

The Components of a Social Science Report

- **An abstract.** A concise summary of the research article.

- **A review of literature.** A survey of published research that has a bearing on the hypothesis advanced in the research report. The review establishes the context for the research essay.

- **A hypothesis.** An introduction to the paper that identifies the assumption to be tested and provides a rationale for studying it.

- **An explanation of method.** A detailed description of the procedures used in the research. Since the validity of the research depends on how the data were gathered, this is a critical section for readers assessing the report.

- **Results.** A section reporting the data, often given through figures, charts, graphs, and so on. The reliability of the data is explained here, but little comment is made on the implications.

- **Discussion/conclusions.** A section in which the research results are interpreted and analyzed.

- **References.** An alphabetical list of research materials and articles cited in the report.

- **Appendixes.** A section of materials germane to the report, but too lengthy to include in the body of the paper.

The Genome Project: Opportunities and Ethics

Gerald J. Reuter

The University of Texas at Austin

CHECKLIST

Title Page for a Paper—APA

APA style requires a separate title page; use the facing page as a model and review the following checklist.

- Use good-quality white bond paper for printed projects. Preferred typefaces (when you have a choice) include Times Roman, American Typewriter, and Courier.

- Arrange and center the title of your paper, your name, and your school.

- Use the correct form for the title, capitalizing all important words and all words of four letters or more. Articles, conjunctions, and prepositions are not capitalized unless they are four letters or more. Do not underline the title or use all capitals.

- Give your first name, middle initial, and last name.

- Number the title page and all subsequent pages in the upper right-hand corner. Place a short title for the paper on the same line, and leave five spaces between the short title and the page number, as shown; the short title consists of the first two or three words of the title. Use the "automatic header" feature of your word processor if available.

Abstract

Begun in 1988, the human genome project intends to map the 23
chromosomes that provide the blueprint for the human species. The
project has both scientific and ethical goals. The scientific goals
underscore the advantages of the genome project, including identifying
and curing diseases and enabling people to select the traits of their
offspring, among other opportunities. Ethically, however, the project
raises serious questions about the morality of genetic engineering. To
handle both the medical opportunities and ethical dilemmas posed by
the genome project, scientists need to develop a clear set of
principles for genetic engineering and to continue educating the
public about the genome project.

CHECKLIST
Abstract for a Paper—APA

Abstracts are common in APA-style projects. (If your instructor does not require an abstract, go to the next page.)

- Place the abstract on a separate page, after the title page.
- Center the word *Abstract* at the top of the page.
- Include the short title of the essay and the page number (2) in the upper right-hand corner, using the "automatic header" feature of your word processor, if possible.
- Double-space the abstract.
- Do not indent the first line of the abstract. Type it in block form. Strict APA form limits abstracts to not more than 960 characters.

The Genome Project: Opportunities and Ethics

If you had the opportunity to rid humanity of the approximately 4,000 genetic diseases, would you do so? What if doing so also meant that millions of people might be deprived of health insurance coverage and that children who didn't meet the physical ideals of a society might not be conceived? These are the opportunities and the dangers we face as a result of the ongoing human genome project. Although the scientific information provided by the project should prove of incalculable benefit to humankind, some of its consequences could be disastrous. The project has already had a major impact on medicine, culture, and society's thinking about genetics and human life. This paper argues that scientists need to educate the public better about the genome project to address the pressing ethical issues it raises.

Goal of the Human Genome Project

The human genome project began a decade ago in 1988 when the Congress of the United States allocated approximately $3 billion to support a 15-year multi-university endeavor to complete the mapping of the human genome (Caskey, 1994). The human genome is the set of 23 chromosomes and 60,000 to 80,000 genes that provide the blueprint for our bodies ("Human genome," 1997). Chromosomes contain DNA made up of four different nucleotides or bases--adenine, guanine, thymine, and cytosine--which, working together, provide the code for different genes (see Figure 1). The genes in chromosomes are arranged in a complex sequence. Mapping these sequences is a highly technical, time-consuming process.

Among the scientific goals of the U.S. Department of Energy genome project is the development of technology to map chromosomes more rapidly and to mark genes more easily. This goal has been partially met; as a result, the first five-year plan, covering 1991-1995, was updated in 1993 to a second five-year plan covering 1993-1998.

Throughout the project, scientists also hope to identify some of the key ethical issues in gene research, to address the societal implications of the research, to bring genetic issues to public

The Body of a Research Paper—APA

The body of the APA paper runs uninterrupted until the separate References page. Be sure to use good-quality bond paper for printed projects. The first page of an APA paper will look like the facing page.

- Repeat the title of your paper, exactly as it appears on the title page, on the first page of the research essay itself.

- Be sure the title is centered and properly capitalized.

- Begin the body of the essay two lines (a double space) below the title.

- Double-space the body of the essay.

- Center first-level heads; do not underline them.

- Use at least one-inch margins at the sides, top, and bottom of this and all subsequent pages.

- Indent the first line of each paragraph five to seven spaces.

- Indent long quotations (more than forty words) in a block five to seven spaces from the left margin. In student papers, APA permits long quotations to be single spaced using the "automatic indent" feature of your word processor, if available.

- Include the short title of the essay and the page number (3) in the upper right-hand corner. Number all subsequent pages the same way.

- Do not hyphenate words at the right-hand margin. Do not justify the right-hand margin.

- Label figures and tables correctly. Be sure to mention them in the body of your text: (See Figure 1).

- Provide copyright/permission data for figures or tables borrowed from other sources.

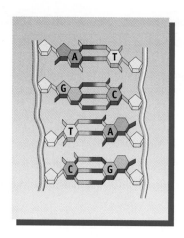

Figure 1. The four bases of the genetic code: adenine
(A), guanine (G), thymine (T), and cytosine (C). Note.
From Your Genes, Your Choice, by C. Baker, 1997.
Copyright 1997 by the American Association for the
Advancement of Science. Reprinted with permission.

attention, and to formulate policy options designed to benefit both
individuals and society (U.S. Department of Energy, 1990). Swinbanks
(1992) observes, however, that since many scientists believe that they
lack expertise in discussing ethical and political issues, they
generally avoid them. So while the genome project five-year plans
identify specific ethical goals, the scientists involved have
sometimes avoided this dimension of their work.

Advantages of the Genome Project

Human genome project researchers believe that mapping the full
set of human chromosomes will benefit society in many ways. Magnus
(1996) argues that gene therapy--curing diseases by manipulating the
genetic code--is likely to revolutionize medicine as much as
antibiotics and vaccinations once did. Matsubara (1993) anticipates
important advances in the treatment of cancer, circulatory diseases,
and even mental conditions, as well as improvements in testing for
diseases and the development of drugs to combat them. Conversely,
Baker (1997) notes that people may be able to select the specific
physical traits and qualities they prefer, from youthful looks and a

thick head of hair to greater height or intelligence. It may even be
possible to modify DNA in ways that give human beings new and useful
traits.

Ethical Dilemmas of the Genome Project

Any research effort with the scientific potential of the genome
project will likely raise serious ethical questions about how and by
whom the new knowledge it creates will be used. Zylke (1992), noting
that the genome project is far from the first attempt to modify and
"improve" the hereditary qualities of human beings, associates the
effort with similar attempts in Nazi Germany to create a superior
race. Even in the United States, Zylke argues, sterilization of the
mentally retarded was common throughout the nineteenth century and not
ruled unconstitutional until years later.

Duster (1996) notes that families at risk for hereditary
conditions such as sickle cell disease and cystic fibrosis already
fear that improved genetic screening may lead to discrimination
against them in employment and loss of health-care benefits. Insurance
companies might deny coverage to individuals with a genetic code that
makes them susceptible to an expensive condition. Davis (1990)
believes that the genome project might also lead to soaring insurance
rates and perhaps to the collapse of the entire medical insurance
industry.

Parents may also be tempted to terminate a pregnancy when an
unborn child does not possess desirable genetic traits, some of them
completely unrelated to concerns for health or well-being. Baker
(1997) notes that some governments already have programs that support
births among some groups of people and not among others. Similar
processes of selection may occur in the future for children with the
"wrong" eye color or body type after parents consult with doctors
furnished with the complete map of human chromosomes the human genome
project will provide. They may be reluctant to accept a child with
markers for any diseases at all, thus demanding an unrealistic
perfection in their offspring. The genome project, some fear, may be
the first step toward a brave new world peopled with beings of dismal

similarity. Furthermore, attempts to control genetic manipulation through legislation may prove futile; Gardner (1995) argues that limits on genetic improvements would quickly collapse once the ban was violated initially.

Living with the Genome Project

Anticipating such ethical dilemmas, the National Center for Human Genome Research and the National Institutes of Health have included an Ethical, Legal, and Social Implications program (ELSI) in the funding of the genome project. The ELSI program, which spends roughly 3% of the project budget annually, is intended both to anticipate and prevent any ethical problems that might develop as a result of the genome mapping (Davis, 1990).

However, advances in genetic research have led other scientists to consider the implications of restructuring the very design of human beings. Independent of the ELSI program, Suzuki and Knudtson (1989) have offered a set of principles for all geneticists to consider. First, geneticists must understand the nature of genes--their origin, their role in the hereditary processes of cells, the possibilities of controlling them--to grasp the difficult issues arising from modern genetics. Second, geneticists must appreciate that it is dangerous to proclaim simple causal relationships between so-called defects in human DNA and human behaviors since human hereditary differences involve the interplay of many genes. Third, information about an individual's genetic constitution ought to guide personal decisions rather than determine them. Fourth, while genetic manipulation of some human cells may lie in the realm of personal choice, tinkering with human germ cells does not. Germ cell therapy ought to be explicitly forbidden without the consent of all members of society. Finally, the accumulation of genetic knowledge alone, however precious it may be, does not guarantee the wisdom to justify decisions about heredity. If such knowledge breeds a false sense of mastery over genes, it can lead to folly. Principles such as these and others articulated by the ELSI project may move scientists to think more deeply about ethical questions than they are accustomed to as the genome project develops.

But as the furor over the cloning of a mammal in 1997
demonstrated, scientists need to press forward with a final
responsibility: the need to educate the press and public about their
work. The ELSI project is already moving in this direction with
components such as the Human Genome Education Project (HGEP) at
Stanford, for which Conn (1996) describes two main goals: development
of a science curriculum for high schools and development of community
outreach programs in genetic science. Clearly, education about human
genetics--both its potential and its limitations--should begin as
early as elementary school since an informed citizenry will ultimately
have to make important decisions in the future. They should be able to
make decisions about their chromosomes without fear or ignorance.

References

Baker, C. (1997). Your genes, your choices. American Association for
    the Advancement of Science [Book on line]. Retrieved July 16,
    1997 from the World Wide Web:
    http://www.nextwave.org/ehr/books/index.html

Caskey, T. C. (1994). Human genes: The map takes shape. Patient Care,
    28, 28-32.

Conn, L. (1996). Human genome education project [Abstract]. 1996 DOE
    Human Genome Program Contractor-Grantee Workshop V. Retrieved
    July 18, 1997 from the World Wide Web: http://www.ornl.gov/
    TechResources/Human_Genome/publicat/96santa/elsi/conn.html

Davis, J. (1990). Mapping the code: The Human Genome Project and the
    choices of modern science. New York: Wiley.

Duster, T. (1996). Pathways to genetic screening: Molecular genetics
    meets the high risk family [Abstract]. 1996 DOE Human Genome
    Program Contractor-Grantee Workshop V. Retrieved July 20, 1997
    from the World Wide Web: http://www.ornl.gov/TechResources/
    Human_Genome/publicat/96santa/elsi/duster.html

Gardner, W. (1995). Can human genetic enhancement be prohibited?
    [Abstract]. Journal of Medicine and Philosophy, 20, 65-84.
    Retrieved July 18, 1997 from the World Wide Web:
    http://www.med.upenn.edu/~bioethic/genetics/articles/
    2.gardner.can.human.html

Human genome project frequently asked questions. (1997, June). Human
    Genome Project information [FAQ posted on the World Wide Web].
    Retrieved July 5, 1997 from the World Wide Web:
    http://www.ornl.gov/hgmis/faq/faqs1.html#q1

Magnus, D. (1996). Gene therapy and the concept of genetic disease.
    Ethics and genetics: A global conversation [Draft of an article
    on the Center for Bioethics electronic discussion site.]
    Retrieved June 28, 1997 from the World Wide Web:
    http://www.med.upenn.edu/~bioethic/genetics/articles/
    12.gen.disease.html

CHECKLIST
References Page—APA

Sources contributing directly to the paper are listed alphabetically on a separate sheet immediately after the body of the essay. For more information about the purpose and form of this list, see pages 277 through 281.

- Center the title "References" at the top of the page.

- All sources mentioned in the text of the paper must appear in the References list, except personal communications; similarly, every source listed in the References list must be mentioned in the paper.

- Arrange the items in the References list alphabetically by the last name of the author. Give initials only for first names. If no author is given for a work, list and alphabetize it by the first word in the title, excluding articles (*A, An,* and *The*).

- The first line of each entry is flush with the left-hand margin. Subsequent lines in an entry are indented five spaces.

- The list is ordinarily double spaced. In student papers, APA style does permit single spacing of individual entries; double spacing is preserved between the single-spaced items.

- Punctuate items in the list carefully. Do not forget the period at the end of each entry, **except those that terminate with an electronic address.**

- In the References list, capitalize only the first word and any proper names in the title of a book or article. Within a title, capitalize the first word after a colon.

- If you have two or more entries by the same author, list them by year of publication, from earliest to latest. If an author publishes two works in the same year, list them alphabetically by title.

Matsubara, K. (1993). Background of human genome analysis. The human
    genome: Toward understanding ourselves [Web site]. Retrieved May
    5, 1997 from the World Wide Web:
    http://www.genome.ad.jp/brochure/english/Background.html#part4

Suzuki, D., & Knudtson, P. (1989). Genethics: The clash between the
    new genetics and human values. Cambridge, MA: Harvard University
    Press.

Swinbanks, D. (1992). When silence isn't golden. Nature, 368, 368-70.

U.S. Department of Energy. (1990). Understanding our genetic
    inheritance: The U.S. Human Genome Project. Human Genome Project
    research [Web site]. Retrieved July 1, 1997 from the World Wide
    Web: http://infosrv1.ctd.ornl.gov/TechResources/Human_Genome/
    project/5yrplan/science2.html#elsihttp://www.ornl.gov/
    TechResources/Human_Genome/FAQ/GOALS.html

Zylke, J. (1992). Examining life's code means re-examining society's
    long-held codes. Journal of the American Medical Association,
    267, 1715-1716.

When founded in 1967, OCLC stood for Ohio College Library Center. But as the library network grew and non-Ohio libraries became members of the group, the name changed in 1981 to Online Computer Library Center, Inc. OCLC, pictured here, reduced library costs and made the sharing of resources more efficient among Ohio university libraries. The regional computer system serving 54 members in 1977 today serves more than 30,000 libraries in the United States as well as libraries in 65 other countries and territories.

OCLC at www.oclc.org provides easy access to library resources. The abundance of printed and electronic materials in the world makes it impossible for any library to hold all of one country's printed materials. OCLC links libraries together from around the world to make locating and disseminating information a fast, easy, and cost-effective process. OCLC's *WorldCat,* for example, is the world's most inclusive bibliographic database. Currently 38 million records are indexed in *WorldCat,* a number that increases by 2 million each year. *FirstSearch* at www.ref.oclc.org:2000 links 70 databases together for searching the world's periodical literature.

305

◎ DON'T MISS . . .

- **The explanation of CMS documentation in Section 25a.** If you are preparing a paper in language, literature, or the humanities, you may want to use CMS documentation—especially if you prefer footnotes or endnotes to in-text parenthetical notes.

- **The index to CMS formats on page 312.** Note that the formats provided include samples of both Works Cited entries and parenthetical notes.

- **The sample CMS paper beginning on page 317.** The sample paper shows how to format CMS-style endnotes.

BOOKMARKS: Web Sites Worth Knowing

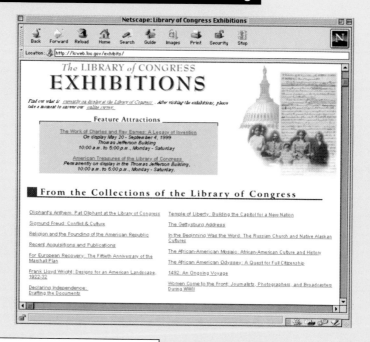

The Library of Congress Exhibitions,
http://lcweb.loc.gov/exhibits/

You can find digital images of thousands of works of art at the Library of Congress Exhibitions site. The Library of Congress is creating digital archives of thousands of photos, illustrations, paintings, books, and other artworks. You can view selected exhibitions of many of these works at this site. If you don't find what you're looking for there, search the library's vast digital image collection at http://lcweb.loc.gov/rr/digital.html, where hundreds of thousands of documents are available online. Please note that the library restricts the "publishing" of many of these documents—even on a student Web page—but always encourages links to them when advance notice is given.

Additional Sites

Argos, "Limited Area Search of the Ancient and Medieval Internet," http://argos.evansville.edu/
ArtSource, http://www.uky.edu/Artsource/artsourcehome.html
The Internet Encyclopedia of Philosophy, http://www.utm.edu/research/iep/
Webmuseum, http://metalab.unc.edu/wm/

CMS Documentation

Writers who prefer full footnotes or endnotes rather than in-text notes often use the "humanities style" of documentation recommended in *The Chicago Manual of Style* (14th ed., 1993). Basic procedures for this CMS documentary-note system are spelled out in the following sections. If you encounter documentation problems not discussed below or prefer the author-date style of CMS documentation, refer to the full manual or to *A Manual for Writers of Term Papers, Theses, and Dissertations* (6th ed., 1996) or check *The Chicago Manual of Style* FAQ at http://www.press.uchicago.edu/Misc/Chicago/cmosfaq.html.

A Note on Citing Electronic Sources

CMS documentation does not currently offer specific forms for many electronic sources, although we do cover several of them on page 316. When citing such items, you may want to use the documentation style recommended by the *Columbia Guide to Online Style;* it was developed explicitly for research in electronic environments. Columbia Online Style (COS) for humanities papers is described in Chapter 22. CMS items that have a Columbia equivalent are marked in the CMS Form Directory (Section 25c) with a distinctive icon: COS p. 000 . Consult your instructor about using Columbia style for electronic sources.

Because notes in CMS humanities style include full publishing information, separate bibliographies are optional in CMS-style papers. However, both notes and bibliographies are covered below in separate sections.

25a CMS notes

25a-1 In the text of your paper, place a raised number after any sentence or clause you need to document. These note numbers follow any punctuation marks, except for dashes, and run consecutively throughout a paper. For example, a direct quotation from Brian Urquhart's *Ralph Bunche: An American Life* is here followed by a raised note number.

```
Ralph Bunche never wavered in his belief that the races in America

had to learn to live together: "In all of his experience of racial

discrimination Bunche never allowed himself to become bitter or to

feel racial hatred."[1]
```

The number is keyed to the first note (see below). To create such a raised, or "superscript," number, select "superscript" from your word-processing font options or, on a typewriter, roll the carriage down slightly and type the figure.

25a-2　**Link every note number to a footnote or endnote.** The basic CMS note itself consists of a note number, the author's name (in normal order), the title of the work, full publication information within parentheses, and appropriate page numbers. The first line of the note is indented like a paragraph.

```
    1. Brian Urquhart, Ralph Bunche: An American Life (New York:
Norton, 1993), 435.
```

To document particular types of sources, including books, articles, magazines, and electronic sources, see Section 25c, the CMS Form Directory.

CMS style allows you to choose whether to place your notes at the bottom of each page (footnotes) or in a single list titled "Notes" at the end of your paper (endnotes). Endnotes are more common now than footnotes and easier to manage—though some word processors can arrange footnotes at the bottom of pages automatically. Individual footnotes are single spaced, with double spaces between them.

Following are some guidelines to use when preparing notes.

1. **When two or more sources are cited within a single sentence,** the note numbers appear right after the statements they support.

```
While some in the humanities fear that electronic technologies

may make the "notion of wisdom" obsolete,[2] others suggest that

technology must be the subject of serious study even in

elementary and secondary school.[3]
```

The notes for this sentence would appear as follows.

```
    2. Sven Birkerts, The Gutenberg Elegies: The Fate of
Reading in an Electronic Age (Boston: Faber and Faber, 1994),
139.

    3. Neil Postman, "The Word Weavers/The World Makers," in
The End of Education: Redefining the Value of School (New
York: Alfred A. Knopf, 1995), 172-93.
```

Observe that note 2 documents a particular quotation while note 3 refers to a full book chapter.

2. **When you cite a work several times in a paper,** the first note gives full information about author(s), title, and publication.

> 1. Helen Wilkinson, "It's Just a Matter of Time," *Utne Reader* (May/June 1995): 66-67.

Then, in shorter papers, any subsequent citations require only the last name of the author(s) and page number(s).

> 3. Wilkinson, 66.

In longer papers, the entry may also include a shortened title to make references from page to page clearer.

> 3. Wilkinson, "Matter of Time," 66.

If you cite the same work again immediately after a full note, you may use the Latin abbreviation *Ibid.* (meaning "in the same place"), followed by the page number(s) of the citation.

> 4. Newt Gingrich, "America and the Third Wave Information Age," in *To Renew America* (New York, HarperCollins, 1995), 51.
>
> 5. Ibid., 55.

To avoid using *Ibid.* when documenting the same source in succession, simply use a page reference—for example, (55)—within the text itself. When successive citations are to exactly the same page, *Ibid.* alone can be used.

> 4. Newt Gingrich, "America and the Third Wave Information Age," in *To Renew America* (New York, HarperCollins, 1995), 51.
>
> 5. Ibid.

Here's how a set of notes using several different sources and subsequent short references might look.

Notes

> 1. Helen Wilkinson, "It's Just a Matter of Time," *Utne Reader* (May/June 1995): 66-67.
>
> 2. Paul Osterman, "Getting Started," *Wilson Quarterly* (autumn 1994): 46-55.
>
> 3. Newt Gingrich, "America and the Third Wave Information Age," in *To Renew America* (New York: HarperCollins, 1995), 51-61.
>
> 4. Ibid., 54.
>
> 5. Wilkinson, 66.
>
> 6. Ibid.
>
> 7. Ibid., 67.

```
8. Osterman, 48-49.

9. Gingrich, 60.
```

Notice that note 4 refers to the Gingrich chapter and notes 6 and 7 refer to Wilkinson's article.

25b CMS bibliographies

At the end of your project, list alphabetically every source you cited or used. This list is usually titled "Works Cited" if it includes only works actually mentioned; it is titled "Bibliography" if it also includes works consulted in preparing the project but not actually cited. Because CMS notes are quite thorough, a Works Cited or Bibliography listing may be optional, depending on the assignment: check with your instructor or editor about including such a list. Individual items on a Works Cited or Bibliography list are single spaced, with a double space between each item (see sample CMS paper, p. 323).

A typical **CMS Works Cited/Bibliography entry for a book** includes the following basic information.

❏ Author(s), last name first, followed by a period and one space.

❏ Title of the work, underlined or italicized, followed by a period and one space.

❏ Place of publication, followed by a colon and one space.

❏ Publisher, followed by a comma and one space.

❏ Date of publication, followed by a period.

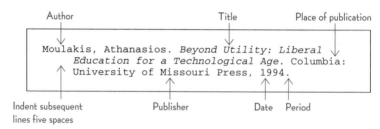

A typical **CMS Works Cited/Bibliography entry for an article in a popular magazine** includes the following basic information.

❏ Author(s), last name first, followed by a period and one space.

❏ Title of the article, followed by a period and enclosed between quotation marks.

❏ Name of the periodical, underlined or italicized, followed by a comma and one space.

❏ Date of publication, followed by a comma and one space. Do not abbreviate months.

❏ Page and/or location, followed by a period. Pages should be inclusive.

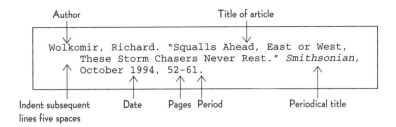

Author   Title of article

Wolkomir, Richard. "Squalls Ahead, East or West,
       These Storm Chasers Never Rest." *Smithsonian*,
       October 1994, 52-61.

Indent subsequent   Date   Pages Period   Periodical title
lines five spaces

A typical **CMS Works Cited/Bibliography entry for an article in a scholarly journal** (where the pagination is continuous throughout a year) includes the following basic information.

❑ Author(s), last name first, followed by a period and one space.

❑ Title of the article, followed by a period (or other final punctuation mark) and enclosed between quotation marks.

❑ Name of the periodical, underlined or italicized, followed by one space.

❑ Volume number, followed by one space.

❑ Date of publication in parentheses, followed by a colon and one space.

❑ Page or location, followed by a period. Page numbers should be inclusive, from the first page of the article to the last, including notes and bibliography.

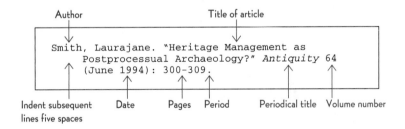

Author   Title of article

Smith, Laurajane. "Heritage Management as
       Postprocessual Archaeology?" *Antiquity* 64
       (June 1994): 300-309.

Indent subsequent   Date   Pages   Period   Periodical title   Volume number
lines five spaces

A typical **CMS Works Cited/Bibliography entry for an electronic source** is arranged and punctuated just like a printed source, with some additions.

❑ Author and title, arranged and punctuated as if for a printed source.

❑ Publication information (if available), including city, publisher, and date for books or volume number/date for periodicals, followed by a period and one space.

❑ A description of the electronic format or computer source (*database online, CD-ROM, journal online, abstract online*), followed by a period and one space.

❑ An electronic address or pathway following the words *Available from.* For World Wide Web sites, give the URL (that is, the address that begins *http*) and follow it with a semicolon and the word *Internet*.

❑ A date of access for online materials. The date of access can appear either before or after the electronic address. If after, it is separated from that address or pathway by a semicolon and followed by a period.

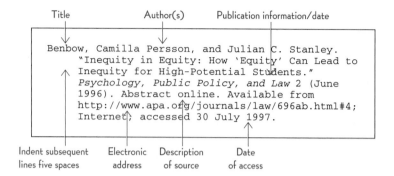

```
Benbow, Camilla Persson, and Julian C. Stanley.
    "Inequity in Equity: How 'Equity' Can Lead to
    Inequity for High-Potential Students."
    Psychology, Public Policy, and Law 2 (June
    1996). Abstract online. Available from
    http://www.apa.org/journals/law/696ab.html#4;
    Internet; accessed 30 July 1997.
```

Title   Author(s)   Publication information/date

Indent subsequent   Electronic   Description   Date
lines five spaces   address   of source   of access

There are so many variations to these general entries, however, that you will want to check the CMS Form Directory below for the correct format of any unusual entry.

When an author has more than one work on the list, those works are listed alphabetically under the author's name using this form.

```
Altick, Richard D. The Shows of London. Cambridge: Belknap-Harvard
    University Press, 1978.

---. Victorian People and Ideas. New York: Norton, 1973.

---. Victorian Studies in Scarlet. New York: Norton, 1977.
```

25c CMS Form Directory

In this section, you will find the CMS notes and bibliography forms for more than twenty types of sources. The numbered items in the list are the sample note forms, often showing specific page numbers as would be the case when you were preparing actual notes; the matching bibliography entries appear immediately after. The "COS" icon next to an entry indicates that a Columbia Online Style (COS) form is available for that source (see Chapter 22 for more on COS).

CMS FORMAT INDEX

143. Book, one author
144. Book, two or three authors or editors
145. Book, four or more authors or editors
146. Book, edited—focus on the editor
147. Book, edited—focus on the original author
148. Book written by a group
149. Book with no author
150. Work of more than one volume
151. Work in a series
152. Chapter in a book
153. Article in a scholarly journal
154. Article in a popular magazine
155. Article or selection from a reader or anthology

143. Book, One Author—CMS

1. Steven Weinberg, *Dreams of a Final Theory* (New York: Pantheon Books, 1992), 38.

Weinberg, Steven. *Dreams of a Final Theory*. New York: Pantheon Books, 1992.

144. Book, Two or Three Authors or Editors—CMS

2. Peter Collier and David Horowitz, *Destructive Generation: Second Thoughts About the '60s* (New York: Summit, 1989), 24.

Collier, Peter, and David Horowitz. *Destructive Generation: Second Thoughts About the '60s*. New York: Summit, 1989.

145. Book, Four or More Authors or Editors—CMS Use *et al.* or *and others* after the first author in the notes, but list all authors in the bibliography when that is convenient.

3. Philip Curtin and others, eds., *African History* (Boston: Little, Brown, 1978), 77.

Curtin, Philip, Steve Feierman, Leonard Thompson, and Jan Vansina, eds. *African History*. Boston: Little, Brown, 1978.

146. Book, Edited—Focus on the Editor—CMS If you cite an edited work by the editor's name, identify the original author after the title of the work.

4. Scott Elledge, ed., *Paradise Lost,* by John Milton (New York: Norton, 1975).

Elledge, Scott, ed. *Paradise Lost,* by John Milton. New York: Norton, 1975.

147. Book, Edited—Focus on the Original Author—CMS

5. William Shakespeare, *The Complete Works of Shakespeare,* 4th ed., ed. David Bevington (New York: Longman, 1997).

Shakespeare, William. *The Complete Works of Shakespeare*. 4th ed. Edited by David Bevington. New York: Longman, 1997.

148. Book Written by a Group—CMS

6. Council of Biology Editors, *Scientific Style and Format: The CBE Manual for Authors, Editors, and Publishers,* 6th ed. (Cambridge: Cambridge Univ. Press, 1994).

Council of Biology Editors. *Scientific Style and Format: The CBE Manual for Authors, Editors, and Publishers.* 6th ed. Cambridge: Cambridge Univ. Press, 1994.

149. Book with No Author—CMS List it by its title, alphabetized by the first major word (excluding *The, A,* or *An*).

7. *Webster's Collegiate Thesaurus* (Springfield: Merriam, 1976).

Webster's Collegiate Thesaurus. Springfield: Merriam, 1976.

150. Work of More Than One Volume—CMS

8. Karlheinz Spindler, *Abstract Algebra with Applications* (New York: Dekker, 1994), 1:17-18.

Spindler, Karlheinz. *Abstract Algebra with Applications.* Vol. 1. New York: Dekker, 1994.

151. Work in a Series—CMS Do not underline or italicize a series name.

9. Grayson Kirk and Nils H. Wessell, eds., *The Soviet Threat: Myths and Realities,* Proceedings of the Academy of Political Science, no. 33 (New York: Academy of Political Science, 1978), 62.

Kirk, Grayson, and Nils H. Wessell, eds. *The Soviet Threat: Myths and Realities.* Proceedings of the Academy of Political Science, no. 33. New York: Academy of Political Science, 1978.

152. Chapter in a Book—CMS

10. Delia Owens and Mark Owens, "Home to the Dunes," in *The Eye of the Elephant: An Epic Adventure in the African Wilderness* (Boston: Houghton Mifflin, 1992), 11-27.

Owens, Delia, and Mark Owens. "Home to the Dunes." In *The Eye of the Elephant: An Epic Adventure in the African Wilderness.* Boston: Houghton Mifflin, 1992.

153. Article in a Scholarly Journal—CMS Scholarly journals are usually identified by volume number or season (rather than day, week, or month of publication). Such journals are usually paginated year by year, with a year's work treated as a volume.

11. Karl P. Wentersdorf, "Hamlet's Encounter with the Pirates," *Shakespeare Quarterly* 34 (1983): 434-40.

Wentersdorf, Karl P. "Hamlet's Encounter with the Pirates." *Shakespeare Quarterly* 34 (1983): 434-40.

154. Article in a Popular Magazine—CMS Magazines are paginated issue by issue and identified by monthly or weekly dates of publication (instead of by volume number). When an article does not appear on consecutive pages (as in the example below), omit page numbers in the bibliography entry.

> 12. Robert Sabbag, "Fear & Reloading in Gun Valley," *Men's Journal,* October 1994, 64.

> Sabbag, Robert. "Fear & Reloading in Gun Valley." *Men's Journal,* October 1994.

155. Article or Selection from a Reader or Anthology—CMS

> 13. Matthew Rohrer, "Found in the Museum of Old Science," in *The Presence of Others,* 2d ed., ed. Andrea Lunsford and John Ruszkiewicz (New York: St. Martin's, 1997), 290-91.

> Rohrer, Matthew. "Found in the Museum of Old Science." In *The Presence of Others.* 2d ed. Edited by Andrea Lunsford and John Ruszkiewicz. New York: St. Martin's, 1997.

156. Article in a Newspaper—CMS Identify the edition of the paper cited (*final edition, home edition, Western edition*) except when citing editorials or features that appear in all editions. Since an individual story may move in location from edition to edition, page numbers are not ordinarily provided. Section numbers are given for papers so divided. Individual news stories are usually not listed in a bibliography.

> 14. Celestine Bohlen, "A Stunned Venice Surveys the Ruins of a Beloved Hall," *New York Times,* 31 January 1995, national edition, sec. B.

157. Encyclopedia—CMS When a reference work is familiar (encyclopedias, dictionaries, thesauruses), omit the names of authors and editors and most publishing information. No page number is given when a work is arranged alphabetically; instead the item referenced is named, following the abbreviation *s.v.* (*sub verbo,* meaning "under the word"). Familiar reference works are not listed in the bibliography.

> 15. *The Oxford Companion to English Literature,* 4th ed., s.v. "Locke, John."

158. Biblical Citation—CMS Biblical citations appear in notes but not in the bibliography. If important, you may mention the version of the Bible cited.

> 16. John 18.37-38 Jerusalem Bible.

159. Computer Software—CMS

> 17. FoxPro Ver. 2.5, Microsoft, Seattle, Wash.

> FoxPro Ver. 2.5. Microsoft, Seattle, Wash.

COS
p. 214

160. Electronic Sources—CMS   The standards for electronic documentation are in flux. CMS follows the style recommended by the International Standards Organization (ISO). But many issues remain unresolved as new sources and formats evolve. In *The Chicago Manual of Style* (14th ed.), the examples of notes for electronic sources generally include three features: a description of the computer source in brackets, such as *[electronic bulletin board]* or *[Web site]*; the date the material was accessed, updated, or cited *[cited 28 May 1996]*; and an electronic address, following the words *available from*. Models 160 through 163 below follow these recommendations as modified in Kate L. Turabian's *Manual of Style for Writers of Term Papers, Theses, and Dissertations* (6th ed., 1996). The resulting citations are quite complex. Some simplification may be in order, or you may wish to consult the chapter on Columbia style for online sources (see pp. 205–220).

```
        18. Sylvia Atore Alva, "Differential Patterns of Achievement
Among Asian-American Adolescents," Journal of Youth and
Adolescence 22 (1993): 407-23, ProQuest General Periodicals
[CD-ROM], UMI-ProQuest, June 1994.

Alva, Sylvia Atore. "Differential Patterns of Achievement Among
        Asian-American Adolescents." Journal of Youth and Adolescence
        22 (1993): 407-23. ProQuest General Periodicals. CD-ROM
        UMI-ProQuest, June 1994.
```

COS
p. 215

161. WWW—Book Online—CMS

```
        19. Amelia E. Barr, Remember the Alamo [book online] (New
York: Dodd, Mead, 1888); available from http://etext.lib.virginia
.edu/cgibin/browse-mixed?id=BarReme&tag=public&images=images/
modeng&data=/lv1/Archive/eng-parsed; Internet; cited 12 May 1997.

Barr, Amelia E. Remember the Alamo. Book online. New York: Dodd,
        Mead, 1888. Available from http://etext.lib.virginia.edu/
        cgibin/browse-mixed?id=BarReme&tag=public&images=images/
        modeng&data=/lv1/Archive/eng-parsed; Internet; cited 12 May
        1997.
```

COS
p. 215

162. WWW—Article Online—CMS

```
        20. Paul Skowronek, "Left and Right for Rights," Trincoll
Journal, 13 March 1997 [journal online]; available from
http://www.trincoll.edu/~tj/tj03.13.97/articles/
comm2.html; Internet; accessed 23 July 1997.

Skowronek, Paul. "Left and Right for Rights." Trincoll Journal,
        13 March 1997. Journal online. Available from
        http://www.trincoll.edu/~tj/tj03.13.97/articles/
        comm2.html; Internet; accessed 23 July 1997.
```

COS
p. 217

163. Email—CMS

```
        21. Robert D. Royer, "Re: Are We in a State of NOMAIL?" Email
to author, 22 July 1997.

Royer, Robert D. "Re: Are We in a State of NOMAIL?" Email to
        author, 22 July 1997.
```

25d Sample CMS paper

The sample CMS paper was written in spring 1996 by Jeremy A. Corley, a student in Joi Chevalier's course "The Rhetoric of Epic Narratives." The paper provides an example of the sort of literary analysis that might be done for a classics or English course. The paper has been lightly edited for style and revised to incorporate CMS-style endnotes and a Works Cited page. The Web site for "The Rhetoric of Epic Narratives" can be viewed at http://www.cwrl.utexas.edu/~babydoll/coursematerial/spring96/index.html.

The sample paper demonstrates how to use both endnotes and a Works Cited page. However, the Works Cited page is optional in CMS style because the endnotes themselves include full bibliographical information. Following the sample paper, we also provide a single page reformatted to demonstrate the use of CMS-style footnotes. If you choose to use footnotes, do not also include endnotes. You may, however, present a Works Cited or Bibliography page. (A Works Cited page lists only those works mentioned in the paper itself; a Bibliography page includes all the works cited in the paper as well as sources you consulted but did not mention in the paper.)

The sample paper shows titles italicized. You may either italicize or underline titles in CMS style, but be consistent. Do not mix italicized and underlined titles within the same paper. In numbering CMS papers, count the title page as a page, but do not number it. Note that footnotes are single spaced. Any indented quotations are also single spaced. (For more on typing student papers in CMS style, see Kate L. Turabian, *A Manual for Writers of Term Papers, Theses, and Dissertations,* 6th ed., 1996.)

[New Page]

THE UNIVERSITY OF TEXAS AT AUSTIN

DIOMEDES AS HERO OF *THE ILIAD*

E 309K--TOPICS IN WRITING
DIVISION OF RHETORIC AND COMPOSITION

BY

JEREMY A. CORLEY

28 FEBRUARY 1996

[New Page]

Diomedes as Hero of *The Iliad*

     Achilles is the central character of *The Iliad,* but is his
prominence alone enough to make him the story's hero? There are many
examples that would say otherwise. One of the most interesting aspects
of the epic is its use of a lesser character, rather than the
technical protagonist, as the tale's benchmark for heroism. This
lesser character is Diomedes, and his leadership skills and maturity
prove to be far superior to those of Achilles. Book V of *The Iliad* is
devoted almost entirely to Diomedes' feats, and there are many scenes
in which he is presented as a leader and hero throughout the rest of
the text. While Diomedes is singled out for his gallantry, Achilles
is, by contrast, noted for his immaturity and selfishness. Homer
depicts Diomedes in a much more positive light than Achilles, despite
the latter's obvious natural superiority as a soldier. It seems
evident that Homer is emphasizing the total use of one's abilities,
rather than just the presence of those abilities, as the basis of
heroism. Diomedes, therefore, is the actual hero of *The Iliad.*
     Achilles is immediately placed at the focal point of the story,
and his pride and immaturity surface almost instantaneously. In Book
I, Agamemnon embarrasses Achilles publicly with an outward display of
his power as the Achaians' commander: "Since Apollo robs me of

Chryseis . . . I will take your beautiful Briseis . . . to show you how much stronger I am than you are."[1] Achilles can hardly be faulted for taking offense at this incident, as it "threatened to invalidate . . . the whole meaning of his life."[2] Achilles' refusal to fight afterward must be looked at from more than one perspective. This is the first example of Achilles acting according to his pride, as proven by his regard for himself as "the best man of all."[3] While it is understandable for a soldier such as Achilles, who "towers above all the other characters of *The Iliad,*" to be hesitant to fight for and under the man who embarrassed him, Agamemnon, it is also folly for a soldier to stop fighting because of anything as relatively unimportant as an insult, even a public one.[4] A soldier's duty is to defend his homeland and fight in its wars, and Achilles misses this greater duty for his own selfishness. This refusal to fight is compounded by his request to his mother, Thetis, to "see if he [Zeus] will help the Trojans and drive the Achaians back to their ships with slaughter!"[5] This is wholly selfish. Achilles is willing to put the fate of the entire Greek army in peril to feed his own wounded ego. Achilles is acting nothing like the leader that his divine gifts give him the power to be. Homer clearly leaves his central character open for some significant character development.

In contrast to Achilles' infantile behavior, which is consistent throughout most of the story, Diomedes is cast in a different light. Athena gives Diomedes "courage and boldness, to make him come to the front and cover himself with glory."[6] While not Achilles' equal as a soldier, "Diomedes was extremely fierce" and proved to be a terrific leader for the Achaians.[7] Diomedes kills off many Trojan warriors in Book V, acting as many hoped Achilles would, and even fighting through an injury suffered from the bow of Pandaros.[8] Rather than back down, Diomedes prayed to Athena for aid and joined the battle even more fiercely than before, slaying even more Trojan soldiers.[9] It is clear at this point that Diomedes is "obviously a paradigm of heroic behavior in Achilles' absence."[10] Diomedes represents a well-behaved, properly subservient soldier in the Achaian army who uses his courage and his honor to accomplish feats that are beyond his natural abilities. Diomedes exhibits self-control above all else, which is the element most wanting in Achilles' character.[11] His courage is further proven when he speaks against Agamemnon at the beginning of Book IX when the Achaian commander is advocating a Greek retreat: "Two of us will go on fighting, Sthenelos and I, until we make our goal!"[12] This is the moment when Diomedes is confirmed as one of the Greeks' greatest leaders, as even in a time when the army was "possessed by Panic,"[13] we see that "all cheered bold Diomedes in admiration."[14] The scene underscores Diomedes' rise to greatness in the Achaian army.

Achilles and Diomedes finally come into direct conflict with one another in Book IX, after Agamemnon has decided to make a peace offering to Achilles in hopes of the latter's return to battle. Agamemnon makes an offer to Achilles that is outrageously generous in exchange for Achilles' return to battle. Achilles' response is far from heroic and borders on cowardly: "If I go home to my native land, there will be no great fame for me, but I shall live long and not die an early death."[15] These words show utter selfishness on the part of the man who is supposedly the greatest warrior in Greek history, and Achilles is certainly not, at this point, living up to his reputation or his potential. Observing that Achilles "shall appear in battle once more whenever he feels inclined or when God makes him go," Diomedes speaks against Achilles for the first time, effectively casting himself as something of an adversary to Achilles in the hopes of bringing him back into the battle, an action that serves the overall good of the Achaians.[16] Once more, Diomedes is doing what is best for his people and his army while Achilles thinks only of himself. Peter Toohey observes that "Homer likes to juxtapose," and here he uses that device to highlight the stark contrast between the protagonist of the story and the true hero of the story.[17]

Homer centers *The Iliad* around Achilles, whose actions are notably selfish and immature. Homer then uses Diomedes, at first a lesser character, as a dramatic foil. Diomedes comes across as an example of the ideal young Greek soldier. Achilles' capacities as a warrior are far superior to those of any man alive, yet Diomedes betters him in both words and actions throughout most of the story.

Achilles is finally brought to realize his supreme military prowess, but it is the death of his friend Patroclos that spurs his fighting spirit, still another example of Achilles' penchant for acting on emotion rather than judgment. Achilles is finally reconciled to Diomedes' example when he meets Priam at the end of the story and responds honorably: "I mean myself to set your Hector free," agreeing to return the corpse of Priam's son for a proper burial.[18] Achilles at last achieves a measure of respect that his abilities could have earned him long before. It is in that time, however, when Achilles was still selfish and immature, that Diomedes shone as the example of leadership and valor. Diomedes is, at least in a measure of consistency, the true hero of *The Iliad*.

NOTES

1. Homer, *The Iliad,* trans. Robert Fitzgerald (New York: Anchor Press, 1974), 14.

2. R. M. Frazer, *A Reading of "The Iliad"* (Lannam, Md.: University Press of America, 1993), 12.

3. Homer, 15.

4. Frazer, 11.

5. Homer, 18.

6. Ibid., 58.

7. Scott Richardson, *The Homeric Narrator* (Nashville: Vanderbilt Univ. Press, 1990), 159.

8. Homer, 59.

9. Ibid., 60-61.

10. W. Thomas MacCary, *Childlike Achilles: Ontogeny and Philogeny in "The Iliad"* (New York: Columbia Univ. Press, 1982), 95.

11. G. S. Kirk, *"The Iliad": A Commentary,* vol. 2 (New York: Cambridge Univ. Press, 1990), 34.

12. Homer, 103.

13. Ibid., 102.

14. Ibid., 103.

15. Ibid., 110.

16. Ibid., 115.

17. Peter Toohey, "Epic and Rhetoric: Speech-making and Persuasion in Homer and Apollonius," *Arachnion: A Journal of Ancient Literature and History on the Web* 1 (1995) [journal online]; available from http://www.cisi.unito.it/arachne/num1/toohey.html; Internet; accessed 21 February 1996.

18. Homer, 293.

WORKS CITED

Frazer, R. M. *A Reading of "The Iliad."* Lanham, Md.: University Press of America, 1993.

Homer. *The Iliad.* Translated by Robert Fitzgerald. New York: Anchor Press, 1974.

Kirk, G. S. *"The Iliad": A Commentary.* Vol. 2. New York: Cambridge Univ. Press, 1990.

MacCary, W. Thomas. *Childlike Achilles: Ontogeny and Philogeny in "The Iliad."* New York: Columbia Univ. Press, 1982.

Richardson, Scott. *The Homeric Narrator.* Nashville: Vanderbilt Univ. Press, 1990.

Toohey, Peter. "Epic and Rhetoric: Speech-making and Persuasion in Homer and Apollonius." *Arachnion: A Journal of Ancient Literature and History on the Web* 1 (1995). Journal online. Available from http://www.cisi.unito.it/arachne/num1/toohey.html; Internet; accessed 21 February 1996.

Sample CMS page with footnotes. In CMS style, you have the option of placing all your notes on pages following the body of a paper, as shown on page 323, or you may locate them at the bottom of each page as demonstrated below.

2

Book I, Agamemnon embarrasses Achilles publicly with an outward display of his power as the Achaians' commander: "since Apollo robs me of Chryseis . . . I will take your beautiful Briseis . . . to show you how much stronger I am than you are."[1] Achilles can hardly be faulted for taking offense at this incident, as it "threatened to invalidate . . . the whole meaning of his life."[2] Achilles' refusal to fight afterward must be looked at from more than one perspective. This is the first example of Achilles acting according to his pride, as proven by his regard for himself as "the best man of all."[3] While it is understandable for a soldier such as Achilles, who "towers above all the other characters of *The Iliad*," to be hesitant to fight for and under the man who embarrassed him, Agamemnon, it is also folly for a soldier to stop fighting because of anything as relatively unimportant as an insult, even a public one.[4] A soldier's duty is to defend his homeland and fight in its wars, and Achilles misses this greater duty for his own selfishness. This refusal to fight is compounded by his request to his mother, Thetis, to "see if he [Zeus] will help the Trojans and drive the Achaians back to their ships with slaughter!"[5] This is wholly selfish. Achilles is willing to put the fate of the entire Greek army in peril to feed his own wounded ego. Achilles is acting nothing like the leader that his divine gifts give him the

---

1. Homer, *The Iliad*, trans. Robert Fitzgerald (New York: Anchor Press, 1974), 14.

2. R. M. Frazer, *A Reading of "The Iliad"* (Lanham, Md.: University Press of America, 1993), 12.

3. Homer, 15.

4. Frazer, 11.

5. Homer, 18.

All research develops from a sense of curiosity. Satisfying such curiosity might involve spending a day, a week, or a career in the Library of Congress (pictured here in all its grandeur). Established by Thomas Jefferson on April 24, 1800, the Library of Congress houses 532 miles of books in three buildings. Anyone over high school age may make use of the library's abundant resources, which include more than 110 million items. Among the collection's treasures is a rare Gutenberg Bible on permanent display in the library's Great Hall.

A library for everyone, the Library of Congress maintains a Web page at http://lcweb.loc.gov that opens its collection to any computer connected to the Internet. The National Digital Library Program provides similar access to the library's programs. Click on Thomas to peruse recent and current legislation, or try the American Memory collection to find archival materials on American history and culture such as Walt Whitman's manuscript notebooks or George Washington's papers. More possibilities are only a click away.

325

◎ DON'T MISS . . .

- **The explanation of CBE documentation on page 327.** If you are preparing a paper in the natural sciences, you may want to use CBE documentation.
- **The explanation of CBE formats on page 329.**

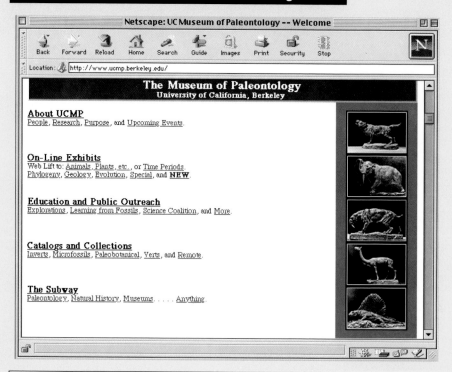

BOOKMARKS: Web Sites Worth Knowing About

Netscape: UC Museum of Paleontology -- Welcome

Location: http://www.ucmp.berkeley.edu/

The Museum of Paleontology
University of California, Berkeley

About UCMP
People, Research, Purpose, and Upcoming Events.

On-Line Exhibits
Web Lift to: Animals, Plants, etc., or Time Periods.
Phylogeny, Geology, Evolution, Special, and **NEW**.

Education and Public Outreach
Explorations, Learning from Fossils, Science Coalition, and More.

Catalogs and Collections
Inverts, Microfossils, Paleobotanical, Verts, and Remote.

The Subway
Paleontology, Natural History, Museums . . . . . Anything.

The Museum of Paleontology, University of California, Berkeley,
http://www.ucmp.berkeley.edu/

A good place to begin pursuing science research on the Web is the Museum of Paleontology at the University of California, Berkeley. Here you can view exhibits that give in-depth coverage of evolution, geology, plants and animals, and, of course, paleontology. Links are provided to other sites that give even more thorough coverage of these subjects. Be sure to check out *The Subway,* UCMP's transit network for the scientific community on the Web.

Additional Sites
Council of Biology Editors Documentation,
    http://www.wisc.edu/writing/Handbook/DocCBE6.html
"The Biology Project," http://www.biology.arizona.edu/
ChemCenter, http://www.ChemCenter.org/
arXiv.org e-Print archive, http://xxx.lanl.gov/
    (a searchable archive of thousands of journal articles in physics, math, and chemistry)

CBE Documentation

Disciplines that study the physical world—physics, chemistry, biology—are called the natural sciences; disciplines that examine (and produce) technologies are described as the applied sciences. Writing in these fields is specialized, and no survey of all forms of documentation can be provided here. For more information about writing in the following fields, we suggest that you consult one of these style manuals.

- ❏ **Chemistry:** *The ACS Style Guide: A Manual for Authors and Editors,* 2nd edition (1997)—American Chemical Society
- ❏ **Geology:** *Suggestions to Authors of Reports of the United States Geological Survey,* 7th edition (1991)—U.S. Geological Survey
- ❏ **Mathematics:** *A Manual for Authors of Mathematical Papers,* revised edition (1990)—American Mathematical Society
- ❏ **Medicine:** *American Medical Association Manual of Style,* 9th edition (1997)
- ❏ **Physics:** *AIP Style Manual,* 4th edition (1990)—American Institute of Physics

A highly influential manual for scientific writing is *Scientific Style and Format: The CBE Manual for Authors, Editors, and Publishers* (6th edition, 1994). In this latest edition of The *CBE Manual,* the Council of Biology Editors advocates a common style for international science but also recognizes important differences between disciplines and even countries.

CBE style itself includes the choice of two major methods of documenting sources used in research: a *name-year* system that resembles APA style and a *citation-sequence* system that lists sources in the order of their use. In this chapter, we briefly describe this second system.

Citing Electronic Sources in the Natural and Applied Sciences

CBE documentation covers many electronic sources (see p. 331 for an explanation), but it does not deal specifically with Web sites and other online environments. When citing such items, you may want to use the documentation style recommended by the *Columbia Guide to Online Style;* it was developed explicitly for newer research situations. Columbia Online Style (COS) for scientific papers, described on pages 222 through 232, is especially adaptable to CBE-style name-year citations. Consult your instructor about using Columbia style for electronic and computerized sources.

26a Include in-text citations

Where a citation is needed in the text of a paper, insert either a raised number (the preferred form) or a number in parentheses. Citations should appear immediately after the word or phrase to which they are related, and they are numbered in the order you use them.

```
Oncologists [1] are aware of trends in cancer mortality [2].
```

```
Oncologists (1) are aware of trends in cancer mortality (2).
```

Source 1 thus becomes the first item listed on the References page, source 2 the second item, and so on.

1. Devesa SS, Silverman DT. Cancer incidence and mortality trends in the United States: 1935-74. J Natl Cancer Inst 1978;60:545-571.

2. Goodfield J. The siege of cancer. New York: Dell; 1978. 240 p.

You can refer to more than one source in a single note, with the numbers separated by a dash if they are in sequence and by commas if out of sequence.

IN SEQUENCE

```
Cancer treatment[2-3] has changed over the decades. But Rettig[4]
shows that the politics of cancer research remains constant.
```

OUT OF SEQUENCE

```
Cancer treatment[2,5] has changed over the decades. But Rettig[4]
shows that the politics of cancer research remains constant.
```

If you cite a source again later in the paper, refer to it by its original number.

```
Great strides have occurred in epidemiological methods[5] despite
the political problems in maintaining research support and funding
described by Rettig[4].
```

26b List sources used

On a separate page at the end of your project, list the sources you used in the order they occurred. These sources are numbered: source 1 in the project would be the first source listed on the References page, source 2 the second item, and so on. Notice, then, that this References list is *not* alphabetical. The first few entries on a CBE list might look like this.

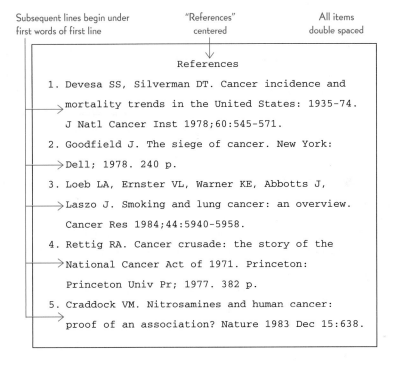

Subsequent lines begin under first words of first line | "References" centered | All items double spaced

```
                          References
1. Devesa SS, Silverman DT. Cancer incidence and
   mortality trends in the United States: 1935-74.
   J Natl Cancer Inst 1978;60:545-571.
2. Goodfield J. The siege of cancer. New York:
   Dell; 1978. 240 p.
3. Loeb LA, Ernster VL, Warner KE, Abbotts J,
   Laszo J. Smoking and lung cancer: an overview.
   Cancer Res 1984;44:5940-5958.
4. Rettig RA. Cancer crusade: the story of the
   National Cancer Act of 1971. Princeton:
   Princeton Univ Pr; 1977. 382 p.
5. Craddock VM. Nitrosamines and human cancer:
   proof of an association? Nature 1983 Dec 15:638.
```

A typical **CBE citation-sequence–style References entry for a book** includes the following basic information.

❑ Number assigned to the source.

❑ Name of author(s), last name first, followed by a period. Initials are used in place of full first or middle names. Commas ordinarily separate the names of multiple authors.

❑ Title of work, followed by a period. Only the first word and any proper nouns in a title are capitalized. The title is not underlined.

❑ Place of publication, followed by a colon.

❑ Publisher, followed by a semicolon. Titles of presses can be abbreviated.

❑ Date, followed by a period.

❑ Number of pages, followed by a period.

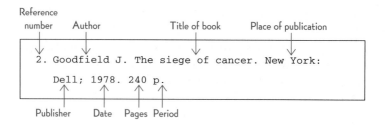

Reference
number · Author · Title of book · Place of publication

2. Goodfield J. The siege of cancer. New York:
   Dell; 1978. 240 p.

Publisher · Date · Pages · Period

A typical **CBE citation-sequence–style References entry for an article in a scholarly journal** (where the pagination is continuous through a year) includes the following basic information.

- ❏ Number assigned to the source.

- ❏ Name of author(s), last name first, followed by a period. Initials are used in place of full first or middle names. Commas ordinarily separate the names of multiple authors.

- ❏ Title of article, followed by a period. Only the first word and any proper nouns in a title are capitalized. The title does not appear between quotation marks.

- ❏ Name of the journal. All major words are capitalized, but the journal title is not underlined. A space (but no punctuation) separates the journal title from the date. Journal titles of more than one word can be abbreviated following the recommendations in *American National Standard Z39.5-1985: Abbreviations of Titles of Publications.*

- ❏ Year (and month for journals not continuously paginated; date for weekly journals), followed immediately by a semicolon.

- ❏ Volume number, followed by a colon, and the page numbers of the article. No spaces separate these items. A period follows the page numbers.

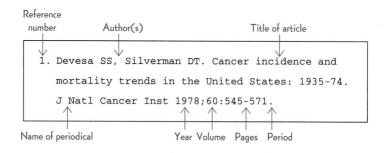

Reference
number · Author(s) · Title of article

1. Devesa SS, Silverman DT. Cancer incidence and
   mortality trends in the United States: 1935-74.
   J Natl Cancer Inst 1978;60:545-571.

Name of periodical · Year · Volume · Pages · Period

A typical **CBE citation-sequence–style References entry for an article in a popular magazine** includes the following basic information.

- ❏ Number assigned to the source.

- ❏ Name of author(s), last name first, followed by a period. Initials are substituted for first names unless two authors mentioned in the paper have identical last names and first initials.

❑ Title of article, followed by a period. Only the first word and any proper nouns in a title are capitalized. The title does not appear between quotation marks. (Where quotation marks are needed, CBE recommends British style. See *CBE Manual,* pp. 180–81.)

❑ Name of magazine, abbreviated. All major words are capitalized, but the journal title is not underlined. A space (but no punctuation) separates the magazine title from the year and month.

❑ Year, month (abbreviated), and day (for a weekly magazine). The year is separated from the month by a space. A colon follows immediately after the date, followed by page number(s). The entry ends with a period.

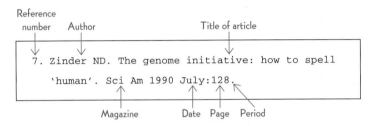

A typical **CBE citation-sequence–style References entry for an electronic item** includes the basic information provided for a print document (author, title, publication information, page numbers) with the following additions.

❑ Electronic medium, identified between brackets. For books and monographs, this information comes after the title *[monograph on-line];* for periodicals, it follows the name of the journal *[serial on-line].*

❑ Availability statement, following the publication information or page numbers.

❑ Date of access, if helpful in identifying what version of an electronic text was consulted.

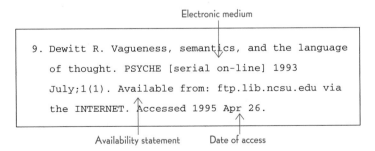

There are so many variations to these basic entries, however, that you will certainly want to check the *CBE Manual* when you do a major CBE-style paper.

CBE Style

- CBE style normally requires a separate title page. The title of the essay can be centered about a third of the way from the top of the page, followed by *by* on a separate line and the writer's name, also on a separate line. Other information such as instructor's name, course title, and date can be included on the bottom third of the page.

- CBE style normally requires an abstract of about 250 words on a separate sheet immediately following the title page. The title "Abstract" is centered on the page.

- Double-space the body of a CBE paper. Avoid hyphenating words at the end of the line.

- Number pages consecutively in the upper right-hand corner, counting the title page as the first page, using the "automatic page numbering" feature of your word processor, if available.

- Take special care with figures and tables. They should be numbered in separate sequences. The *CBE Manual* includes an entire chapter on handling illustrative material.

- The References page follows the text of the CBE essay on a new page. Remember that the items on this page are *not* listed alphabetically. References pages can also be titled "Literature Cited" or "References Cited."

- All works listed on the References page should be cited at least once in the body of your paper.

- Entries on the References page are single spaced, with a space left between the entries.

Credits

American Psychological Association. *Publication Manual of the American Psychological Association,* Fourth edition, 1994.

"Atlantic Unbound Roundtable: Life, Liberty, and the Pursuit of Copyright?" at http://www .theatlantic.com/unbound/forum/copyright/intro.htm. Copyright 1998 by The Atlantic Monthly Company. Reprinted with permission.

Baker, C. From *Your Genes, Your Choice* by C. Baker, 1997. Copyright 1997 by the American Association for the Advancement of Science. Reprinted with permission.

"Bartlett's Familiar Quotations" at http://www.columbia.edu/acis/bartleby/bartlett. Reprinted with permission.

Bishop, J. Michael. "Enemies of Promise." *The Wilson Quarterly,* Summer 1995.

"Boolean Searching on the Internet" at http://www.albany.edu/library/internet/boolean.html. Reprinted with permission. Permission granted by AltaVista for second screen shot on using Boolean logic to narrow a search.

Bork, Robert H. "Give Me a Bowl of Texas." *Forbes,* September 1985, p. 184.

Carter, Stephen L. "The Culture of Disbelief" from *The Culture of Disbelief: How American Law and Politics Trivialize Religious Devotion,* Basic Books, 1993.

College Composition and Communication. Home page for CCC (College Composition and Communication) at http://ncte.org/ccc/nx.html. Web Design by Todd Taylor. Copyright by the National Council of Teachers of English. Reprinted with permission.

Council of Biology Editors. *Scientific Style and Format: The CBE Manual for Authors, Editors, and Publishers,* Sixth Edition, 1994.

"Excite Power Search" web page. Excite and the Excite Logo are trademarks of Excite, Inc., a subsidiary of At Home Corporation, and may be registered in various jurisdictions. Excite screen display copyright 1995-1999 by Excite, Inc. Reprinted by permission.

eZines Ultimate Magazine Database at http://www.dominis.com/Zines/. Reprinted with permission.

Grafton, Anthony. "The Death of the Footnote." *The Wilson Quarterly,* Winter 1997, pp. 76-77.

Hoberman, Barry. From "Translating the Bible." *The Atlantic Monthly,* February, 1985, vol. 255 no. 2. Reproduced by permission of the author.

Hofstadter, Douglas. *Gödel, Escher, Bach: An Eternal Golden Braid.* Vintage Books/Random House, 1979, p. 603.

"IPL Online Literary Criticism Collection" at http://www.ipl.org/ref/litcrit/. Reprinted with permission.

The Library of Congress. "African American Odyssey" home page and source code at http://memory.loc.gov/ammem/aaohtml/exhibit/aointro.html

The Library of Congress Exhibitions at http://www.lcweb.loc.gov/exhibits/. Reprinted with permission.

Libweb index of "Library Servers via WWW" at http://www.sunsite.berkeley.edu/Libweb/. Reprinted with permission.

The Museum of Paleontology, University of California, Berkeley, at http://www.ucmp.berkeley.edu/. Reprinted with permission.

National Center for Supercomputing Applications (NCSA). "A Beginner's Guide to HTML" at http://www.ncsa.uiuc.edu/General/Internet/WWW/HTMLPrimerAll.html. Reprinted by permission of NCSA/University of Illinois at Urbana-Champaign.

Netscape. Portions copyright 1999 by Netscape Communications Corporation. All Rights Reserved. Netscape, Netscape Navigator, and the Netscape N Logo are registered trademarks of Netscape in the United States and other countries.

PsychCrawler at http://www.psychcrawler.com. Reprinted with permission.

Roland, Alex. "Leave the People Home." *USA Today Online,* July 7, 1997. Reprinted by permission of the author.

Shrum, Robert. From "The Nikes Jumped Over the Moon" by Robert Shrum in *Slate,* December 13, 1996. First published in Slate, www.slate.com. Reprinted with permission. Slate is a trademark of Microsoft Corporation, copyright © 1996.

Stern, Barbara Lang. "Tears Can Be Crucial to Your Physical and Emotional Health." *Vogue,* June 1979, Condé Nast Publications.

The Modern Language Association Style Manual. "Rules." Thanks to the *MLA Style Manual and Guide to Scholarly Publishing,* Second edition, 1998, and the *MLA Handbook for Writers of Research Papers,* Fifth edition, 1999.

University of Texas at Arlington. The University of Texas at Arlington web home page, http://www.uta.edu/index.old.html. Reproduced by permission.

Urquhart, Brian. *Ralph Bunche: An American Life.* New York: W. W. Norton & Co., 1993, p. 435.

"Using Cybersources" at http://www.devry-phx.edu/lrnresrc/dowsc/integrty.htm. Web Design by the DeVry/Phoenix Web Administrator. Copyright 1997-1999 by DeVry Institute of Technology/Phoenix. Reprinted with permission.

"UT Library Online" web page at the University of Texas at Austin. Provided courtesy of The General Libraries, The University of Texas at Austin.

van der Plas, Robert. *The Mountain Bike Book.* San Francisco: Bicycle Books, 1993, p. 106.

Walker, Janice R., and Todd Taylor. *The Columbia Guide to Online Style.* Copyright © 1998 by Columbia University Press.

Web Developer's Virtual Library, Tutorials for Web Developers at http://www.wdvl.com/Authoring/Tutorials. Reprinted with permission.

Williams, Terry Tempest. "The Clan of One-Breasted Women" from *Refuge: An Unnatural History of Family and Place,* Pantheon Books, 1990. Originally published in *Northern Lights,* January 1990.

Yahoo! Web page. Text and artwork copyright © 1998 by Yahoo! Inc. All rights reserved. YAHOO! and the YAHOO! logo are trademarks of YAHOO! Inc.

Yankelovich, Daniel. "The Work Ethic Is Underemployed." *Psychology Today,* May 1982. Ziff-Davis Publishing Co.

PHOTO CREDITS

Unless otherwise acknowledged, all photographs are the property of Addison Wesley Longman.

Tabbed-Divider Guide: *(top left)* The Granger Collection. *(top middle)* Corbis-Bettmann. *(top right)* The Granger Collection. *(middle)* Corbis-Bettmann. *(bottom left)* UPI/Corbis-Bettmann. *(bottom middle)* Joel Gordon. *(bottom right)* Stan Ries/International Stock.

Interior photographs: Page 3: AP/Wide World Photos. Page 4: Photofest. Page 22: Don Hamerman/Folio, Inc. Page 36: Bonnie Kamin/Photo Edit. Page 41: Corbis-Bettmann. Page 63: The Granger Collection. Page 66: David Young-Wolff/Photo Edit. Page 73: Michael Newman/Photo Edit. Page 78: Jason Laure. Page 84: Michael Newman/Photo Edit. Page 89: Rhoda Sidney/Photo Edit. Page 95: The Granger Collection. Page 121: The Granger Collection. Page 129: T. Charles Erickson/Theatre Pix. Page 153: UPI/Corbis-Bettmann. Page 161: Corbis-Bettmann. Page 183: The Granger Collection. Page 203: Joel Gordon. Page 233: UPI/Corbis-Bettmann. Page 273: David Young-Wolff/Photo Edit. Page 305: Courtesy, Online Computer Library Center (OCLC). Page 325: Stan Ries/International Stock.

Index

Glossary

address. The route or path followed to access a specific file. An email address usually consists of a log-in name and a domain name. A WWW address usually includes a domain name, a directory or directories, and a file name.

asynchronous. In Internet communication, electronic mail and other communication wherein messages are not dependent on timing.

BBS. Bulletin board service. A service that provides dial-in access to remote users, enabling them to access files and information and to communicate with other users. Many also offer varying levels of Internet access.

bookmarks. Called "Favorites" in some browsers, bookmarks are a way of marking a specific file, online address, or location within a file for later retrieval.

Boolean operators. Search terms based on logic that allow you to limit and define search criteria. The most commonly used Boolean operators are AND, OR, and NOT.

browser. Software that allows users to access files on the World Wide Web and move through hypertext links. Some browsers such as *Lynx* offer text-only access, while browsers such as Netscape *Navigator* and Microsoft *Internet Explorer* use graphical interfaces and point-and-click technology.

chat room. A virtual room; an address where multiple users may communicate with each other in real time, usually by inputting text on a keyboard.

database. A collection of files containing related information or records which can be organized and manipulated for use in various ways.

directory. A structure for organizing files on a computer or host, similar to a file folder containing individual files.

disk. Various forms of media designed for storage of electronic data, including *floppy diskettes* (usually contained in a $3\frac{1}{2}$-inch-square plastic case), *hard disks* (the computer's internal hard drive), and *CD-ROMs* (compact disc, read-only memory).

domain name. The unique name assigned to an individual host address, such as www.whitehouse.gov.

download. The act of moving a file from a host or server directory to a local storage medium such as your diskette or hard drive.

FAQ. Frequently asked questions. A file providing information about a newsgroup, listserv, or other online service, including details of membership, discussion topics, and rules or netiquette guidelines.

FTP. File transfer protocol. A means of transferring files between machines.

Gopher. A menu-driven system for organizing and accessing remote files on the Internet.

HTTP. HyperText Transfer Protocol. The process by which hypertext files are transferred between remote computers on the Internet using browser software.

hypertext. Designated text, graphics, or files that are linked together, as designated by the hypertext author, using a special system of tags called HyperText Markup Language (HTML).